BATTLEFIELD CYBER

*How China and Russia Are Undermining Our Democracy
and National Security*

MICHAEL G. MCLAUGHLIN AND

WILLIAM J. HOLSTEIN

 Prometheus Books

Essex, Connecticut

*This book is dedicated to our wives, Theresa and Rita,
for enduring the agony of living with authors.*

Ⓟ Prometheus Books

An imprint of Globe Pequot, the trade division of
The Rowman & Littlefield Publishing Group, Inc.
4501 Forbes Blvd., Ste. 200
Lanham, MD 20706
www.rowman.com

Distributed by NATIONAL BOOK NETWORK

British Library Cataloguing in Publication Information Available

Library of Congress Cataloging-in-Publication Data

Names: McLaughlin, Michael (Michael J.), author. | Holstein, William J., author.
Title: Battlefield cyber : how China and Russia are undermining our democracy and national security / William J Holstein and Michael McLaughlin.
Description: Lanham, MD : Prometheus Books, [2023] | Includes bibliographical references and index. | Summary: "The United States is being bombarded with cyber-attacks. From the surge in ransomware groups targeting critical infrastructure to nation-states compromising the software supply chain and corporate email servers, malicious cyber activities have reached an all-time high. This book discusses this and more."—Provided by publisher.
Identifiers: LCCN 2022053668 (print) | LCCN 2022053669 (ebook) | ISBN 9781633889019 (cloth) | ISBN 9781633889026 (epub)
Subjects: LCSH: Cyberterrorism—United States. | Cyberterrorism—Government Policy—United States. | Information warfare—United States. | Computer networks—Security measures—United States.
Classification: LCC HV6773.15.C97 H65 2023 (print) | LCC HV6773.15.C97 (ebook) | DDC 363.325/1720973/eng/20230130—dcundefined
LC record available at https://lccn.loc.gov/2022053668
LC ebook record available at https://lccn.loc.gov/2022053669

∞™ The paper used in this publication meets the minimum requirements of American National Standard for Information Sciences—Permanence of Paper for Printed Library Materials, ANSI/NISO Z39.48-1992

Contents

Introduction

All Hands on Deck

It was a moment of supreme geopolitical drama. Chinese president Xi Jinping took advantage of the opening of the Winter Olympics in Beijing in February 2022 to greet Russian president Vladimir Putin. Together they declared that they would start a deeper pattern of cooperation with one another with "no limits." Even though deep mutual distrust persists, they have found common cause in challenging the supremacy of American democracy—and democracies throughout the world. Putin's invasion of Ukraine and China's brazen military pressure on Taiwan are the two primary manifestations of their testing of America's alliances with other democracies.

But there is a deeper, perhaps even more malicious strategy afoot—one that is much less visible. China and Russia are each exploiting cyberspace and all the digital highways the United States has taken a lead in building. The interests and methods of these two authoritarian regimes appear to be aligning. Increasingly, they are attacking the very foundations of our democracy and national security.

As Americans, we thought we had created the technology of the internet and therefore would dominate and control it. But these adversaries have learned how to penetrate American systems for espionage, data and intellectual property theft, and criminal gains, and how to position themselves for future cyberattacks against our critical infrastructure. Unlike Western democracies, which closely adhere to international norms in cyberspace, these adversaries understand cyberspace for what it truly is: a battlefield.

The rise of the internet and social media has changed the way nation-states compete and altered the very definition and boundaries of war. As technology advances, its use generally becomes safer. But, ironically, our increasing reliance on sophisticated information technology and communications networks has made us more vulnerable rather than more secure. The internet is one of the biggest technological changes in human history—on par with the printing press and the steam engine. While Americans have been excited by new possibilities, our rivals have been quicker to understand the total nature of the new competition the internet has ushered in.

This battlefield is not limited to network penetrations. Our opponents have also mastered the use of our own social media platforms to deepen the dangerous illusion that different sets of Americans are fighting among ourselves in to-the-death struggles for ideological supremacy. Our adversaries have learned how to fan the flames of ethnic and racial tension and how to either interfere in our elections or cause us to question their legitimacy. They use our own social media platforms to pit our political parties against each other and to sow confusion among our populace about the origins of COVID-19 or the Chinese government's ethnic cleansing of its Uighur population. They cooperate in promoting Putin's crazed notion that the United States and its NATO allies forced him to invade Ukraine to depose its "neo-Nazis." And they do all of this legally. While some narratives are pushed through fake accounts and bots, many are propagated through the expenditure of billions of dollars in advertisements on our social media platforms. Chinese entities, doubtlessly coordinated by the Communist Party and the state, spent $10 billion on Facebook advertisements in 2021 alone—a massive propaganda blitz.[1] The Chinese Foreign Ministry recently boasted that it has published more than nine thousand posts on social media outside China and attracted almost 500 million views.

The Chinese government, in particular, is also engaged in a massive campaign of technology theft targeting American companies and organizations. It relies on penetration of American telecommunication and computing platforms to do that in combination with old-fashioned human espionage. This comes in many forms—from network exploitation by state-sponsored hackers, to predatory investment in U.S. technology startups, to the insertion of backdoors in technology that is "Made in China" and installed in our systems. Technology theft amounts to denying economic gains to the very people whose tax dollars are supporting advanced research in U.S. laboratories and universities. Most Americans do not understand that products developed in China—and the wealth created—accrue to the benefit of China, not the United States. China's multipronged approach to reap the rewards from America's technical prowess and innovation places both private-sector corporations and U.S. national security in peril.

Although our adversaries opt for illicit cyber activities, their strategies have been carefully calibrated to prevent a forceful U.S. military response or cyber onslaught on their own computer systems or critical infrastructure. China and Russia know that if we are galvanized as a nation—as we were by the attack on Pearl Harbor or the terrorist attacks of September 11, 2001, we are capable of stunning achievements. That is why they pursue a long-term numbing strategy, not sudden and obvious assaults, such as shutting down the electrical power system of Washington, DC. If we are waiting for a cyber Pearl Harbor or a cyber 9/11, we are fatally misunderstanding how our adversaries wage cyber warfare.

The Russians have been willing to walk right up to the line of what would be considered an act of war, and the United States has caught them in the act. In a stunning indictment in March 2022, the U.S. Department of Justice accused one member of the Russian Ministry of Defense and three officers of Russia's Federal Security Service of penetrating critical energy infrastructure in multiple countries, including a nuclear power plant in Kansas. There was no purpose behind this type of activity other than to preposition cyber weapons for a future attack. In an open conflict scenario, Russian hackers could turn a small town in Kansas into the next Chernobyl.[2]

These types of attacks and penetrations are not onetime occurrences. Simply put, our adversaries have "graduated" from the occasional assault targeting individual companies and agencies and now have established a permanent presence in America's computers. The experts call this "persistent access," and it appears from recent software supply-chain attacks that our opponents can lurk inside some of our systems for years without being detected. According to a defense intelligence source, "the Russians make more noise, which is why they get caught, but the Chinese are completely embedded in these systems." The Russians seek to disrupt; the Chinese seek to colonize.

The combination of these different types of cyber strategies is corrosive because it undermines our faith in our own institutions. It is only when one adds up the different threads that the overall pattern becomes clear. If Americans have to wait in lines for gasoline because of a ransomware attack against an oil pipeline company, they do not necessarily understand *why* it is happening. They just know that something in our society and economy is not working. At the same time, they are suffering from health concerns, supply-chain disruptions, mass shootings, and weather-related disturbances such as wildfires. The combination has resulted in what the *New York Times* called a "national funk." One of its columnists, Michelle Goldberg, suffered a near nervous breakdown in print, warning in the same column about "political despair," "growing hopelessness," "dystopia," and "democratic unraveling."

Our adversaries have studied how democracies work and have found their true vulnerability—their very openness. Americans fundamentally believe in pluralism and checks and balances among different interest groups. The private sector is different from government and does not expect to stand on the front line in a battle to protect America's national security. Business leaders genuinely feel they bear no responsibility for national security. But the battlefield is shifting.

The way the experts have traditionally defined cyber warfare is much too narrow. They underestimate the impact of the theft of data—China's Ministry of State Security is widely presumed to construct profiles of prominent Americans using health, travel, financial, and other data it has stolen over the years. They understand and follow the decision-making processes inside an unknown number of American companies and government agencies. The traditional definitions of cyber warfare miss the fact that the combination of different types of attacks and penetrations is aimed at subverting the very concept of democracy, which seems to be a central goal for both Xi and Putin. They want to make the world safe for their increasingly authoritarian systems, and so long as the world's democracies demonstrate that democracy can flourish, their systems are at risk.

For the purposes of this book, we define "cyber warfare" as follows: state or nonstate actors, their proxies, or criminal actors operating either at the behest of or with impunity within the sovereign territory of a nation-state, who engage in cyber-enabled malicious activities at or below the level of armed conflict with the strategic aim of inflicting harm to the government or private sector of another nation. This type of cyber-enabled malicious activity has clear political, psychological, and societal impact meant to render democracies less capable of managing their own internal affairs or projecting power internationally.

The recent ransomware blitz is merely the latest manifestation of our adversaries' broad campaigns. Under traditional definitions, ransomware groups acting in concert to target organizations would not necessarily qualify as cyber warfare. Does that make Russia's enabling of ransomware actors any less a potent weapon in its cyber arsenal to destabilize the United States? Obviously not.

One thing is clear: We are at war—a new kind of war we have been slow to comprehend.

In this war, the battle space is limitless. Combatant and noncombatant status is irrelevant. If you operate a network connected to the internet, you are on the cyber battlefield. And we, as a nation, are actually increasing our vulnerability by expanding the interconnectivity of our networked devices and relying increasingly on cloud computing. Without a significant change of course, the coming Internet of Things, which will connect millions of new devices to the internet, combined with 5G and 6G wireless communications, virtual reality and artificial intelligence, and the metaverse, will create vulnerabilities that touch every part of our lives.

There is plenty of blame to go around for this sad state of affairs. Even though the evidence has mounted that China, in particular, is turning the digital tables on us, our own companies continue to enable it because short-term quarterly profits drive decision making. Major companies such as Microsoft and Amazon Web Services gave away access to their systems to operate in China[3] and have become part of the Chinese party-state's influence and penetration operations. Apple is also at risk because the vast majority of its products are manufactured in China, including a large facility in Zhengzhou that was shut by a COVID lockdown.[4] American tech companies have continued to pretend that cloud computing—in which companies such as Microsoft, IBM, and Amazon Web Services manage a client company's IT systems, data, and software—is some sort of cybersecurity panacea. Yet cloud computing is far from impenetrable.

The U.S. government, for its part, has been slow, poorly organized, and at times outright naive. President Obama made an agreement with President Xi not to conduct cyber intrusions into U.S. commercial networks. But Xi soon violated that agreement. Obama was naive to trust him. The Trump administration believed in "naming and shaming," holding press conferences to reveal pictures of suspected Chinese hackers. The assumption was that going public with the information would somehow change Chinese behavior. That was naive as well. And under the Biden administration, officials have identified Russian criminal ransomware groups and appealed to the Russian government to act against them. That is also naive—the Russian government recently shut down one, but on balance it *wants* ransomware groups to disrupt American infrastructure.

Simply put, the American government has not yet organized itself for the internet era. "The digital environment around us has changed so dramatically in the last 25 years, while our government hasn't kept up," former director of the Cybersecurity and Infrastructure Security Agency Chris Krebs told a conference in August 2022. "It's time to rethink the way government interacts with technology."

Individual Americans are also part of the problem. They continue to click on phishing emails, allowing attackers to enter their personal computers and their companies' networks. They have intermingled corporate and personal devices, increasing security risks for their companies—particularly in the COVID-induced era of more widely distributed workforces. They have flocked to Zoom and TikTok even though those applications were written in China, and the data they generate is, by law, accessible to China's authoritarian party-state. In addition, most Americans have not sufficiently educated themselves about the power of their data. "If you allow another country to gain access to really critical data about your society, over time that will erode your sovereignty," says Richard Moore, the head of Britain's highly secretive intelligence agency, MI6.[5]

So far, the discussion about all these issues has just been the experts talking to other experts, but we aim in this book to explain the issues in language every reader can understand. It has been nearly impossible for Americans and our allies to put these issues in context, partly because cyber threats are largely invisible to the public. People cannot see the attacks, and companies are reluctant to report them. We've had Americans ask us, "Is all this really hurting us?" Our answer is emphatically yes. The very foundations of our democracy and national security are being eroded.

What is the way forward? In the second half of this book, we will attempt to help Americans chart a path out of this digital morass.

The United States has never found itself in a confrontation like the one it faces today. In our entire history, we have never before simultaneously competed against adversaries like China, a technologically advanced power of 1.4 billion people, and Russia, a nuclear-armed regime bent on combining eighteenth-century geopolitics with the weapons of modern warfare. The Chinese government has operationalized a conflict and cooperation pattern that we have never before witnessed. "The supreme art of war," Sun Tzu wrote in his famous book *The Art of War*, "is to defeat the enemy without fighting." Because they have such a long history, consisting of five thousand years of written history, the Chinese are masters of subtle, long-term conflict. Russia, as well as North Korea and Iran, is part of the autocratic alliance of convenience, with China as the driving force. Cyberspace, our adversaries have come to recognize, is at the center of this struggle.

What this means is that we and our allies have to shift our thinking in truly historic ways. We must galvanize ourselves to respond. Many Americans have believed that our values and democratic ideals are universal and that it was only a matter of time before the peoples of China, Russia, and other autocratic states recognized that. We believed that the internet would, by definition, expand freedom in China. Millions of Chinese did seem to enjoy the freedoms they won throughout the decades following their opening to the world in 1979. But under President Xi, they have been forced to conform to his rigidly Marxist, nationalistic vision of the future. He has imposed Communist Party control over almost every aspect of life in China, creating the world's first digital dictatorship and installing himself as emperor for life.

We will say some things that may seem radical—for instance, in the face of pervasive threats, we need to expand the internet and our information ecosystem, rather than seeking to retreat from open engagement with the world. There are some signs that the internet is becoming the "splinternet," with Russia and China both building their own digital walls.[6] That's bad for the good guys. We must find ways to better protect our internet and the computing and communications platforms it supports rather than seeking to shutter them from the world—an incredibly difficult balancing act.

Corporate leaders also need to rethink their traditional notions of globalization, where they have historically borne no responsibility for U.S. national security or technological strength. Entire generations of CEOs have fervently believed that they were stateless and owed no responsibility to the preservation of U.S. national security or its democracy. Their sole responsibility has been to seek to increase their earnings each quarter, as University of Chicago economist Milton Friedman prophesized and celebrated by President Ronald Reagan. The profit motive is one of the most powerful engines of the American system, but it may have to be moderated or rechanneled. That alone is a huge ideological and political fight, with obvious consequences for the markets and the economy. But geopolitics is clearly colliding with business interests—look no further than the Chinese government's threats to launch military action when House Speaker Nancy Pelosi visited Taiwan in August 2022 and then sending live ballistic missiles over the island, some landing in waters claimed by Japan. That had to send chills down the spine of any CEO doing business in or with China.

America's social media giants—the likes of YouTube, Facebook, Twitter, LinkedIn, and others—also must become part of the solution, not part of the problem. They are making billions of dollars from their platforms that our adversaries have effectively hijacked to our national detriment. We agree with Emily de La Bruyère, a fast-rising China analyst who produced a report for the National Bureau of Asia Research called "A New Type of Geopolitical Power: China's Competitive Strategy for the Digital Revolution," published in March 2022. "We live in a world of absolutely inter-tangled markets," she told us. "The entire U.S. private sector is exposed to China in some way, shape or form, whether they depend on Beijing for production or depend on it for markets or both. If the United States is going to compete, it's going to need a strong, more patriotic tech sector to lead the process."

We do not argue that it is necessary to "decouple" from China, because the two economies have essentially been integrated. It is impossible to put the genie back in the bottle. We think a better goal is to "rebalance," meaning easing our dependence on manufacturing in China and easing our dependence on the Chinese market so that American companies and institutions can maintain critical distance from Beijing and cease being platforms that the Communist Party seeks to exploit.

We have to push for stronger cooperation among our European and Asian allies who are strong in technological fields, the so-called techno-democracies. We need a collective strategy to safeguard our technological advantages, particularly in the semiconductor industry, while seeking to minimize China's digital intrusions and technology theft. If we cannot make progress in that direction, we will be picked apart. The Chinese are masters at playing one nation-state against another.

We need to learn from the Europeans, who have enacted privacy and antitrust laws and established models for how large internet-based platforms should be managed. Some countries also are enacting laws that allow authorities to examine the algorithms that social media giants have created. We also need to rethink how we write software and how we configure the architecture of our computing systems.

For its part, the U.S. government has made some progress by appointing a national cyber director for the first time and is seeking to statutorily require companies to report cyber intrusions. The creation of the Cybersecurity and Infrastructure Security Agency (CISA) within the Department of Homeland Security was also a positive step, but much more work remains to be done. The government has not yet created a full-fledged, integrated approach to cybersecurity challenges. To this end, a Department of Digital Services must be established at the cabinet level. Just as the 9/11 attacks spurred creation of the Department of Homeland Security, the development of the internet and associated systems is an epochal event that demands a similar response. In general, government agencies must work better together rather than compete with one another. We have not yet established mechanisms that would allow the military, the intelligence community, homeland security officials, and law enforcement agencies such as the Federal Bureau of Investigation to rapidly and fully share cyber threat information with each other, much less share it with the civilian sector. We have not yet established sufficient coordination between the government and the private-sector companies that own and control much of the nation's critical infrastructure, such as electricity grids, banking systems, food distribution systems, and the like. We also have to overcome persistent gaps in trust between the military and the civilian sector.

Elsewhere, we need our universities to generate the best ideas and the necessary skill sets to prevail in this competition rather than simply accepting tuition money from hundreds of thousands of Chinese students. We need a stand-alone Cyber Force modeled on the Coast Guard, with a reserve component available to state governors that can coordinate cyber assistance for both federal agencies and state governments. And we need changes to the international legal framework governing cyber warfare.

It has now become a cliché to argue that a "whole of government" or "whole of society" response is necessary to respond to this crisis, but that concept has never been more important. It will take many years and billions of dollars to even begin to secure our IT systems and prevent the slow rot that is destroying America. We wish to educate Americans about what has happened and inspire them to seek solutions.

We need all hands on deck.

PART I

WE ARE AT WAR

CHAPTER I

Cyber Warfare

The Enemy inside the Gates

ONE OF THE FIRST IDENTIFIABLE ACTS OF CYBER WARFARE BY A NATION was executed by the United States and Israel. In 2010, the Stuxnet worm attacked a computer network at the Iranian nuclear enrichment facility at Natanz—a windswept desert town two hundred miles south of Tehran. A fully digital assault launched from half a world away caused significant damage to the facility and temporarily halted Iran's nuclear weapons program. In the end, Stuxnet resulted in the total loss of nearly a third of the six thousand centrifuges then in operation at Natanz.

The hallmark of the Stuxnet attack was the method by which the worm was able to penetrate the network, which was not connected to the internet, and covertly strike its target with exacting precision. Centrifuges inside a nuclear enrichment facility spin at extremely precise speeds—between seventy and one hundred thousand revolutions per minute—and for extremely specific periods of time. Any alteration in speeds or durations can cause these precision instruments to burn out, resulting in unusable fissile material. This is not something that can be monitored and maintained by humans, which is why the centrifuges are controlled by computers. At Natanz, these systems—called programmable logic controllers—used computers running Microsoft Windows–based operating systems and software made by Siemens, the German industrial giant.

Importantly, the Iranian systems were not connected to the internet—or any outside network. To compromise this isolated network,

American and Israeli intelligence agencies targeted the software supply chain that provided updates to these systems. This is an important concept and bears some explanation, as this early software supply-chain attack was a harbinger of the tactics used in modern cyber warfare. When software companies issue their software, it is rarely perfect. Because software developers often "borrow" code from multiple publicly available online repositories, when the final program—possibly consisting of millions of lines of code—is issued commercially, it will frequently contain vulnerabilities. The software companies must periodically issue updates, called patches, to their software as vulnerabilities are discovered or as new threats are identified. Software developers also issue updates when they feel they have made improvements. Once developed, these patches are then signed by the manufacturer using unique certificates for authentication and delivered to customers.

The first victory for Stuxnet's creators was to compromise the certificate authority used by the targeted software developer. Certificate authorities are critical to the functioning of the internet because they manage and issue the digital certificates required to encrypt and authenticate communications. These certificates are small packets of data that contain the identity credentials necessary for authenticating users, websites, and manufacturers online. By compromising a certificate authority, cyber actors are able to masquerade as a software manufacturer and deliver malware packaged as legitimate software. This is the digital equivalent of lacing Tylenol with cyanide, replacing the tinfoil safety seal on the bottles, and placing them back on the drugstore shelf. In other words, the recipient of such a software package would inherently trust the code because it had signed certificates.

But the Stuxnet creators went further. Stuxnet relied on a "zero-day" exploit to compromise the network—meaning there was no known fix for the vulnerabilities it targeted. The people who defend computer systems constantly scan their networks looking for unauthorized or malicious software, or malware. But zero-day exploits defeat these scans because the software that network defenders use to identify and block malware does not recognize the exploit as a malicious program. In other words, because Stuxnet was brand new, there was no way for an Iranian network defender to identify it as malicious. This zero-day was covertly inserted into a legitimate software update before being saved to a thumb drive and delivered to the Natanz facility.

At no point as the worm was snaking its way through the Iranian network during the initial compromise was it discovered. According to one report, Stuxnet even programmed the centrifuges to communicate to the operators that they were functioning smoothly. Only when the Stuxnet operators ramped up their operation and significantly altered the speeds, causing the centrifuges to fail at an alarming rate did the technicians and International Atomic Energy Agency inspectors suspect foul play. In terms of damage, this covert operation—which likely constituted an act of war under international law—set the Iranian nuclear weapons program back at least two years.[1]

Fast-forward.

In late June 2017, cyber actors working for the Russian government unleashed upon the world the most destructive cyberattack in history.[2] Initially taking aim at targets inside Ukraine, the malware rapidly became a global digital pandemic.[3] The goal of this attack was to inflict significant damage on Ukrainian computer systems on the eve of Ukraine's Constitution Day, which commemorates the establishment of a democratic Ukraine free from Moscow's rule.[4] Combining multiple potent cyber weapons—including an open-source tool that steals usernames and passwords, ransomware that both renders the victim's system inaccessible and infects connected devices, and a highly sophisticated zero-day exploit stolen from the National Security Agency (NSA)—the Russian malware, dubbed "NotPetya," rapidly spread worldwide.[5] Neither recognizing geographic borders nor distinguishing between government and civilian targets, NotPetya brought the country of Ukraine and some of the largest companies in global commerce to a standstill.[6] Like Stuxnet, NotPetya began with a compromise of the software supply chain.

On the outskirts of Ukraine is a small software company called Linkos Group, which develops and maintains a tax software called M.E.Docs. M.E.Docs is similar to the American accounting software tool TurboTax. Everyone who does business in Ukraine uses M.E.Docs to file their taxes. Amid the ongoing crisis in Ukraine, Russian military hackers compromised Linkos Group's update servers and installed backdoors into thousands of computers that had M.E.Docs installed. Through this backdoor, the Russians deployed NotPetya, which quickly spread worldwide, encrypting data and destroying computers with an ultimate result of more than $10 billion in damages.

Fast-forward again.

In the spring of 2020, U.S. software developer SolarWinds issued an update for its Orion software to more than eighteen thousand of its customers. Orion is a network-monitoring tool that allows IT departments to look on one screen and monitor activity across their whole network. It provides unfettered access and visibility to the entire system. However, this update had been modified by Russian hackers to compromise the Orion platform loaded onto the affected systems. Similar to Stuxnet, the compromise occurred *before* SolarWinds signed the digital certificates for the Orion software. Thus, when SolarWinds issued its update containing the malicious code, the recipients inherently trusted the update.

As a result, cyber actors assigned to Russia's foreign intelligence service, or SVR, obtained access to the networks of thousands of Solar-Winds' customers, including Microsoft, Intel, and Cisco, as well as the U.S. Departments of Defense, Treasury, Justice, and Energy. For nine months, Russian hackers were able to comb through these networks, likely establishing a permanent presence and potentially modifying other software destined for critical infrastructure and military weapon systems. To this day, no one knows the full extent of the compromise or the damage to national security. One likely goal of this supply-chain attack was to establish persistent access to critical infrastructure for future cyberattacks.[7]

There are myriad examples of cyber operations that could constitute cyber warfare. For instance, partly in response to Stuxnet, Iran targeted the U.S. financial sector multiple times from 2011 to 2013 using distributed denial-of-service (DDoS) attacks. DDoS attacks involve victims' servers being targeted with such high volumes of traffic from so many "distributed" computers that the servers crash. North Korea offers another example. In response to the impending release of the comedy film *The Interview* in 2017, North Korean hackers attacked Sony Pictures to prevent the film's showing and caused millions of dollars in physical and reputational damage in the process. These examples form the traditional notion of cyber warfare—stand-alone cyberattacks by one nation-state against another nation-state as a tool of geopolitics.

Software supply-chain attacks are something different. In addition to being far more potent—as evidenced by SolarWinds and NotPetya—this type of attack is designed to look like espionage or criminal activity. This serves the dual purpose of creating access for future destructive cyber-attacks as well as injecting ambiguity into the legal analysis of victims. While targeting a nuclear enrichment facility or an electric grid with a destructive attack may be an act of war, merely accessing a network to steal data is not.

Russia and China have evolved their cyber warfare capabilities to be executed almost exclusively in the digital gray zone of international law—the area where traditional rules and principles do not apply clearly. By conducting operations below the level of armed conflict, China and Russia brush against the boundary of international law without clearly breaking it. Victim states may fail to respond because they fear that any countermeasures or use of force in self-defense might itself be viewed as a violation. It is in this zone that the vast majority of cyber conflicts now occur, precisely because it prevents an effective response.

That is, until a conflict goes *hot* and the access achieved through gray-zone activities is used to launch attacks that shut down systems critical to national security.

This is the new face of cyber warfare.

RUSSIA

In 2013, General Valery Gerasimov, chief of the Russian General Staff, published an article in a little-known Russian trade paper that went on to serve as the basis for the doctrine that bears his name. The Gerasimov doctrine describes Russia's particular brand of warfare: a hybrid model that combines statecraft, spy craft, cyberspace operations, and covert military action to asymmetrically advance the goals of the Russian government. To Russia, these activities fall on a spectrum—on the left is propaganda, followed by fake news, publication of stolen documents, and manipulated election results, with damage or destruction of physical infrastructure on the far right.

Russia's military and intelligence services conduct complementary operations across this spectrum to achieve a single goal: to undermine the internal affairs of and sow fear in their targets. For example, in 2015, as part of Russia's ongoing open conflict in Ukraine, Russian cyber actors penetrated the networks of three Ukrainian energy distribution companies and disrupted the power supply for 225,000 customers. David Sanger, chief Washington correspondent for the *New York Times*, described Russia's cyber operations in Ukraine in his 2020 book *The Perfect Weapon*: "This attack was about sending a message and sowing fear. . . . [It] demonstrated in the cyber realm what the Russians had already demonstrated in the physical world[:] they could get away with a lot, as long as they used subtle, short of war tactics." Sanger continued: "What happened in Ukraine confirmed the corollary to the Gerasimov doctrine: As long as cyber-induced paralysis was hard to see, and left little blood, it was difficult for any country to muster a robust response."[8]

Firing at the heart of Ukraine's critical infrastructure, Russian cyber actors deployed the destructive malware BlackEnergy, KillDisk, and Industroyer against companies in Ukraine's energy sector, its Ministry of Finance, and the State Treasury Service. But Russia's premier destructive cyber operations team that targeted Ukraine's power grid and election system did not limit its operations to within the borders of Ukraine. Self-styled after the colossal wormlike creatures in Frank Herbert's *Dune* novels, the elite Russian military intelligence cyber team, dubbed "Sandworm," has executed a campaign of malicious cyber activities targeting the Hillary Clinton presidential campaign (hack and leak), the country of Georgia (defacement of fifteen thousand websites), France's elections (interference and malign influence), and the 2018 Winter Olympics (hack on Olympic IT infrastructure).[9]

More recently, in the hours before Russian forces launched their invasion of Ukraine in February 2022, Russia's military intelligence agency, or GRU, launched a cyberattack that took down Ukraine's satellite communications in an attempt to sever the country's ability to control its armed forces.[10] While the U.S. and European governments reported the attack without attributing it to any specific actor, other sources told the *New York Times* that responsibility lay with the GRU. The malware used in the attack, known as AcidRain, is a tool previously associated with Russian military intelligence and has been used to great effect. In this instance, Russian hackers exploited the land-based modems maintained by the California satellite company ViaSat, which operates satellite-based internet in parts of Ukraine. While the attack did not spill over to American targets, it nonetheless frightened American defense strategists, because it suggests what the Russians could do to communications systems inside the United States.

Outside of strictly government actors, Russia also incorporates its criminal enterprises into its strategic cyber warfare campaigns. Some of the most notorious hacking groups in the world are criminal organizations that have connections with Russia's three intelligence agencies—albeit while maintaining a certain degree of autonomy (and plausible deniability for the Kremlin). On the whole, Russian hackers are far more prolific than those from any other nation. In 2021, 58 percent of cyberattacks worldwide—at least the ones that can be seen—originated in Russia. Further, the vast majority of ransomware attacks originate in Russia or former Soviet republics.

To understand how Russia employs its cyber underworld, it is helpful to draw an analogy. In the sixteenth century, England and France issued letters of "marque and reprisal" to enterprising private sea captains as a way to augment their nations' foundering navies in the face of a much better resourced and equipped Spanish fleet. Letters of marque were the legal mechanism authorizing private vessels to target and capture ships of a named foreign country. Letters of reprisal authorized those private vessels to take the captured ships back home for a reward. Combined, letters of marque and reprisal converted pirate vessels into naval auxiliaries, authorized to engage in acts of war on behalf of the sponsoring country.

While Spain plundered immeasurable wealth from the New World, English, Dutch, and French privateers attacked Spanish ships transporting treasure back to Spain from the Americas. By the end of the seventeenth century, Spain was no longer an unrivaled sea power. England and France developed world-class navies while Spain battled privateers.

Though privateering on the high seas was largely abolished by international law in the mid-nineteenth century, cyberspace bears no such prohibition. Cyberspace offers America's adversaries the ability to destabilize and inflict significant economic and sociopolitical damage on the United States with few repercussions, because international law has not evolved sufficiently to address this modality of combat.

Despite both sanctions by the U.S. government and public attribution by the United Kingdom, Canada, New Zealand, and Australia, malicious cyber activities conducted by actors both tightly and loosely affiliated with the Russian government have continued unabated. While individual operations executed by Russian cyber forces or proxies may be strategically framed to stop short of an "act of aggression," "use of force," or "armed attack" under international law, the consequences of the totality of Russia's cyber campaigns have had far-reaching effects on the peace and security of the international community. Russia's continuous and concerted campaign has undermined the political institutions of global democratic states, created societal discord, and interfered with the governmental functions of other nations.

Like the United States, global victims of such cyber-enabled malicious activities have struggled to identify an effective extraterritorial response using existing rubrics of international law. While these low-intensity cyber operations may be in violation of a victim state's domestic laws—and may violate the traditional rule of state sovereignty—they do not inherently violate international law. This is the primary challenge to waging effective cyber warfare: The United States struggles to effectively defend itself and deter adversary aggression without itself violating international law. And this is precisely the gap America's adversaries are exploiting.

CHINA

During the past decade, China has developed a particularly sophisticated digital footprint. This is a direct result of President Xi Jinping's methodical reorganization of the country's military and intelligence cyber forces to support his ambitions. Beginning in 2012, Xi began reducing the size of China's land army—a huge force China has for decades held out to the world as a strategic deterrent. In the process, China established within the People's Liberation Army a new Strategic Support Force, which focuses on cyber, space, and electronic warfare. "This reorganization has accelerated a shift in military posture from land-based territorial protection to extended power projection, with joint forces and technology as key enablers," Winnona DeSombre, a research fellow at the Atlantic Council, testified before the U.S.–China Economic and Security Review Commission in February 2022. "The CCP [Chinese Communist Party] believes that the U.S. is more vulnerable in cyberspace, and that they can develop asymmetric capabilities that would give them a distinct wartime advantage."[11]

Before Xi consolidated power in 2012 and 2013, the Chinese were not particularly skilled at penetrating the world's communications and computing infrastructure. "Back in the early 2000s, their hackers were so noisy. They were so loud," Mandiant principal analyst Scott Henderson told us. "Their footprint was just massive. We could see them recycling aliases that had been exposed in previous operations to register new operational infrastructure. They would list their cities. They had no recognition that they should be avoiding attribution." Attribution is the word used to describe how cybersecurity firms such as Mandiant or government agencies seek to make a positive identification of hacking groups. Now after years of effort, Henderson adds, "the Chinese have become masters of the game."[12]

While many policy papers refer to China as a "near-peer" competitor in terms of military capabilities, China's sprint in cyberspace has raised its capabilities to be on par with the United States. "The country's offensive cyber capabilities rival or exceed those of the United States, and its cyber defensive capabilities are able to detect many U.S. operations—in some cases turning our own tools against us," DeSombre testified. Moreover, Chinese cyber actors are not constrained by the many self-imposed restrictions the United States and other Western nations place on their cyber operations. Where the U.S. intelligence community is prohibited from using its considerable collection capabilities to steal intellectual property and economic data for the benefit of U.S. companies, the Chinese government openly encourages and rewards such activities. The

U.S. Department of Defense sees the fruits of China's efforts in the near carbon copies of U.S. defense technologies being fielded by the Chinese military, as we will describe in chapter 8. "I like to think of this as being part of the historical cycles of war," Henderson's fellow principal analyst, Cristiana Kittner, told us. "A lot of the activity we see is traditional espionage, but it's conducted over the internet. It's not unprecedented intelligence gathering. It's just a different means of getting it."[13]

China also rewards the front-end development of cyber weapons. For instance, each year, the Chinese government hosts a series of hack-a-thons—competitions wherein hackers use tools they have developed to exploit unknown vulnerabilities in networks for cash prizes. But instead of reporting these vulnerabilities to the software developers to fix them, the Chinese government stockpiles the newly acquired cyber weapons for use by its cyber actors against the world. Though these weapons have not yet been used in destructive cyberattacks, the U.S. intelligence community assesses that China "possesses substantial cyber-attack capabilities . . . [and] can launch cyberattacks that, at a minimum, can cause localized, temporary disruption to critical infrastructure within the United States."[14]

In general, the visible way that nation-states attack one another is through sophisticated hacking groups identified by the cybersecurity industry as advanced persistent threats (APTs). But the connections between APTs and their government sponsors are rarely clear cut. In China's case, most of the identified APTs are affiliated either with the Ministry of State Security (MSS), which is China's equivalent of the U.S. Central Intelligence Agency, or with the Strategic Support Force within the People's Liberation Army. In 2021, Mandiant was tracking thirty-six of these individual Chinese entities conducting cyber operations worldwide. But the number of Chinese APTs likely far exceeds Mandiant's count.

This is due to the nature of China's cyber activities. Though China employs a significant number of hackers throughout its military and intelligence services, it also leverages contractors with more tenuous ties to the state. According to Mandiant, many more of the recently established Chinese assailants appear to be hybrids—hackers who work on one set of targets on behalf of the Chinese government during business hours but then at night use their tools to target others, seeking personal financial gain. This creates challenges for victims because these actors, like the ransomware groups supporting the Russian government, inject further ambiguity, thus slowing down the ability of a victim to respond.

China's cyber operations have become so sophisticated that in some cases its hackers are able to maintain access to a network for years. For instance, an advanced piece of malware called Daxin gave Chinese hackers a backdoor into government networks throughout the world for more than a decade before it was identified in 2022 by the cybersecurity firm Symantec. "The newly discovered malware is no one-off," the *MIT Technology Review* concluded. "It's yet another sign that a decade-long quest to become a cyber superpower is paying off for China. While Beijing's hackers were once known for simple smash-and-grab operations, the country is now among the best in the world thanks to a strategy of tightened control, big spending, and an infrastructure for feeding hacking tools to the government that is unlike anything else in the world."[15]

Chinese efforts to swamp U.S. systems have been obvious. In September 2020, the U.S. Cybersecurity and Infrastructure Security Agency (CISA) and the Federal Bureau of Investigation (FBI) revealed that China's MSS was engaged in a massive operation on U.S. soil. The ministry took advantage of the fact that a unit of the Department of Commerce called the National Institute of Standards and Technologies (NIST) routinely publishes an openly available list of thousands of "known vulnerabilities" in U.S. software systems. NIST's goal is to encourage companies and government agencies to fix the vulnerabilities by applying patches. However, even under the best of circumstances, those patches take time and human resources to install. As a result, too many companies and agencies are slow to implement them—or do not implement them at all. The end result was that the MSS took advantage of information disclosed by the U.S. government to identify and compromise countless American computing systems.

These threats notwithstanding, the United States continues to have one key advantage over China in cyberspace. This is due in large part to the early innovation and investments made by American companies in the nearly endless miles of the fiber-optic backbone. The internet, the most commonly used electronic devices, and the most frequently accessed web search engines all ride on those fibers. However, the Chinese Communist Party is well aware of these shortcomings and is investing heavily to overtake America's digital hegemony. As a result, Chinese cyber actors have zeroed their laser focus on companies in the U.S. technology and innovation base. All of China's actions in cyberspace point to the strategic goal of establishing China as the sole global superpower—militarily, economically, and ideologically.

LOOKING INWARD

In 2018, secretary of defense and retired four-star Marine Corps general James Mattis signed his name to the Department of Defense Cyber Strategy. This document outlined the "Defend Forward" strategy that has come to define how the Department of Defense executes cyber operations in defense of the homeland. In the publicly released summary of the strategy, the Defense Department emphatically states, "We will defend forward to disrupt or halt malicious cyber activity at its source, including activity that falls below the level of armed conflict . . . by leveraging our focus outward to stop threats before they reach their targets."[16] In other words, since 2018, the United States has been on a war footing in cyberspace.

The 2018 strategy "set an important tone stressing just how serious these threats have become," said U.S. Army general Paul Nakasone, the dual-hatted commander of U.S. Cyber Command and director of the National Security Agency. "It acknowledged that defending the United States in cyberspace requires executing operations outside the U.S. military's networks."[17]

In response to this bold strategy, U.S. Cyber Command began executing a much wider array of cyber operations. These operations included offensive cyber operations designed to disrupt and degrade adversary networks under new authorities granted by President Trump in a now hotly debated national security presidential memorandum, or NSPM, as well as less controversial—but far more impactful—defensive cyberspace operations executed worldwide.

The latter form of cyber operations goes by the apt moniker "Hunt Forward Operations," wherein teams of military defensive cyber operations specialists deploy to foreign nations to harden their networks against penetration by adversaries. In other words, teams of U.S. network defenders are given unfettered access by a host nation to their government networks known to be compromised by nation-state actors to root out their tools, backdoors, and malicious programs. This includes hunting for active intrusions by adversary cyber actors or other indicators of compromise, as well as applying patches and updates to software and operating systems running on the host network. "The objective of the Hunt Forward Operations is to observe and identify malicious activity that threatens both nations and use those insights to bolster homeland defense and increase the resiliency of critical networks to shared cyber threats," the U.S. Cyber Command public affairs office said in an official statement.[18]

The end result of Hunt Forward Operations is both operational and strategic. During and after Hunt Forward Operations are conducted abroad, U.S. Cyber Command publishes malware developed and used by adversary hackers to public repositories, such as VirusTotal.com, wherein the diaspora of antivirus companies worldwide can access the data to create defenses for their customers. This effectively renders America's adversaries' most potent cyber weapons inert before they can be used to target U.S. networks. "For us, it isn't just about hunting on our partner's networks for similar threats to our networks and then bringing that back home to defend our nation's networks," said a hunt-forward team leader, whose name is withheld for security reasons. "It was also about the personal relationships we built, and the partnership we can grow."[19] The strategic impact of these operations is that they send the clear message that the United States will not permit its adversaries to have freedom of movement in the networks of sovereign nations in their near-abroad.

These operations began in 2018 shortly after the publication of the Defense Cyber Strategy and ahead of the 2018 U.S. midterm elections. As of August 2022, U.S. Cyber Command had conducted thirty Hunt Forward Operations across the globe in 16 countries, including Estonia, Lithuania, Montenegro, North Macedonia, and Ukraine.[20] Importantly,

Hunt Forward Operations function as both an effective tool to bolster domestic cyber defense as well as a bulwark against adversaries targeting America's allies. In the battle for hearts and minds, a pound of sugar goes much further than a pinch of salt.

But while U.S. Cyber Command is notching victories abroad, America's domestic cyberspace continues to face an uphill battle. The primary challenge in the federal government's ability to protect American systems is the legal lines of demarcation that separate domestic space from foreign space. For example, the NSA, with its incredible signals intelligence and cyber collection capabilities, is not legally permitted to collect information on citizens of the United States. For the NSA to turn its considerable capabilities inward, it must do so pursuant to a warrant issued by a special court in accordance with the Foreign Intelligence Surveillance Act, more widely known by its acronym, FISA. The CIA is governed by the same restrictions. For the FBI to collect information domestically, it generally does so pursuant to a warrant or subpoena consistent with its law enforcement role, or with the consent of the network owner pursuant to the Wiretap Act. No warrant? No consent? No collection.

The Cybersecurity and Infrastructure Security Agency, or CISA, falls within the Department of Homeland Security and is designated as the lead agency for protecting U.S. critical infrastructure and federal government networks. But CISA lacks the authority to conduct offensive cyberspace operations or law enforcement functions beyond issuing administrative subpoenas. It is not yet empowered to hunt for threats beyond government networks. For other response actions, CISA must work hand in hand with the FBI, which serves as the lead for both federal law enforcement and counterintelligence work inside the United States, and U.S. Cyber Command, which is the lead military organization for cyberspace operations.

Attackers understand and regularly exploit these inherent gaps and institutional differences. When the SolarWinds compromise was revealed in 2020—at the same time that Microsoft's Exchange email service was being exploited by Chinese hackers—the attackers were able to escape scrutiny by the NSA because they launched their attacks from virtual servers located inside the United States. They actually took advantage of American law to protect themselves from scrutiny by the NSA or other U.S. government entities for long enough that they could carry out their attacks and then disappear by shutting down their operations and vanishing into the ether.

In a public congressional testimony, General Nakasone stressed that the SolarWinds hackers had taken advantage of the intelligence community's "blind spot"—internet activity that occurs in domestic cyberspace. "Our adversaries understand that they can come into the United States and rapidly utilize an Internet service provider, come up and do their activities, and then take that down before a warrant can be issued, before we can actually have surveillance by a civilian authority here in the United States," he told the Senate Armed Services Committee.[21]

To further compound the issues, most government agencies rely on private-sector networks for the entirety of their supply chains. But the lack of trust between the public and private sectors is such that companies resist efforts by government agencies to fully vet their cybersecurity posture or audit their networks to make sure no foreign entities are present.

The Department of Defense, for example, contracts with more than three hundred thousand American companies in its defense industrial base. There are multiple tiers of these contractors with many small and medium-sized companies making key components that larger contractors then assemble into more complete systems. Chinese entities, such as Unit 61398 of the People's Liberation Army—which we will discuss in detail later—are known to have penetrated the systems of smaller companies that do not employ sufficient numbers of IT personnel or buy the most secure systems.

The federal government is further hamstrung because each agency attempts to impose its own cyber rules on the industry it regulates. Glenn S. Gerstell, the former general counsel at the NSA, explained the problem in a *New York Times* essay in March 2022. "In just the past few months, the Department of Homeland Security's Transportation Security Agency (TSA) announced new cyber requirements for pipelines and railroads; the Securities and Exchange Commission voted on rules for investment advisers and funds; and the Federal Trade Commission threatened to legally pursue companies that fail to fix a newly detected software vulnerability found in many business applications. And on Capitol Hill, there are approximately 80 committees and subcommittees that claim jurisdiction over various aspects of cyber regulation." Then, in one of history's great understatements, he added, "These scattered efforts are unlikely to reduce, let alone stop," cyberattacks.[22]

The reason is that Chinese and Russian cyber actors are actively burrowing into the networks of U.S. federal agencies, corporations, and critical infrastructure and are gaining and maintaining persistent access for when it is needed most. Make no mistake, America's adversaries are fully engaged in a cyber war, and it is raging all around us.

Water and Oil

Weaponized Ransomware, Digital Proxies, and the Threat to Critical Infrastructure

ARRIVING EARLY TO THE OFFICE, THE NETWORK ADMINISTRATOR FOR A large U.S. corporation sets her bag down on a rarely used swivel chair and stands at her VariDesk. She taps the spacebar on her keyboard to wake the four black monitors staring back at her. An image of a blue sky with white, puffy clouds spreads across her screens.

She types the administrator username and password and takes a sip of coffee as she waits for her profile to load. But instead of loading, the screens return to black. Swallowing hard, she puts down her coffee and moves her cursor from one dark screen to the next. As she does, a pop-up window appears at the center of each screen, emblazoned with skull and crossbones and the crimson words: "YOUR FILES HAVE BEEN ENCRYPTED." Beneath those ominous words is a payment key and a clock—counting down to when the files will either be leaked to the world or lost forever. Helplessly, she tries to restart her computer. As she does, the phone on her desk begins to ring—the first of a deluge of calls from frantic employees seeing the same crimson pop-up on every screen across the network. *Her* network.

This nightmare scenario is playing out every single day across the globe. In recent years, ransomware has become one of the most prolific forms of cyberattack targeting U.S. and Western organizations. Ransomware is a type of malicious software—or "malware"—used to encrypt data on a computer or server with the intent of extracting payment from the victim in exchange for either the decryption key or a promise not to leak the data.[1]

Hackers operating in Russia are the most prolific. Despite Russian government overtures that it is cracking down on ransomware actors, as of 2021, 74 percent of all ransomware revenue ultimately went to accounts affiliated with Russia.[2] One of the most notorious Russian groups—Conti—is alone responsible for more than one thousand ransomware attacks against the networks of U.S. and international organizations.[3] And as the world braced for the Russian invasion of Ukraine in the winter of 2022, Conti publicly pledged its allegiance to the Kremlin. On February 25, the day after the invasion, the Conti ransomware group formally announced its support for the Russian government, issuing a dire warning: "If anybody will decide to organize a cyberattack or any war activities against Russia, we are going to use all our possible resources to strike back at the critical infrastructure of an enemy."[4]

In 2021, ransomware attacks increased by 105 percent from the previous year, totaling 623.3 million attacks worldwide.[5] That's an incredible number. But it is not only the Russians. In September 2019, the U.S. Department of the Treasury Office of Foreign Asset Control, known more commonly as OFAC, issued an advisory naming North Korea's Lazarus Group as responsible for the 2017 WannaCry ransomware attack that affected more than three hundred thousand computers in more than 150 countries.[6] Lazarus Group is an advanced persistent threat (APT) affiliated with North Korea's main spy agency, the Reconnaissance General Bureau.[7]

Moreover, since September 2020, Microsoft's Threat Intelligence Center—shortened to MSTIC and aptly pronounced "mystic"—has been tracking at least six Iranian APTs targeting Western organizations with ransomware to advance Iranian strategic objectives.[8] Notably, the Chinese are much less active in this sphere than they are in other cyber realms. While ransomware has been a method of attack for more than three decades, the evolution of ransomware-as-a-service and the wide adoption of cryptocurrencies have fueled the meteoric rise of this attack vector and the crippling effect it has had on private industry.

The United States has not yet been able to mount an effective defense against ransomware attacks, partly because the private sector and academic community are often reluctant to share details of attacks with government agencies that might possess the technical means to help them. One reason is that company executives and university leaders are leery of granting the FBI or the Department of Defense access to their networks out of fear of prosecution or discovery of contract fraud. Instead of partnering with the government to halt the attacks, the private sector has developed an entire industry of ransomware attack advisers, negotiators, and security experts to engage in "mitigation," backed up by lawyers and insurance companies. The prevailing strategy has been to transfer the cost of the attacks to the insurance industry, not halt the attacks altogether. The lack of effective cryptocurrency regulation has further enabled ransomware because that is the standard means of payment.

The Russians, in particular, have more than just money on their minds when they launch these attacks. The hacks are part and parcel of Moscow's strategy to degrade Americans' trust in their own institutions and their own society. "When these private entities (the hackers) act, the outcomes align suspiciously well with the Kremlin's objectives," Kiral Avramov, director of the Global (Dis)Information Lab at the University of Texas at Austin wrote. "The result is a proliferation of confusion and chaos [and] erosion of social trust."[9]

At its inception, ransomware appeared to be a flash in the pan. At a time when there were more inhabitants of the city of Providence, Rhode Island, than there were internet users worldwide, an AIDS researcher took hostage thousands of computers used by the global medical community.[10] The year was 1989. The number of AIDS cases in the United States had just reached one hundred thousand, and panic was beginning to take hold.[11] At thirty-nine years of age, Dr. Joseph L. Popp was a Harvard PhD whose doctorate in primatology and evolutionary biology suited well his studies of the origins of the AIDS virus.

However, for reasons that remain unclear, Dr. Popp decided that year to try his hand at another profession: cybercrime. Between December 8 and 12 of 1989, Popp packaged and mailed more than twenty thousand 5.25-inch floppy disks to delegates from more than ninety countries who had attended the 1988 World Congress on the AIDS Virus in Stockholm, Sweden. Labeling the disks "AIDS Information Introductory Diskette," Popp advertised his program to the recipients as a computer-based questionnaire to determine a person's likelihood of contracting AIDS as a consequence of a number of risk factors. While the questionnaire was real, laden in the file was a malicious executable program that Popp designed to lay dormant through eighty-nine restarts of the infected computer. On restart number ninety, a blood-red pop-up appeared on the screen alerting victims that their files had been encrypted. Though the attack did not affect the files themselves, it changed and encrypted the name of each file extension on the victim computer, preventing files from being opened.

Popp's digital ransom note demanded $189 for a one-year "lease" of the files or $378 for a permanent lease. To pay this nominal fee, victims were required to mail either a cashier's check or international money order to a post office box in Panama registered to "PC Cyborg Corporation." This rudimentary ransom scheme using the postal service proved too clumsy to yield Popp the riches he sought, and it did not take long for the nascent cybersecurity antivirus community to develop a decryption tool that rendered Popp's encryption schema ineffective. However, while the antivirus community scrambled to develop a fix, many victims panicked and preemptively wiped their hard drives, erasing decades of research into the AIDS virus.

The Computer Unit from Britain's famed Scotland Yard investigated the case for months with no leads. That is, until Popp's unruly behavior on a flight to Amsterdam spurred Dutch authorities to search his bags. In his luggage was a business logo sporting the name "PC Cyborg Corp." Shortly thereafter, Popp was taken into custody by the FBI at his family home in Ohio and ultimately was extradited to Britain. However, in 1991, he was deemed unfit to stand trial for his crime. Sporting a prophylactic over his nose, a box on his head, and hair curlers in his beard during questioning, the court doubted his mental stability.[12] In the end, the man regarded as the father of ransomware ultimately derived no benefit from nor faced any penalty for his crime. But this stunt set in motion the future use of far more advanced encryption as leverage to extort funds from victims using financial mechanisms unimaginable in the early 1990s.

Affecting nearly every industry, modern ransomware actors have come to indiscriminately target small and large organizations alike. Traditionally characterized by Western governments as nonstate criminal activity, ransomware poses an outsized risk to organizations in every sector. Most alarming from a national security perspective are potential threats against critical infrastructure. Private-sector companies are responsible for nearly everything Americans require in their everyday lives, as Jen Easterly, director of the Cybersecurity and Infrastructure Security Agency, told *60 Minutes*. "Everything that you do, hour by hour, is largely dependent in some way on the critical infrastructure," Easterly said. "How you get gas at the local pump, how you get food at the grocery store, how you get money from your ATM, how you get your power, how you get your water, how you communicate—all of that is our critical infrastructure. And that's what we're saying is at potential risk to a Russian malicious cyberattack."[13]

Easterly added in a post on LinkedIn: "This is not a problem we're going to 'solve'; rather it's a persistent challenge that requires all of us— across industry, state & local government, academia, non-profits, and the federal government—to work together for the collective cyber defense of the nation." Easterly is positioning her relatively new agency as the lead cybersecurity organization in the federal government and the focal point for coordinating the government's response to cyber threats to critical infrastructure.

But critical infrastructure is not the only sector at risk. From hospitals to higher education and from governments to individuals, ransomware groups exploit targets of opportunity to exert maximum pressure for maximum reward in the shortest amount of time. What began as a Harvard PhD individually packaging thousands of floppy disks and mailing them to unsuspecting AIDS researchers has exploded into a multibillion-dollar industry. Today, ransomware groups have corporate headquarters in Moscow skyscrapers, twenty-four-hour answering services, and even incentives and bonuses for top performers. To recruit top talent, ransomware groups pay top dollar. But who are these ransomware groups, and how do they operate? Strap in.

When we think of organized crime, it's natural for scenes from *The Godfather*, *The Sopranos*, or *The Irishman* to come to mind. In each of these fictionalized versions of the American mafia, there is a head of the family who runs his territory, while his lieutenants (usually relatives) carry out the family business. The intrigue of these stories focuses on feuding families, broken loyalties, and power. "Keep your friends close but your enemies closer," Michael Corleone famously quips in *The Godfather, Part II*. Unfortunately, the mafioso model our society has glamorized does not capture its digital counterpart. It is far more appropriate to liken these groups to ride-sharing apps like Uber than to the Corleone family.

Modern ransomware groups have taken to various models to maximize their profitability; however, the most common model—and most prolific—is ransomware-as-a-service, or "RaaS." This is what happens when the gig economy meets cybercrime. RaaS is a business model whereby digital organized crime groups provide tools and a platform to anyone seeking to conduct a ransomware attack in exchange for a fee or a percentage of the ransom.

Think of it like Uber. To drive for Uber, there are a few basic requirements: first, you need to have a car; you also need a license, registration, and insurance; and finally, you need the Uber app on your phone. That's it. Uber conducts a cursory screening of a driver's driving record to make sure you aren't a destruction derby enthusiast on I-95—but, for the most part, if you are a licensed driver with access to a vehicle, you can drive for Uber. You download the app, attach it to your bank account, and you're Ubering. Fire up the app, and the platform's map feature will direct you to nearby fares awaiting you to ferry them off to untold destinations.

For all of this, Uber takes a 25 percent commission from each fare as well as a small "booking fee" on the front end. For drivers, this is a fast and easy way to put their free time to use and earn money on the side, which is why the number of drivers has ballooned to more than 1 million Uber drivers in the United States alone.[14] And for Uber? In 2019, just before the COVID-19 pandemic sent the country into lockdown, Uber clocked in 6.9 billion trips worldwide and total revenue of $4.1 billion.[15]

As Uber has created steady income for millions of drivers, the gig model is also partially driving the recent surge in ransomware attacks. Like Uber, ransomware groups using a RaaS model offer a suite of easy-to-use services for hackers, such as access to malware and encryption tools, a platform for accepting payments, ransom negotiation specialists, and cryptocurrency tools. Much like Uber, ransomware groups value both efficiency and specialization across their organizations. Employees—those who work directly for the leadership of modern ransomware groups—are exceedingly rare. Far more numerous are individuals paid on an ad hoc basis, such as malware or encryption developers, penetration testers, and ransomware affiliates.

Ransomware affiliates are typically the actors who first compromise a company's networks. Experts refer to that process as the "first mile" of an attack. Affiliates are the Uber drivers of ransomware. These are hackers with varying degrees of skill who leverage RaaS platforms to attack organizations. A ransomware affiliate can theoretically be anyone from the kid next door to a Chinese spy. The only barrier to entry is the affiliate's ability to initially compromise a target network. In hacker-speak, RaaS gives "script kiddies" a seat at the table. Script kiddies, who are held in low regard by the hacker community, are unskilled hackers who use existing exploits to conduct an attack, often without understanding how the exploit itself works.

While the benefit of the RaaS model from the criminal perspective is that it allows relatively unsophisticated hackers to conduct devastating attacks, the sophistication required of an affiliate depends largely on the target. For instance, a script kiddie may be able to compromise a local school district through a generic phishing campaign, but this same tactic likely would be totally ineffective against a major financial institution like Goldman Sachs, which pours millions of dollars into network security each year. As a result, some RaaS groups are selective about the affiliates they permit to use their services to protect their brand—bigger targets yield greater exposure, which yields more demand for their services, which yields greater profits.

How do RaaS groups screen their affiliates? In this regard, digital organized criminal groups are a *bit* like Hollywood mafiosos. Where traditional criminal groups require that their members have "skin in the game"—generally by committing a crime—RaaS groups require their members to prove their bona fides by compromising a network of some importance. This recruitment process generally takes place on a number of different hacker forums hosted on the dark web.

What is the dark web? To understand the different layers of the internet, imagine for a moment that you are on an aerial tour of Manhattan. Out your window, you can see busy streets, hundreds of buildings, and thousands of people and cars moving about. You can pick out notable buildings and landmarks; you can see that there is an opening night on Broadway; you can even see an arrest in progress. What you are seeing from your window is the surface web. This is the internet as you know it. The World Wide Web that you use on a daily basis—that which is "Google-able"—comprises only about 10 percent of the information that is available on the total internet. The surface web is everything that is indexed and discoverable as publicly available information. When you type "liberty" into Google and get 1.1 billion results—everything from Liberty Mutual, to Liberty Cannabis, to images of the Statue of Liberty in New York—you are scouring the surface web.

But there is far more to Manhattan than what you can see by flying overhead. From the window of your helicopter, you can see each and every building, but no matter how hard you try, you cannot see what is happening inside. You can't see the floor of the New York Stock Exchange, the stage of the Apollo Theater, or inside the clinic at Sloan Kettering. To see these spaces, you need access badges or special tickets. This is the deep web. Unlike the surface web, the deep web is that which is not discoverable as publicly available information. The deep web houses your banking information, university library databases, health records, and much, much more. The deep web is information that is accessible through the internet but requires certain credentials to access. This information is not indexed by major search engines and will never (or should never) show up in a Google search.

Then there is the criminal underground. Flying high above, you can't see the clandestine activities occurring on the street. And even if you were at ground level, you wouldn't see the jeweler purchasing blood diamonds in a back room, or the drug trafficker distributing cocaine to his dealers in a basement, or the FBI agents on a stakeout in a florist van outside a high-rise. This is the dark web. The dark web consists of dark nets that sit on top of the accessible internet. To access the dark web, you need to have specific software and configurations on your computer, and you need to know where to look. Dark nets are either closed peer-to-peer exchanges for direct file sharing and social networking or anonymized proxy networks, such as the Onion Router—or Tor.

To surf the dark web, you need to download specialized software, such as the Tor browser, which is specifically designed to access the dark web and preserve the anonymity of its users. Tor was originally developed in the 1990s by the U.S. Navy as a means for intelligence officers to securely communicate with their clandestine assets online. However, since its inception, it has been used by intelligence agencies, political dissidents, journalists, and criminals the world over. Tor has been instrumental in social uprisings such as the Arab Spring in 2010 and as a means of sidestepping authoritarian censorship such as China's Great Firewall and Russia's surveillance laws.[16]

Tor works by routing web traffic through multiple computers and servers—known as "hop points"—and encrypting both the content and the metadata at each step along the way. Communications metadata is data about data—the information required to route communications traffic from one place to another. If I, Michael McLaughlin, am in Washington, DC, and communicating with my coauthor in New York via Tor, the information I send will go from my computer, through an encrypted tunnel, to a server in, say, Toronto. There, all information about where the communication came from before it hit that hop point will be encrypted. The communication will then be transmitted through another encrypted tunnel to a server in London, then Casablanca, then Marseilles, before finally reaching the ultimate destination in New York City. At no point along the way can anyone read the contents of the communication nor see where it has come from or where it is going other than along that segment of the journey. There is also no way of telling if any one hop point is the originator, the recipient, or just another stop along the way.

In 2002, the U.S. Navy released the code for the Tor network under a free and open software license to enable volunteers worldwide to serve as hop points. In 2004, the Electronic Frontier Foundation—an international nonprofit digital rights group based in San Francisco—took over funding for the project. And in 2006, the Tor Project established itself as a 501(c)(3) nonprofit organization.[17] Major donors contributing annually to the project include the *New York Times*, ProtonMail, and Duck-DuckGo.[18] Today there are more than 3 million users accessing the dark web through Tor across more than ten thousand volunteer hop points.[19]

So now you've installed the Tor browser. Unfortunately, that does not give you carte blanche access to the dark web, because it is not indexed or easily accessible through a search engine. To access sites on the dark web, you need to have the host name of the site you are trying to reach. Where, on the surface web, a domain name server (or DNS) will automatically translate "www.google.com" to its IP address ("8.8.8.8") to enable your computer to communicate with the Google server and whisk you off to the Google splash page, the dark web requires that you know the exact address. These addresses are alphanumeric values derived from the virtual handshake required to authenticate your secure communication. Dark web addresses use the .onion top-level domain (as opposed to the traditional top-level domains, such as .com, .org, or .edu) and are very complex, to make them difficult to find. For example, if you wanted to hire a hit man, Dark Mamba offers services at http://darktvh74jnxqjco.onion.[20] For more wholesome dark web adventures, BBC maintains a dark web mirror of its news service to provide access to its services in areas otherwise censored by authoritarian governments—such as China and Russia. The BBC's dark web site in Russian is https://www.bbcweb3hytmzhn5d532owbu6oqadra5z3ar726vq5kgwwn6aucdccrad.onion/russian.[21] Many RaaS groups prefer their privacy and seek to keep their forums hidden by frequently changing their host name.

Important to the ransomware ecosystem are both dark web forums and marketplaces. Throughout the dark web, there are forums tailored to specific topics that allow users to anonymously discuss diverse topics—typically related to illegal activities, such as drugs, child pornography, extremist content, hacking, and much more. Each forum has its own unique set of rules, but in general there are moderators—paid or well-established members—who preserve the sanctity of the forums and enforce the rules. Some forums are open only to those approved by the moderators or administrators. Typically, this requires some action on the part of the person requesting access—either to have a well-established member vouch for you or to provide some other credential, such as proof of ability to compromise a network of significance.[22] On forums, users exchange information about vulnerable networks or planned activities, hype their latest conquest, or offer cyber tools or compromised databases for sale.

Marketplaces, by contrast, exist as a platform specifically to buy and sell illicit goods. One notorious marketplace that garnered significant infamy before it was seized by the FBI was the Silk Road. Founded and operated by a twenty-something with a physics degree from the University of Texas, the Silk Road brought the buying and selling of illegal goods and services into the twenty-first century. Ross Ulbricht, known by the pseudonym "Dread Pirate Roberts"—a nod to the character in the 1987 cult classic *The Princess Bride*—built and operated one of the most successful dark web marketplaces of all time. When he was arrested in 2013 and charged with narcotics-trafficking conspiracy, computer-hacking conspiracy, and money-laundering conspiracy, his Silk Road website had garnered more than $1.2 billion in sales for narcotics and other illicit goods.[23] Dark web marketplaces such as the Silk Road offer a veritable bazaar of cyber tools such as exploit kits (tools used by penetration testers and red teams to assess vulnerabilities), ransomware, botnets (zombie computers used to flood a target with bogus traffic), crypters (tools to encrypt malware to fool antivirus software), binders (tools to trojanize legitimate software and lace it with malware), zero-day exploits, cryptocurrency tools, and more. Just about anything worth buying in the hacker's arsenal can be purchased on the dark web.

To get into a target company's systems, ransomware affiliates most frequently use spear phishing or social engineering to trick victims into clicking on a link or opening an attachment. This can be done through email, SMS text messaging, direct messaging through any social media platform, or even over the phone. Irrespective of the medium of communication, this vector of attack comprises some form of social engineering. Christopher Hadnagy, founder and CEO of Social-Engineer. com and author of the seminal book on the subject, *Social Engineering: The Art of Human Hacking*, defines social engineering as "the act of manipulating a person to take an action that may or may not be in the 'target's' best interest. This may include obtaining information, gaining access, or getting the target to take a certain action."

Aside from social engineering schemes, ransomware affiliates frequently exploit weaknesses in network authentication to gain initial access to a network. For instance, if your organization uses single-factor authentication (only username and password), and your users are permitted to create their own passwords, there is a good chance that at least one user will use his or her email address and that same password to sign up for newsletters, giveaways, or other third-party services. As soon as one of these third-party databases is compromised, thousands of usernames and passwords are immediately offered for sale on the dark web. With access to this trove of information, ransomware affiliates can triage the most lucrative targets for exploitation and simply log into a user's organizational accounts, search for a means by which they can elevate their privileges—meaning the level of control they have over the system—and completely compromise the entire network.

While there are dozens of similar tactics through which ransomware affiliates can gain initial access to your network, it is important to remember that your network defenders must be successful *every single time* to prevent compromise; a hacker only needs to be successful *once*. When a ransomware affiliate does gain a foothold in your network, they are generally patient and methodical. Distinct from the "smash-and-grab" tactics of some other criminal actors, modern RaaS affiliates are seeking to understand the type of data that is most important to an organization so that they can exert maximum pressure. Microsoft terms this threat "human-operated ransomware" to capture the meticulous decision-making process that goes into each stage of an attack.[24] According to Microsoft, "unlike the broad targeting and opportunistic approach of earlier ransomware infections, attackers behind these human-operated campaigns vary their attack patterns depending on their discoveries—for example, a security product that isn't configured to prevent tampering or a service that is running as a highly privileged account like a domain admin. Attackers can use those weaknesses to elevate their privileges to steal even more valuable data, leading to a bigger payout for them—with no guarantee they'll leave their target environment once they've been paid."[25]

The initial goal of a ransomware affiliate is to obtain administrative privileges to your network. More important than malware, the golden tickets for ransomware affiliates are administrative credentials. For a ransomware attack to be successful, an attacker must be able to access a domain admin-level account to effectively exfiltrate and encrypt all critical databases. Once this access is achieved—what hackers refer to as getting "root"—the RaaS affiliates generally have complete access to all network databases. At this point, the affiliate's role is complete upon exfiltration of critical data and deployment of the ransomware. And this is where the ransomware service comes in.

Once the ransomware payload is deployed on a victim network, the RaaS group notifies the victim. This is generally through a digital ransom note, either sent via email to the system administrator or executives of the target organization, or as a pop-up on affected devices. The notification informs the victim of the ransomware attack and provides a payment option, a deadline, and a means by which the organization can communicate with the RaaS group. One of the major distinguishing features of RaaS groups is that they handle all negotiations and payments on behalf of their affiliates. These negotiations occur through private messaging forums on the dark web for which many organizations hire professional ransomware negotiators or attorneys to engage with the ransomware group. During these negotiations, it is common for RaaS groups to provide a sample of the type of information that was stolen, such as internal emails, financial statements, trade secrets, or other proprietary information not otherwise available. Increasingly, if ransom demands are not met in a timely manner, RaaS groups also notify media outlets and publish samples of stolen data on social media or through their dark web sites. In a recent trend to apply additional pressure to victims, ransomware groups also replace the victim's public-facing website with an image of the ransomware note. The publicity ensures that targeted organizations are pressured to bring the matter to a speedy resolution.

RaaS groups take their reputations very seriously. These groups are constantly vying for talented affiliates and seeking to establish themselves as honest brokers. These goals are equally important to RaaS groups for one simple reason: branding. If a RaaS group gets a poor reputation among affiliates for charging too high a fee or for having low-quality customer service, the affiliates can easily choose from any number of other RaaS groups all competing for top talent among affiliates. Similarly, if a ransomware group gets a reputation for withholding decryption keys or publishing stolen data even after payment, future victims are far less likely to pay the ransom to restore their systems. In this regard, honor among thieves is at a premium.

Take the DarkSide group, for example. In May 2021, DarkSide targeted the Colonial Pipeline Corporation, which transports nearly 45 percent of the fuel consumed on the United States' eastern seaboard, and stole nearly one hundred gigabytes of data from Colonial's network.[26] The result of this attack was a complete shutdown of Colonial's 5,500 miles of pipeline for five days.[27] This shutdown resulted in "panic buying" of gasoline, causing shortages at more than one thousand fuel stations across America's Southeast.[28]

This single event cemented in America's collective psyche two things: first, that DarkSide is a major player in the ransomware game and is able to extort high-value targets, including critical infrastructure, and second, that if the ransom is paid, DarkSide will hold up its end of the bargain and release the data. In the end, Colonial paid $4.4 million in Bitcoin to DarkSide in exchange for the decryption key.[29]

Ransomware groups deal exclusively in cryptocurrencies, such as Bitcoin, for payments. Cryptocurrency is a digital medium of exchange that uses blockchain technology to enable financial transactions. While so-called "cyber currencies" and other electronic transaction mechanisms were established in the 1990s, modern cryptocurrencies using blockchain technology took hold shortly after the 2008 global financial crisis. Bitcoin was originally theorized as an alternative to centralized control of money. Shrouded in mystery, an individual known only by the pseudonym

Satoshi Nakamoto penned a white paper describing a public blockchain ledger as a means to exchange funds without using a centralized third party.[30] From this modest start, Bitcoin—and the trillion-dollar crypto-currency market—was born.

Bitcoin works like this. If you want to purchase this book online using Bitcoin, you first need to have a Bitcoin wallet. A Bitcoin wallet is a program on your computer or mobile device that generates a digital address from which and to which funds can be paid. In addition to this digital address, the wallet creates a private key and a signature that is unique to each transaction. Rather than "sending" funds in the traditional sense, Bitcoin works on a ledger system. When you agree to pay a seller for this book, funds are deducted from your Bitcoin wallet, and the corresponding amount is added to the seller's wallet—without going through an intermediary, such as a bank.

But this is no ordinary ledger; this ledger is comprised of every Bitcoin transaction worldwide and forms immutable links in a long chain of similar transactions, called a blockchain. In order for transactions to be added to the blockchain, they must be validated. This is how new Bitcoin is minted. Bitcoin miners race to have their computers solve a cryptographic hash—a difficult and irreversible math problem—to place your transaction on the blockchain. This takes up a considerable amount of memory and power, but miners are rewarded for each transaction they validate with new Bitcoin. Once your transaction is validated and the transaction is logged on the blockchain, the ledger reflects that the seller's wallet has now increased by the price of this book.

Importantly, the Bitcoin ledger is publicly available. This means that every transaction is subject to inspection. And though each transaction has a randomly generated signature, it is possible to determine the identity of a wallet owner through other investigative means. This was demonstrated when the FBI successfully obtained the private key to DarkSide's Bitcoin wallet following the Colonial Pipeline attack and returned $2.3 million in ransom payment to Colonial.[31]

As a result of the widespread adoption of Bitcoin and other digital currencies, coupled with technologically advanced money-laundering options, RaaS groups are not only able to execute ransomware attacks at scale but are able to reap the rewards of their misdeeds with relative ease. Because there is no centralized third-party entity managing transactions, very large sums can be exchanged worldwide both instantaneously and irreversibly. The importance of cryptocurrency's role in fueling the ransomware ecosystem and enabling it to explode into a multibillion-dollar industry cannot be overstated. Even though the cryptocurrency world has recently been rocked by financial losses, it still plays a pivotal role in ransomware.

While DarkSide's attack on Colonial Pipeline brought the impact of ransomware home for a lot of Americans, this pattern has since repeated itself several times across myriad sectors. For instance, shortly after Colonial paid the ransom to DarkSide, REvil, another Russia-based ransomware group, breached JBS Foods, the largest meat supplier in the world, forcing it to temporarily shut down operations in the United States, Australia, and Canada.[32] To decrypt its data, JBS paid the REvil group an $11 million ransom.[33] Shortly thereafter, in September 2021, NEW Cooperative, the Iowa-based grain co-op, suffered a cyberattack at the hands of the BlackMatter ransomware group.[34] Like the ransomware attacks against both Colonial Pipeline and JBS, NEW Cooperative was forced to take its systems offline, resulting in degradation of its operating system, in addition to business and reputational losses.[35] And in December 2021, Lincoln College in Illinois, named in honor of America's sixteenth president, was forced to permanently shutter its doors after 157 years when an Iranian ransomware attack left it financially insolvent.[36]

Ransomware attacks continue unabated and are increasingly targeting organizations in critical infrastructure sectors, supply chains, and academia. At this point, the economic incentives far outweigh any risk these groups run. Further, because the vast majority of ransomware groups are harbored by nations adverse to Western interests, there is little incentive for Russia, China, Iran, and North Korea to police these groups. As a result, the ransomware pandemic is likely to get worse before it gets better.

As Russian troops streamed across the border into northern Ukraine, nations throughout the world set in motion a series of unprecedented sanctions against both the Russian government and sectors critical to

Russia's military-industrial complex.[37] Sanctioned entities include significant portions of Russia's information technology (IT) sector, which is expected to decline by 39 percent this year.[38] Without access to Western software, hardware, and system updates, Russia's robust IT sector faces considerable challenges to both its innovative edge as well as its employment levels.[39] As sanctions deepen the internal economic crisis in Russia—particularly affecting cyber professionals in the IT sector—there exists the real risk of a coincidental surge in Russia-based ransomware activity.[40] The reduction in economic opportunities for highly skilled technology workers may actually incentivize these workers to engage instead in cybercrime targeting Western organizations and individuals.[41] In other words, the unintended consequence of heightened sanctions aimed at bringing the Kremlin to heel may be an even greater number of ransomware attacks targeting U.S. organizations.

To make matters worse, it is not the criminal actors alone who pose a threat to U.S. companies. On March 24, 2022, the U.S. Department of Justice unsealed an indictment charging an individual affiliated with the Russian government with executing a cyberattack against a Saudi Arabian oil refinery.[42] Using specially designed malware, Evgeny Viktorovich Gladkikh and unnamed coconspirators hacked into the Saudi refinery and compromised an engineering workstation.[43] On two separate occasions, Gladkikh and his coconspirators unsuccessfully attempted to gain control over the industrial control system to cause physical damage.[44] These systems are responsible for controlling the refinery's operations and ensuring the facility's safe functionality.[45] On both occasions, a safety override mechanism prevented the Russian actors from taking control, instead automatically triggering an emergency shutdown of the entire refinery, damaging equipment and halting the shipment of oil products.[46]

Following this indictment, on April 13, 2022, cybersecurity agencies from across the U.S. government issued a joint cybersecurity advisory warning that certain state-sponsored hackers have the ability to take control of the industrial control systems of companies in the U.S. energy sector.[47] The malware detailed in the advisory is able to manipulate critical equipment used in nearly every type of industrial facility.[48] Similar to the unsuccessful cyberattack described in the Gladkikh indictment, the threat this joint advisory warns of is one that could cause catastrophic damage to all systems, as well as other physical property. Amplifying the reported threat, Sergio Caltagirone, vice president of threat intelligence at Dragos and a former global technical lead at the U.S. National Security Agency, characterized the malware as "the most expansive industrial control system attack tool anyone has ever documented" and concluded that the risk of damage to property and systems will persist for many years.[49]

Shortly after the Conti ransomware group's pledge of allegiance to Moscow at the outset of the Russian invasion, a Ukrainian cybersecurity researcher published a cache of more than sixty thousand leaked internal conversations and files. This leak provided a rare glimpse into the inner workings of the group and its relationship with the Russian government. Throughout the files, Conti group members discuss the umbrella of protection they enjoy from interference by Russian law enforcement so long as they follow the "rules." "There appeared to have been at least some lines of communication between the Russian government and Conti leadership," Allan Liska, an analyst for the cybersecurity firm Recorded Future, told *Wired* magazine.[50] "The impression from the leaked chats is that the leaders of Conti understood that they were allowed to operate as long as they followed unspoken guidelines from the Russian government." In January 2021, Russia's Federal Security Service (FSB)—comparable to the American FBI—arrested and dismantled REvil, a notorious ransomware group whose members had participated in the attack on Colonial Pipeline.[51] This demonstration of Russia's ability to stop ransomware groups at will was intended as a message to the United States: ransomware groups are a tool of the Kremlin, and one that can be ratcheted up or tamped down at will.

At the time of writing, the United States and its NATO allies are inflicting significant damage on the Russian economy through sanctions while arming Ukrainian forces to defeat Russia's war machine. As China weighs its options for a forceful takeover of Taiwan, the Communist Party leadership in Beijing is certainly taking note. Aside from the economic harm that ransomware groups inflict on private industry, these groups also represent a potential digital militia that could be used with devastating effect either in response to Western actions vis-à-vis Ukraine or to preempt interference in Beijing's plans for Taiwan.

In a nightmare scenario, Russia and China are postured to share the highly sophisticated tools they have developed to target critical infrastructure with the ransomware groups operating from their soil. Injecting ambiguity into attribution and legal analysis regarding countermeasures and uses of force under international law, our adversaries could arm these ransomware groups with zero-day exploits and other advanced tools and turn them loose against targets across critical infrastructure sectors and in critical supply chains. Once considered merely a criminal threat, ransomware groups are becoming a significant threat to national security and a key player on the cyber battlefield.

CHAPTER 3

Chinese Cyber Espionage

The Greatest Transfer of Wealth in History

As one millennium gave way to another in the year 2000, Canada's Nortel Networks was a superstar of the fiber-optics industry and associated technologies, such as wireless networks. The company's headquarters dominated the otherwise sleepy Canadian capital of Ottawa, employing ninety thousand people globally and enjoying a market value of about $250 billion. It seemed poised to lead the world in building advanced 4G (fourth generation) and then 5G wireless telecommunications networks. 5G would become the wireless technology on which all Internet of Things (IoT) devices and services operate—from self-driving cars to robotic vacuums to remote surgery. 5G is about one hundred times faster than the previous generation.

But starting in the late 1990s, the Canadian Security Intelligence Service became aware of unusual traffic on Canadian telecommunications networks, suggesting that Chinese hackers were stealing data and documents from someone in Ottawa. The obvious suspicion was that Nortel, formerly named Northern Telecom, was the target. "We went to Nortel in Ottawa, and we told the executives, 'They're sucking your intellectual property out,'" the head of the security agency's Asia-Pacific unit said. "They didn't do anything."[1] It has never been established precisely who at Nortel the Canadian government service briefed.

What followed was a textbook case of how the Chinese were able to penetrate the email accounts of chief executive officer Frank Dunn and six other senior executives, not only to steal enormous amounts of technology but also to surveil the company's internal decision-making processes. The company obviously made a mistake in not responding to the government's warnings, most likely out of hubris, and it also made bad business decisions. In 2009, the company declared bankruptcy, and only then did the reports of a Chinese hack begin to surface.

Perhaps because the company was Canadian, few Americans have heard about the bankruptcy. The company's nationality was also a reason the Chinese would dare to penetrate it so thoroughly—Canada is not known for playing geopolitical hardball. A full decade later, journalists and other researchers were still trying to make sense of what happened.

The purpose of telling the story here is that Chinese computing and communications sophistication has exploded since the Nortel hack, and some American companies almost certainly have been penetrated in even more sophisticated ways than Nortel was. In other words, the People's Republic has a playbook that it uses against the world's corporations. "Make no mistake—the Chinese have hurt a lot of American companies," Brian Shields, who was a senior systems security adviser and part of the five-person team that investigated the Nortel breach, told us. "You can be absolutely certain there is a very high level of thievery going on against U.S. and other companies around the world, especially if they are an industry leader."[2]

Part of the confusion surrounding what happened—and why the Chinese role was not spotlighted at the time—stems from the fact that Frank Dunn, Nortel's CEO, was caught up in an accounting scandal, and the company had to restate its earnings. This highly embarrassing event led to significant churn within the company that culminated with Dunn being fired. "While it's true that management may have made some bad decisions, it's far too easy to just blame bad management," Shields said.

"The real truth is no company can survive a nation-state effort to get technology to start up their own industry that spans more than a decade of stealing," he added. "No company is going to do well when faced with such unfair competition, especially when [the Chinese] know your every move, and they are underbidding you on everything where they suddenly have products that can compete." Shields is now a cyber threat investigator working for the U.S. government in Raleigh, North Carolina.

The Nortel hack became known after Shields was assigned to an investigating team in April 2004. It erupted when one Nortel executive in Ottawa, Brian McFadden, head of the company's highly sophisticated optical networking group, received an email from a Nortel employee in Maidenhead, England, about the company's internal library of important documents—which were stored online in something called Livelink. Executives, engineers, and other employees had access to Livelink and could trace any activity involving their own documents. One day, McFadden got an email from the England-based employee saying, "I noticed you looked at my documents last night and downloaded them. Can I help you in any way?" That was a routine business follow-up email.

The only problem was that McFadden said he had not downloaded anything. The employee in Maidenhead provided what he considered proof of the download made by McFadden. The Livelink logs, or records of activity, were obtained from the computer that hosted them, and these showed that the download was made by a remotely connected personal computer using a virtual private network (VPN). This is a secure connection tool that lets employees obtain access to the corporate network from anywhere in the world. Shields looked in the remote access server logs for McFadden's user ID. To his surprise, it was not there for the date and time the England-based employee had specified.

Shields then looked at the remote access log to get the Internet Protocol address—or IP address, which functions like a mailing address for internet traffic—to determine where the VPN connection came from. He expected to see an address in the Ottawa area. To his surprise, the IP address was registered in Shanghai, China. "How the hell did that happen?" Shields recalls thinking. "That's messed up. We have been hacked."

The hacking continued for years until the drama reached a crescendo: the board of directors was in the process of firing their CEO while Chinese hackers were prowling through Nortel's global network. At a moment when Dunn and other top executives were distracted because the company's board of directors was meeting to decide what to do about the accounting scandal, corporate emails would have revealed that Dunn was on the verge of departure. At that precise moment, the hackers sent nearly eight hundred sensitive documents to the Shanghai IP address using the account of no less a person than the CEO. Dunn's account had been penetrated and his passwords stolen, and with his attention diverted with the scandal and his unceremonious departure, he never noticed anything amiss.

The stolen documents were extensive, including design details for an American communications network. "It was a vacuum cleaner approach," Shields said. "I had been watching them take fifty or seventy-five documents a day and maybe one hundred on a busy day, but now they took 775 documents using Frank Dunn's user ID. They were on his system for six to eight hours. Maybe they did it because he was the CEO and he had access to everything. That's why they used his account. The reality was that they weren't worried about getting caught. I think they knew he was going to be fired before the news was made public, so they thought it was a perfect opportunity to steal a large batch of documents. That was the level of compromise."

Precisely who did it was a mystery, at least initially. The documents were flowing to a tight cluster of IP addresses registered to Shanghai Faxian Corp., an obvious front company for someone else. Investigators later gave the attacking group the name Advanced Persistent Threat 1 (APT1) because it was the first such massive assault on a Western company's computing systems from China. The suspicion was that the People's Liberation Army was behind the attack—partly because one of its premier hacking units, Unit 61398, was based in Shanghai, and partly because of the sophistication with which the hack was carried out. The sophistication was beyond what any private entity could achieve—it had to have been carried out at the nation-state level. The hackers hid spying software so deeply within some Nortel employee computers that it took investigators years to realize how persistent the compromise was.[3]

The hack was part of a conscious strategy. Every five years since 1953, the Chinese Communist Party has published "Five-Year Plans" that establish the near-term goals for the party's national strategy for social and economic development. The Chinese government had stated in its 1986 five-year plan that China needed to develop its own telecom equipment manufacturing industry. Huawei Technologies was founded just a year later in 1987 by Ren Zhengfei, a former military engineer, who was highly aware of the strategic and military value of information and telecommunications networks. The company was led by retired officers of the People's Liberation Army and received as much as $75 billion in subsidies and other forms of financial assistance from the central government according to an estimate by the *Wall Street Journal*.[4]

As a result, Huawei won the race to 5G wireless communications. Endorsed by the Chinese Communist Party, subsidized by Chinese taxpayers, and spoon-fed stolen research and development by Chinese intelligence services, Huawei rapidly became China's global telecom juggernaut.

This is an example of a Chinese strategy to leapfrog the West in terms of technological sophistication. Huawei's creation was part of an effort by the Chinese government to overcome the country's near complete dependence on foreign communications equipment makers. The Chinese suspected, and leaker Edward Snowden much later confirmed, that American and other foreign intelligence agencies, including the National Security Agency, had penetrated that equipment—though the NSA has never responded to those accusations.

Over the past two decades, Chinese manufacturing and engineering prowess across many key industries—from pharmaceuticals to stealth fighter jets—has reached near parity with that of the United States. Online espionage accounts for a large part of the explanation. In 2012, U.S. Army general Keith Alexander, then director of the National Security Agency and the first commander of U.S. Cyber Command, described the Chinese theft of American intellectual property as the "greatest transfer of wealth in history."[5]

Since then, the cost of theft to U.S. companies has ballooned. According to the Intellectual Property Commission report published by the National Bureau of Asian Research, the cost of trade secret theft alone "is between 1% and 3% of GDP."[6] And in 2022, following a detailed report into an ongoing Chinese cyber espionage campaign, Lior Div, CEO of Cybereason—a Boston-based cybersecurity firm—estimated that the total annual cost to U.S. companies could now be measured in the trillions of dollars.[7]

"The real impact is something we're going to see in five years from now, ten years from now, when we think that we have the upper hand on pharmaceutical, energy, and defense technologies," Div told *Breitbart News* in May 2022. "We're going to look at China and say, how did they bridge the gap so quickly without the engineers and resources?"[8] Huawei strenuously denies that it works with the Chinese government or the Chinese military, but its denials are simply not credible. The evidence to the contrary is overwhelming.

The exact mechanism through which Huawei obtained the intellectual property from the PLA remains unknown, but Shields said it was likely the PLA specialists who conducted the initial attacks in the 1990s eventually turned the hacking operation over to civilians whose role was to look for and steal documents and monitor Nortel executives to understand every move the company was making. Civilians, including people working at Huawei, would have known what type of secrets to look for. "You don't need to keep your front-line people in there anymore," Shields explained. "They can move on to breaking into other companies with technology the Chinese government wants as part of its five-year growth plans. You can turn the operation over to other people to harvest the data."

There is no denying that Huawei was a major beneficiary of the hack. Huawei was not even a close competitor of Nortel's when the penetration started. It was merely a reseller of equipment made by foreign companies to Chinese customers. But as a result of inside information that allowed Huawei to make rapid gains in its products and underbid Nortel (and also Britain's Marconi) for major contracts in Britain in 2004 and in Canada in 2008, Huawei was able to establish itself as a giant of the telecommunications world—which both the Chinese government and the People's Liberation Army clearly supported. The fact that both Nortel and Marconi lost out on big networking upgrades in their home markets to Huawei led to their bankruptcies within a year afterward.

There were other fronts in the Chinese attack on Nortel. As in most of these cases, the Chinese attack from multiple directions all at once, overwhelming the defender. If one attack vector does not work, another will. The use of electronic listening devices found planted throughout Nortel's vast research facility strongly suggested direct Chinese government involvement.

Then there was the human dimension. Huawei opened a recruitment office near a Nortel facility in Richardson, Texas, to start enticing key employees. And Huawei quietly hired about twenty Nortel scientists as the company was collapsing. These employees had been developing the groundwork for 5G technology. One of them was Wen Tong, originally from China, who emigrated to study at Montreal's Concordia University. Tong, who had generated more than one hundred patents in wireless research, became the chief technology officer for Huawei's wireless business. "The real problem for Huawei was they lacked legitimacy without the highly qualified R&D personnel staff," Shields told us. Tong served as the 5G chief scientist and led Huawei's 5G research and development starting in 2011.[9]

"They gained legitimacy once they ran competitors like Marconi and Nortel out of business and then hired their personnel," he said. "It really is eye-opening when you look at what happened to Nortel and how that strategic move (the hiring of key personnel) gave Huawei greater legitimacy."

The Nortel scientists became heroes within Huawei. In 2020, more than a decade after the bankruptcy, Tom Blackwell, a reporter for Canada's *National Post*, attempted to put the pieces together, partly because, in a huge irony, Canada was then debating whether to buy Huawei's advanced 5G systems for its telecommunications system.[10] Blackwell interviewed Jonathan Calof, a University of Ottawa business professor who took his students to Huawei's corporate headquarters in Shenzhen in southern China, just across the border from Hong Kong.

On a wall of fame for Huawei's star scientists and researchers, Calof recognized the faces of several former Nortel employees he had known back in Ottawa. "These are (now) Huawei employees associated with great technological accomplishment," he said, "and I recognized so many of them."

After years of agonizing about whether to use Huawei equipment in its new 5G networks, the Canadian government in May 2022 announced it would not use any Huawei or ZTE gear and would gradually force them out of other networks. No mention was made of Nortel.

The failure of Nortel to respond to the hacking is illuminating because it speaks to the challenges that all companies face in the cyber realm. Beginning in 2004, Shields forwarded his research up the management chain, but two levels above him was an assistant vice president (AVP), which is how we'll identify the individual. He was a specialist in physical security, not cybersecurity.

Shields said he presented a report about the hacking to the AVP. But years later, he was told by mutual acquaintances that the AVP had expressed "discomfort" with the report because it was outside his area of expertise. He also might have been risking his career. "If he had forwarded the report up the management chain, all the big guys (top executives) would have been looking at him and asking, 'What are you doing about it?'" Shields recalled. "But he had no experience with this type of problem, which was true of most organizations at the time."

Three months after Dunn's departure, Shields was still investigating the hackers, trying to determine how far they had penetrated and just what they had stolen. But the AVP wanted to "stop the bleeding" of more documents being stolen. Shields said that companies typically have a mistaken policy of immediately changing a password if it has been compromised. If that had been done, it would have alerted the hackers that Nortel knew they were in its systems. There would have been no time to investigate how the user accounts were compromised and no time to try to see what systems the hackers had broken into.

Trying to turn the corner on the whole episode, the company decided to reset the six remaining compromised passwords and rebuild the operating system of the PCs that had been involved. Shields said there was no way this remediation could rid the company of the hackers. There were no failed login attempts for these six user accounts nor any new abuses after the passwords were reset—for the next six months. All leads temporarily dried up, and the hackers stopped abusing the employee accounts, but Shields suspected the game was not over. His budget started getting cut, however. Management was, in effect, trying to bury the hack. Shields thinks this reflects just how little senior management understands IT security and the ramifications of their decisions. And this is true of other companies as well. There is always pressure on the chief information officer (CIO), who is in charge of all IT systems, to do whatever the top management team says they need. There is little to be gained for a CIO in seeking a big budget increase or creating alarm for his or her bosses.

Half a year after the changing of the passwords, Shields got a break. He noticed a pattern. One of the ISPs the hackers were using had stopped completely for six months. This was, in fact, a small mistake that Shields was able to take advantage of. If the hackers were posing as off-site employees working from home, why would one ISP go completely dark for six months? No employee would simply stop working for that long.

This mistake is what then led Shields to find beacon signals the hackers were using. Nortel's firewall logs showed that a Nortel computer periodically sent out about fifty bytes of data (equivalent to about twenty-five typed words) to an address on the internet, but the device on the other end did not respond to confirm it had received the data. Sending data in this way means the sender has no idea whether the data was ever received. This way of sending data creates a security concern because IT specialists, as a general rule, prefer to know that a particular piece of data was accurately and completely received. "Typically, the hackers wanted to send a short burst to their main server that was monitoring the operation," Shields explained. "The beacon might say, 'This is the IP address I'm on, this is the machine I'm using, and this is the operating system that's running. It was like sending a note back home, saying, 'Here's where I am.'"

So, the Chinese were still inside Nortel's systems. Shields kept on investigating. He had learned from industry sources that hackers went after the Microsoft domain servers that managed a company's login process. These servers store the passwords for all user accounts in what is known as a hashing format. Passwords need to be kept on the server system but not in the plain text the user types to log in. A piece of software scrambles them into unrecognizable patterns called hashes.

Since Nortel had worldwide operations, there were forty-eight of these Microsoft domain servers, meaning that any one of these servers could have been compromised and given the hackers the master file holding all the user account passwords in the hashed format. These servers were using the very first version of the hashing algorithm Microsoft came out with in 1999. This first version was very weak, and Microsoft issued upgrades; but Nortel did not update its hashing software—another critical decision that left the company vulnerable. The attackers had, in effect, carte blanche to roam through the company's systems. Shields said he is certain this is how the hackers originally broke into Nortel's computers.

In 2008, Shields learned about a field of computer science called memory forensics. Like DNA forensics work in a TV crime series, memory forensics allowed technicians to look at a computer's memory to discover what had taken place in it. That took him on a journey that ultimately found hard proof that the hackers were still in Nortel's computers. "They had names because they used social media, like their Internet internal bulletin board site, to talk to their buddies while they were in our systems," he said. "I caught them red-handed. I was on two machines just after they had gotten off. I did memory dumps." That means he could reconstruct some of the hackers' activity.

But by this time Nortel was deep in crisis as bankruptcy loomed. Shields's results were never shared up the management chain because they were too explosive. Too many careers were at risk. As incredible as it sounds, Shields says there were never any urgent requests from any CEO or the board of directors for updates on the hack. "There was no push-down from management," Shields continued. "The shit should have been hitting the fan over something like this. It was serious."

The moral of the story seems to be that lower-level managers on the front lines are reluctant to inform top management about hacks because they may not possess the right skill sets to deal with the problem, and their jobs would be on the line if they were to get blamed for not properly dealing with it. Stopping a hack requires resources, personnel, and expertise, taking away from the company's primary purpose of generating revenue. For many companies, cybersecurity is looked at as simply a money pit—a cost center that provides no tangible benefits to the organization's primary operations.

Nortel did not have a chief information security officer (CISO), a relatively new corporate position. A CISO is the senior data and cyber-security executive in any company and is incredibly important to an effective cybersecurity program. These executives typically report to a chief information officer, whose primary job, by contrast, is to ensure that the company's IT systems are operational. For Nortel, it was an obvious oversight not to have a CISO. Frequent corporate reorganizations and a rotation of CEOs through the corner office complete the picture of dysfunctionality.

Nortel is hardly alone. Our experience with the workings of major companies is that they wish to maximize the profit and performance that can be achieved by large IT systems, but most are not sufficiently organized, staffed, or equipped to respond to security breaches. In fact, what Nortel did was to look at the percentage of dollars that its competitors budgeted for IT and use that as the basis for deciding how much Nortel should spend. The problem with this approach was that it did not make cybersecurity a priority. The question, Shields believes, really needs to be, "If this were my personal company and these were my assets at risk of being hacked, what would my security strategy be and how much would that cost?"

For all these reasons, Shields told us, "There's no Fortune 500 company that cannot be compromised by a targeted, foreign government–sponsored cyberattack." Shields was laid off from the company after the bankruptcy filing in 2009.

News of the hack did not surface until it was first reported by the *Wall Street Journal* in February 2012 when Shields first revealed it to cyber technology reporter Siobhan Gorman.[11] Then-CEO of Nortel Mike Zafirovski said he did not recall seeing any reports from Shields. He said some security managers told him that Shields was smart but that he had a reputation as someone who would "cry wolf." In response, Shields says today: "Isn't it sad that I was labeled this way when in fact there were wolves in our network stealing the most valuable secrets from Nortel for over a decade?"

Not long after news surfaced about the hack, in 2013 the cybersecurity firm Mandiant produced a report about just who APT1 was.[12]

The firm was clearly taking a risk because going public could trigger a punishing counterattack. Mandiant concluded that APT1 was in fact Unit 61398 of the People's Liberation Army, also known as the Second Bureau within the General Staff Department's Technical Reconnaissance Department, or Third Department. The General Staff Department is similar to the U.S. Joint Chiefs of Staff.

Mandiant located a twelve-story headquarters building in the Pudong section of Shanghai, which is the area that once consisted of marshes and fishing villages but has now been completely transformed with factories, hotels, and many other appurtenances of modernity. Unit 61398's headquarters were physically big enough to accommodate thousands of workers, with other offices and facilities in the area.

The unit operated a vast global network of computers and seemed to specialize in targeting English-speaking countries. Mandiant said Unit 61398 had established at least 937 command-and-control servers hosted on 849 distinct internet addresses in thirteen countries. This allowed Unit 61398 to constantly switch between the IP addresses and geographies of its attacks so that any system administrator would be challenged to identify a pattern.

Mandiant was able to document that, starting in 2006, Unit 61398 had targeted 141 companies in twenty major industries, mostly in the English-speaking world, achieving persistent access to these networks. The longest of these sustained penetrations was four years and ten months. The average duration of its penetrations was 356 days—almost a full year.

Some of the industries targeted were information technology, aerospace, satellites and telecommunications, transportation, navigation, and metals and mining—all critically important industries. Unit 61398 compressed the information they wanted into archives and then deleted them once they had been sent back to China, or "exfiltrated." That left little evidence because the files were usually overwritten during normal business activities.

Unit 61398 was extremely clever in how it tried to get Mandiant executives to click on dangerous links that would have given them access to Mandiant's systems. On April 18, 2012, they sent an email in the name of Mandiant's CEO, Kevin Mandia, to Mandiant employees. They saw an email from Mandia, saying, "Hello, shall we schedule a time to meet next week? We need to finalize the press release. Details click here."

But the email was not from a Mandiant address. It was from rocket-mail.com. If anyone had clicked on the fake link, they would have downloaded a malicious piece of malware that would have given the hackers a backdoor into Mandiant's systems. This practice is called spear phishing, using a spoofed email account.

Stop to contemplate the implications of all this. In 2021, the Chinese operated thirty-six APTs and less fully understood groups called UNCs, for "uncategorized," according to Mandiant. They have hundreds of targets. And they have been conducting these penetrations for years, relying on global infrastructures of computers and servers and vast budgets.

Although some American CEOs have responded well, Shields says CEOs simply do not understand what they are up against. One particular problem is that many companies have built large presences in China over a period of decades, and only recently has it become clear that the Chinese government has penetrated many of them. "What executives do not even consider is the risk of having manufacturing or research or other offices physically located in China," Shields said. "The risk of loss of information contained on those systems is all but guaranteed because now the government will have physical access to the facilities as well as in the cyber realm. Executives should operate under the assumption that everything on the systems located in China can be stolen if the Chinese government wants the information. Besides the physical access concern, there will be networking connections for the offices in China to be connected back into the corporate network."

To think one can easily control these connections from inside China to the outside world is sorely mistaken according to Shields. He said that at first, Nortel had a firewall to manage access from its Chinese offices to the main corporate network. A firewall would have prevented unwanted intruders from using Nortel's China-based systems to reach out into its global network. But eventually the firewall was removed because requests were always approved; they were rubber-stamped. The company did not see the point of maintaining the firewall, another critical mistake.

No CEO is going to acknowledge that his or her company's systems have been severely compromised due to his or her poor decisions, because that would almost surely result in his or her forced departure. Boards of directors would be irate. Shareholders would sue. Similarly, if a company quietly tried to extricate itself from China's grip, profits would take a hit because it would be a hugely expensive problem to fix. It would require a major effort to establish that each and every one of thousands of users of a large corporate IT system is legitimate. If a company got serious about shutting the Chinese out of its systems, the Chinese government would find a way to retaliate, and sales in China would almost certainly be hurt. The Faustian bargain appears to be, if the Chinese operate with stealth and do not disrupt the daily operations of a company, why bother rooting them out? Let's hit our quarterly earnings predictions.

The problem is compounded by the fact that both the Chinese and the Russians have learned to crack the software supply chains of many systems, leaving them essentially defenseless. And the trend toward cloud computing and distributed computing in general has also created complex systems that are often vulnerable. We turn now to China's massive collection of data, which sometimes goes hand in hand with the theft of intellectual property but is put to very different uses.

CHAPTER 4

The New Oil

Data and China's Digital Silk Road Strategy

Data is the new oil. It's valuable, but if unrefined it cannot really be used. It has to be changed into gas, plastic, chemicals, etc., to create a valuable entity that drives profitable activity; so data must be broken down, analyzed, for it to have value.

—CLIVE HUMBY, 2006

CHINA'S BELT AND ROAD INITIATIVE HAS ATTRACTED A GREAT DEAL OF attention around the world because Chinese companies and state-owned enterprises are building ports, railroads, bridges, highways, housing complexes, and other types of physical infrastructure everywhere from Cambodia and Pakistan to Italy and Greece. In some cases, governments have borrowed too much money from Chinese banks, state-owned enterprises, and agencies and have become ensnared in "debt traps." In several cases, these debtor states have been forced to cede control of the projects, as in the case of a port in Sri Lanka, which has obvious military implications for China's forward naval basing in the Indian Ocean. If China can leverage debt to exert control over a foreign port, they can use it to support their rapidly expanding navy.

But China is also building what it calls its Digital Silk Road. When the Chinese talk about the Silk Road, they are referring to the era when caravans of traders and merchants from Europe and the Middle East (such as Marco Polo) made the long trek across Central Asia to buy Chinese silk, fine teas, porcelain vases, and other products they could not manufacture themselves. China had a technological advantage and created much wealth for itself as a result.

That's the kind of dominance the Chinese are in the process of recreating today, only this time the key commodity is data. Very few Americans, or other peoples for that matter, understand the power of data. Sufficient amounts of data, when mined or combined with other data, offer deep insight into a person's life or into the decision-making processes of a government agency or private company, and hence provide a measure of influence or outright control. This is a central goal of the Chinese Communist Party—not only does it wish to control its own population of 1.4 billion, but it also seeks to employ similar tools to influence and control the world. Democracy and social justice reforms anywhere in the world are seen as a threat to the party's domination at home.[1]

Huawei Technologies is the absolute lynchpin to this effort. Huawei has taken the lead among Chinese companies and state-owned enterprises in building the telecommunications systems at the heart of the Digital Silk Road strategy. Other technologies Beijing wishes to dominate are listed in what China used to call its Made in China 2025 program, but it has now dropped all public references to that plan because it triggered so much concern in other world capitals.

In this chapter, we will describe the different ways China steals or otherwise obtains data. Russia does much the same but seemingly on a smaller, less comprehensive scale. The Russians concentrate more on espionage, provocative actions, and denial-of-service attacks (in which a website is flooded with so much traffic that it crashes), as well as support to ransomware groups—and they don't seem to mind getting caught. They might even prefer to be caught to create maximum embarrassment for and loss of confidence in American and Western institutions. There is no danger that any of the people who commit these crimes will be arrested so long as they don't leave Russia. The Chinese have a very different style and prefer to remain invisible. They do not tend to disrupt. After surveying China's and Russia's data theft patterns, we will turn to the important and largely unanswered question: what exactly are these adversaries doing with all the data they accumulate?

A variety of Chinese entities have been engaged in stealing massive amounts of American data, such as the APT groups. Some of them operate from the provincial units of the central ministry to better conceal their origins. Others operate from technical universities. The Ministry of State Security also trolls through American computer systems taking advantage of software vulnerabilities. The People's Liberation Army has multiple attack units, including Unit 61398 as described in the previous chapter.

But even nonmilitary, nonintelligence agencies are involved in the attacks on the world's IT systems. "A huge amount of this [data collection] is carried out by elements of the Chinese government that are not explicitly in the surveillance business," Emily de La Bruyère of Horizon Advisory told us. "We can't underestimate how much the Ministry of Commerce or any ministry in charge of an industry might be collecting. That's part of why this is a different kind of competition and one the United States might not be prepared for. Data collection isn't being undertaken by just the conventional arms of the security apparatus or the military. This is a competition that's playing out on the commercial playing field. All these other agents of state oversight and power matter even if they have not been thought of as intelligence competitors."

Wherever these hacks originate, they typically make headlines for a day or two, and then the American attention span moves on to the next headline. But stop for a moment to consider the sheer scale and duration of these attacks.

The attacks have been occurring for at least a decade, but the first large-scale theft of data that shook the consciousness of the American public might have been the attack on the systems of the federal government's Office of Personnel Management (OPM) in 2014–2015.[2] This was where the personal information of virtually every federal employee was stored. The attackers, linked to the Chinese government, got away with stealing the security clearance information of 22 million employees, including agents of the Federal Bureau of Investigation and service members across the Department of Defense, including the coauthor of this book, Michael McLaughlin.

At the time, OPM managed the repository of the federal government's Special Form 86. These forms contain all of the personal information of anyone applying to the federal government for a security clearance. To obtain these security clearances, government employees and contractors are required to reveal foreign contacts, relationships (including extramarital affairs), health histories, drug use, criminal records, and information about their children.

The information held by OPM was extremely personal and could be used by itself for all sorts of malicious activities, from outing undercover agents, to blackmail and coercion of senior officials, to password cracking. ("What's your mother's maiden name?" and "What street did you grow up on?" are common password recovery questions—answers to both of which can be found on a Special Form 86.) After the breach, the CIA had to cancel assignments for undercover officers because some of those individuals work undercover in other government agencies. Well before the breach, the CIA made the unilateral decision to store its officers' information on its own systems rather than with the OPM due to security concerns.

A year later, the same group hacked United Airlines, resulting in the theft of personally identifiable information of more than 20 million passengers. Once again, the CIA and other federal government agencies, including the U.S. military's equivalent of the CIA, the Defense Intelligence Agency, or DIA, may have been affected because Dulles International Airport, a major hub for United, is one of the primary transportation hubs for federal government employees. Government personnel who have used the airport or visitors from other countries could have had their identities revealed, particularly if the Chinese were able to match the travelers' passport numbers and destinations with other data stores.[3]

In 2016, Chinese hackers compromised Starwood Hotels and Resorts prior to its acquisition by Marriott International. Much to its chagrin, Marriott discovered this hack after the acquisition was completed. This substantial breach resulted in the further compromise of 130 million travel records, which in many cases involved passport numbers. And in 2017, a group from the Chinese army's Fifty-Fourth Research Institute compromised Equifax—an American multinational credit-reporting agency—resulting in the capture of the credit histories of more than 145 million Americans. That means the personal financial details of these Americans now reside in a Chinese government database, including such compromising information as whether they were behind on paying any of their bills or had gambling problems.[4]

In 2018, National Security Adviser John Bolton explicitly attributed the attacks on OPM, Marriott, and Equifax to China.[5] In 2020, the U.S. Department of Justice unsealed an indictment against four hackers working for the Chinese military for the Equifax breach.[6]

Chinese hackers have proven proficient at gaining initial access and covering their tracks to maintain access to a network for years, patiently waiting and watching. If a user clicks on the link in a spear-fishing email or opens the attachment, malware is downloaded into the computer system, and the Chinese can capture the keystrokes that the legitimate user is making and therefore obtain that user's log-in and password information or enable a remote desktop protocol session where the hacker can remotely access the user's device. A security expert observing or monitoring an IT system would see only legitimate users doing legitimate tasks. In the Equifax hack, the attackers used encrypted communications to hide their tracks and routed their internet traffic through thirty-four different computer servers in nearly twenty countries.

One of the best-documented examples of the Chinese operating style was what the APT10 group was able to accomplish, as revealed by the federal government in December 2018.[7] This was an attack against managed service providers (MSPs) such as IBM. The term "managed service provider" refers to a major technology company such as IBM, Microsoft, Amazon Web Services, or Oracle whose service offerings allow them to manage customers' IT systems, whether on the company's premises or off-site. It's easy to see the appeal to a CEO—why should we spend the money to defend and maintain all these expensive systems when IBM or Microsoft can do it better and for less money?

When this outsourcing is done away from a company's physical premises, it is called "cloud computing." A customer company's data and software are thus "in the cloud." Cloud services come in many different forms. The most common is software-as-a-service, or "SaaS" applications. SaaS allows users to run applications that are entirely hosted in the cloud. When you log into Gmail, you are accessing a SaaS application. Other examples are Netflix, Amazon Prime, and Pandora. With SaaS, the user is just that, a user of an application that is created, hosted, and managed by someone else. The cloud service provider typically hosts dozens of companies.

But ironically, if the Chinese can penetrate a cloud service provider, it appears to make it easier, not harder, for them to "hop" from one company's systems to another. Through the campaign revealed in 2018, APT10 penetrated the computing systems of companies in at least twelve countries over a period of four years. The victim companies were engaged in banking and finance, telecommunications, consumer electronics, medical equipment, packaging, manufacturing, consulting, health care, biotechnology, automotive, oil and gas exploration, and mining.

The U.S. Navy was one target. APT10 was able to steal the personally identifiable information of more than one hundred thousand personnel, including names, Social Security numbers, dates of birth, salary information, personal phone numbers, and email addresses. That obviously would give the Chinese military important information about who is aboard the ships of the Seventh Fleet patrolling the South China Sea or the Taiwan Straits. They also stole maintenance records from the Seventh Fleet, so they know when U.S. ships need to return to port to be serviced—and they also learned how to maintain their own equipment based on stolen U.S. designs.

The federal government did not reveal which tech companies were involved in the APT10 case, but the *Wall Street Journal* identified one as IBM. When asked about the breach, the company said it had seen no evidence that sensitive data was compromised. That's because the Chinese were so skilled at copying data and exfiltrating it, or transmitting it back to Chinese-controlled computers, that IBM apparently never saw it happen.

Another major avenue of penetration for the Chinese are the computer systems that American companies have built in China to help them manage sales and billing and all the functions involved in selling goods or services in any country, as discussed by Brian Shields in the previous chapter. We shone a spotlight on this issue in our 2020 article in the *National Interest* titled "Is China Seeking a Secretive, Permanent Presence in America's Computers?"[8]

The Chinese have passed a series of laws that require all foreign companies operating in China to share their encryption codes and other sensitive information with the government. As we noted in our article, this has set the legal groundwork for the Chinese Communist Party to access all network activity that occurs in China or in communications that cross its borders. The culmination of this legal maneuvering was the updated Multi-Level Protection System (MLPS 2.0), which came into effect in December 2019.

Consisting of more than one thousand pages and published only in Chinese, MLPS 2.0 sets out the technical and organizational requirements to which every company and individual in China must adhere. MLPS 2.0 gives "the legal authority to go in and ensure that a foreign company's system is completely open to inspection and retrieval of information by the Communist Party," Steve Dickinson, an attorney formerly with Harris Bricken, a Seattle-based international law firm with offices in Beijing, told us. In other words, China has stripped away the legal grounds for an American company operating in China to protect its network from inspection by the Ministry of Public Security—the country's feared domestic law enforcement agency.

While no Chinese law grants the authority to install malware or backdoors in corporate networks, under MLPS 2.0, "anything the company would install on its Chinese system to prevent that will be neutralized," Dickinson said.

America's top tech companies have had no choice but to cooperate. Microsoft, for example, has given the source code for its Windows operating system to the government, as it has to other governments and partners.[9] The government has also required companies such as Microsoft and Apple to build data centers in China that the government manages.[10]

Government agents knock on the doors of U.S. corporate data centers at any time of day or night and demand access to the systems. It is assumed that they have total access.

What we do not know for sure is how well the Chinese are able to use that, in effect, control of U.S. computing systems in China to leapfrog to the rest of the world. Have American companies erected sufficiently strong barriers to seal off their Chinese operations? As Brian Shields argued in the previous chapter, the answer is almost certainly not.

Samantha Hoffman, one of the world's smartest China technology watchers, who is based at the Australian Strategic Policy Institute, shares our concerns. "No assurances from any individual China-based company—no matter how loud or compelling they may be—can mitigate the political, security, and supply-chain risks that now come with operating in China," she wrote in July 2021.[11] "The Chinese Communist Party has absolute power over China-based companies, which its laws—like the 2021 Data Security Law, 2015 National Security Law, 2016 Cybersecurity Law, and 2017 National Intelligence Law—have reinforced. For companies that host massive amounts of data, especially data that originated from other parts of the world, including the United States, the risks are now even greater."

Hoffman has also warned about a company controlled by the Communist Party's Central Propaganda Department that is engaged in global bulk data collection. She says the company, called Global Tone Communications Technology (GTCOM), accumulates two to three petabytes of data per year, much of it from Twitter and Facebook. That's a staggering amount. That information is in the public sphere, but the collection of it and China's ability to mine the torrent of data provides GTCOM with real-time insights about people and companies. It would, for example, allow GTCOM to map out a target's entire social and professional networks, which then could be monitored.[12]

If one adds up all these strands, it's clear that the Chinese have had access to enormous amounts of American data. *Wired* magazine calls it the largest accumulation of data by any country of an adversary in history, one whose implications will play out for decades.[13] These are not just random, periodic attacks. The People's Republic of China has achieved a permanent, ongoing presence in at least some parts of America's computer and communications networks. And America's own inability to come up with legislation about how personal data should be protected compounds the problems. "People in the corporate IT world don't care about data," one specialist told us. "They care more about performance."

We suspect that the pattern of China's data theft is even deeper than what has been revealed publicly. The exploding use of TikTok, Zoom, and WeChat during the pandemic has dramatically enhanced China's ability to gather the world's data. More than 130 million Americans are quite literally addicted to TikTok, and the use of Zoom exploded as people worked from home during the pandemic. Both TikTok and Zoom run on algorithms that were written in China, transmit data through servers that can be accessed from China, and hence are fully accessible to Chinese intelligence services due to China's legal framework.

However, as ubiquitous as TikTok and Zoom have become, the amount of data accessible to the Chinese government resulting from these platforms is dwarfed by that of WeChat, which its boosters call the world's "first superapp."

Wholly owned by China's mega–tech conglomerate Tencent Holdings, WeChat is an incredibly powerful multifunction platform that combines the social media features of Facebook, the chat features of WhatsApp, the e-commerce features of Amazon, and the payment features of PayPal. On a single platform reside all data points about an individual's daily life—where they work, what they buy, with whom they communicate, what they say, and where they sleep. WeChat is an indispensable part of life in China and for Chinese nationals living abroad.

At the direction of the Chinese Communist Party, WeChat implemented a requirement that all users in China register with a digital ID for authentication and to tie WeChat accounts to individuals' social credit scores. China's social credit scores are similar to U.S. Social Security numbers, but they are used to give Chinese citizens a rating based on their loyalty to the Communist Party. This score affects their ability to travel, find work, hold public office, and even purchase a home. The system varies from province to province and has not been fully integrated on a national level, but that clearly is the end goal.

Beyond the social credit score, everything on WeChat is available to Chinese intelligence and security services, feeding both China's massive databases and enabling worldwide censorship. In 2020, the *New York Times* reported the personal story of Joanne Li, a Chinese expatriate who had returned to China after living in Canada for several years.

Upon her return, she posted an article from Radio Free Asia to her WeChat account about the deteriorating relationship between China and Canada. The next day, armed police officers wielding riot shields banged on the door of her family's apartment, arrested Joanne, and proceeded to interrogate her for days while she sat manacled in a police holding cell. Joanne was finally released only after signing a confession and a statement avowing loyalty to China.[14] Stories like this are hardly a rarity in China and lead to self-censorship for Chinese residents as well as the Chinese diaspora worldwide.

Establishing legal backing for its censorship and data collection efforts, China enacted the Hong Kong National Security Law in June 2020 in the wake of protests in the special administrative region. The law, which allows the Chinese government to impose a maximum penalty of life imprisonment for extremely vague offenses, such as "subversion" and "collusion with foreign forces," applies to everyone on the planet. In other words, if you publish a damning social media post anywhere in the world condemning China's treatment of the citizens of Hong Kong, this sweeping criminal statute could subject you to extradition to mainland China and life imprisonment should you travel anywhere China exerts jurisdiction. Amnesty International described the effect of this statute: "This draconian law is so vague, it prevents anyone from knowing how and when they might transgress it and has consequently had an instant chilling effect across the territory (Hong Kong)."[15]

While WeChat has extensive reach in China (78 percent of Chinese residents actively use the platform), only a minuscule 1.48 million of the total 1.3 billion monthly active users worldwide reside in the United States. That is still a useful tool for Chinese authorities because they can monitor parts of the nonresident Chinese and Chinese American community and communicate with their intelligence agents. One of America's significant disadvantages in the intelligence field is that it cannot communicate with its agents in China as easily as Chinese intelligence services can communicate with theirs in the United States. The Chinese conversations can start on WeChat, but quickly move to encrypted channels.

TikTok is a very different animal and has achieved much greater penetration into American society. It appears to be particularly pernicious because it is so personal. TikTok has more than 1.4 billion active monthly users worldwide—and roughly 40 percent of the total American population. The short-form video hosting service is owned by one of China's largest technology companies, ByteDance, and is based on a similar service in China, called Douyin. ByteDance specializes in developing AI and machine learning to interpret what it sees on social media, video feeds, and other inputs.

TikTok is so addictive because its algorithms serve up video clips to a viewer and then measure how much time the viewer spends on each clip. It also gains access to information such as a user's search history, location, and contact list, and it can form a profile or understanding of the user's personal likes and dislikes. In fact, TikTok can circumvent Apple and Google privacy policies and obtain full access to user data, *The Wrap* reported in 2022 on the basis of two studies by "white hat" hackers.[16] These are individuals who attack computing systems in hopes of helping them rectify their vulnerabilities to earn a payment from the owners of such systems. *The Wrap* confirmed the findings in interviews with five other security experts. Apple and Google denied the report, as they routinely do.

While TikTok's addictive quality has generated controversy because of its impact on young peoples' brains, one of the real issues from our point of view is what happens to the data it has access to. It may seem perfectly harmless that TikTok has access to a teenager's complete online life, but that teenager could be the child of an American government decision maker, someone in the U.S. intelligence community, or someone at a university with access to critical technology that the Chinese party-state is targeting.

All the teenager's contacts are accessible to TikTok, including family contacts, and a portrait of their lives is easy to extrapolate. If the teenagers complain about their parents or talk about private family issues, that information could be powerful in understanding the sorts of pressures their parents are facing. The more you know about an individual, the better able you are to tailor an approach that elicits his or her interest. As noted, spear-phishing emails work best when they are tailored to an individual's interests. If you can get targets to open an attachment or click on a link, you've just penetrated their network. If an intelligence agency or hacker is making an approach to a prominent American individual, how better than to create a false identity and claim some affiliation with family members?

It gets worse. Each time a user opens up TikTok on their devices, they are automatically linked to a computer server that is almost certainly accessible to the Chinese government that can update the application and continue to "improve" it from the user's perspective, to make it even more personally attuned. (It's much like how Apple can remotely update an iPhone's operating system.) But it also means that millions of American young people could be directly connected to ByteDance's servers, at least some of which are based outside the United States and therefore beyond U.S. control. "These dynamic properties allow TikTok carte blanche access to your device within the scope of what the application can see," said Frank Lockerman, a cyber threat engineer at cybersecurity firm Conquest Cyber, who reviewed the two white-hat studies.

TikTok, in a move that was widely overlooked, also announced in 2021 that it can collect biometric identifiers and biometric information as defined under U.S. laws, meaning faceprints and voiceprints. It said it may "share all of the information we collect with a parent, subsidiary, or other affiliates of our corporate group"—which obviously could be in China and subject to Chinese laws. Biometric information could also include health and exercise data recorded by smart phones and other devices.[17] The collection of facial images could mean that TikTok can literally see what makes a user laugh or smile and then provide more of the same. That has not yet been documented, but the possibility exists.

But wait, there's more. Whenever a user accesses a webpage through TikTok's mobile application—by clicking on a link to Amazon, for instance—TikTok inserts code that can monitor the user's activity on those outside websites, including harvesting usernames and passwords. While third-party tracking is not unheard of, logging a user's keystrokes *is*. "This was an active choice the company made," Felix Krause, a software researcher based in Vienna who identified TikTok's code insertion, told *Forbes*. "This is a non-trivial engineering task. This does not happen by mistake or randomly."[18]

TikTok responded to all these concerns by telling *The Wrap* that "the security and privacy of our global community is always a top priority." That's the standard denial. India, which boasts a very sophisticated technology base, did not buy that version of the truth and banned TikTok and other Chinese applications in 2020 over national security concerns.

Under fire from President Donald Trump in 2020, TikTok sought to portray itself as an American company based in California with an American CEO. It argued that all the data it collected was stored on computers not accessible from China. A TikTok executive, in sworn testimony to a Senate hearing in October 2021, said that a "world-renowned, US-based security team" decided who got access to the data.

But it was all a deception, as BuzzFeed reported in June 2022 on the basis of leaked audio from eighty internal TikTok meetings. China-based employees of ByteDance repeatedly obtained access to nonpublic data about U.S. TikTok users. It turned out that the "world-renowned" security team had to turn to their colleagues in China to determine how U.S. user data was flowing. The American staff did not have permission or knowledge of how to access the data on their own according to the leaked audiotapes. "Everything is seen in China," said a member of TikTok's Trust and Safety Department in a September 2021 meeting.[19]

The BuzzFeed reporting triggered an angry response from Brendan Carr, a commissioner for the Federal Communications Commission (FCC). He tweeted that TikTok "is pulling biometric data, face recognition, voice print, browsing history, keystroke patterns, location information. What we know is that if the CCP (Chinese Communist Party) . . . gets all this data, they have all sorts of ends they can achieve." He wrote a letter to the CEOs of Apple and Google demanding to know why they did not remove TikTok from their app stores. Carr, a Republican, is not the chairman of the FCC, and the FCC does not regulate the app stores.[20] Meanwhile, Senators Marco Rubio and Mark Warner, who lead the Senate Intelligence Committee, wrote to the Federal Trade Commission urging an investigation of TikTok's data handling.[21]

The damage to TikTok was compounded in July 2022 when Internet 2.0 published a report from consulting firm Penetrum which alleged that the TikTok app "had a server connection to mainland China." Further, TikTok checks its users' device location at least once an hour, which would allow it to track the physical movements of a user, plus it maps all the applications that a device is running or has installed.[22] Clearly, the pressure on TikTok was mounting.

There are still other flows of data moving to China. Whenever Huawei or one of its Chinese competitors builds a "smart city" (also known as a "safe city"), in which city managers may have real-time control over water, traffic, and garbage, the surveillance cameras in use generate videos and images, much of which is transmitted through servers controlled by Chinese corporations. Facial-recognition software, which relies on artificial intelligence trained by this massive pool of images and videos, is then sold by Chinese companies to police departments and law enforcement agencies throughout the world. This creates a cycle where more and more data is piped back to China as Chinese tech companies expand their offerings worldwide. The more Chinese tech companies establish an international presence, the more data the Chinese government has access to. The Internet of Things, in which everything becomes interconnected through 5G mobile technology, creates untold opportunities for data acquisition.

And that data can be accessed anywhere it sits at rest or where it travels. When information traverses the internet, in does so as electronic signals riding predominantly on physical wires. When oceans separate communicants, the signals ride on any of the more than 380 lines comprising the 745,645 miles of submarine cable encircling the globe. Near landing stations on the coast, these cables are buried and hardened to prevent them from being accidentally cut by ships' anchors or fishing vessels, as well as to prevent sabotage and espionage attempts at shallow depths.

However, as the miles of cable stretch into the deepest parts of the world's oceans, telecommunications companies cease to apply the hard outer surface to the cables and simply lay them on the sea floor. According to the U.S. Patent and Trademark Office, the fiber-optic cables transmitting 99 percent of the world's data communications are no thicker than a garden hose.[23]

These cables are an incredibly lucrative target for spies and saboteurs. Both the Chinese and Russians target the undersea cables that carry the world's international communications from one continent to another. But they do it differently.

The Chinese try to divert traffic through China and build their own undersea communications cables linking continents. If you own the cables or can lawfully obtain the information, there is no need for tapping. The information that flows through these cables is organized in the form of what are called "packets." The Chinese, in particular, are known for their ability to "sniff" the packets, meaning to look for key phrases or names. Because much of the global traffic is business related, the Chinese can identify company names or the name of a technology that interests them and possibly direct that intercept to a Chinese entity that could benefit.

The Russians, by contrast, have a well-documented history of using their naval vessels and submarines to find and tap into the undersea cables. A war game hobbyist named H. I. Sutton, who produces the *Covert Shores* blog, has revealed in great detail how the Russian spy ship *Yantar*, which is based in the far northern Kola Peninsula as part of Russia's secretive GUGI (Main Directorate of Underwater Research), is used to target cables around the world. *Yantar*, which the Russians officially classify as an oceanographic research vessel, is equipped with submersibles that can dive to depths of over twenty thousand feet. Since it launched in 2015, *Yantar* has loitered and conducted submarine "survey" operations off Syria, in the Arabian Gulf, and throughout the Atlantic Ocean. This ship's primary purpose is likely to tap into underwater cables owned by foreign companies and identify critical cables that would be most damaging if severed during a conflict.[24]

It is not known whether they have been able to successfully intercept communications, but it is not for lack of trying. And it's not clear what they would do with the information if they could get it. They could make use of it militarily, to inform the Russian navy about U.S. ship movements, for example. But Russia does not possess the economic and technological sophistication to rapidly absorb and exploit sensitive intellectual property the way the Chinese can.

In short, the world has never before witnessed systematic data collection on such a massive, global scale. "A new global digital architecture is taking shape," de La Bruyère wrote in "China's Digital Ambitions." She continued: the new order "is disrupting the existing hierarchy and creating the foundation for a new kind of geopolitical power. China intends to define this digital architecture by building its physical infrastructure and corresponding virtual networks and platforms, setting the technical standards that govern them, and shaping the emerging global digital governance regime. In doing so, it is cementing Chinese control over the international flow of data—and, as a result, resources."

We caught up with de La Bruyère from her base in Washington, DC. Originally from the suburbs of New York City, she started studying Chinese in school but realized she was going to have to spend time in the Chinese-speaking world to truly master the language. So she spent two years in Taiwan and China. "I started reading the things the Chinese were writing and sensed a gap between what Beijing was saying they wanted to do and what was commonly understood here in the United States," she said. She cofounded a consulting company called Horizon Advisory, mentioned previously, and is a senior fellow at the Foundation for Defense of Democracies.

We asked whether China had caught up with or surpassed the United States in any way. "I think Beijing has not caught up in terms of the best, flashiest cutting-edge technologies," she said. "But that's not the only thing that matters. China can access what is developed here because of the general openness of our ecosystem and because of their influence in the U.S. What they are very good at—and better than us at—is commercializing what comes out of our labs.

"5G is a test case of this. China did not have the best 5G technology. But China was the country that was going to invest a lot of money to build out these systems, which are expensive. Those are things that the

Chinese system is uniquely suited to do because of its size and because of its centralized nature. It's also something the U.S. is very bad at doing because we're fragmented and because of how our private sector works. I think in that sense, which is pretty core to the competition, China has leapfrogged us."

It may also have leapfrogged the United States in terms of the amount of data it holds, de La Bruyère believes. "If you think about emerging technological capabilities, part of it is the skills and the innovative algorithms that are developed, but also part of it is how much data do you have," she said. "That's somewhere that China has been putting in effort and probably has overtaken us there as well."

How did all this happen? "I think a lot of it is a function of intellectual cultures," she said. "Being a socialist or at least semi-socialist state, China thinks about things in terms of industrial policy and in terms of the how goods are produced and states compete for goods. In the United States, we tend to be a lot less deliberate about how we think about resources and production of them and the competition for them. We are not strategic, and we are not long-termists."

Larry Clinton, president of the Internet Security Alliance, explained the Chinese strategy this way in August 2022: "The Digital Silk Road strategy integrates what we in the U.S. think of as cybersecurity with China's military, geo-political, economic, and totalitarian philosophy and is already successfully creating fissures in the foundation of the post–World War II, US/Western European world order—which is China's stated goal." He added, "The U.S. has nothing remotely similar to this sort of modern digital strategy."[25]

Let's turn now to the question of what the Chinese do with all the data they are acquiring. It appears they are much more sophisticated than the Russians are.

Different pieces of the Chinese party-state have stolen or obtained these different flows of data. That suggests that the stolen data is not all in some centralized warehouse—partly because no entity in the world could house all that data—but rather it resides in "data lakes" that different elements of the government, tech sector, and military control.

Our sources tell us that the Communist Party organizes committees of different sizes to coordinate with government agencies and the PLA on most policy issues. If the party says to the Ministry of State Security and to a unit of the PLA that it wants to target a certain foreign institution or set of individuals, the different organizations can query their data lakes for any number of identifiers to aggregate what is known about a target.

The party-state clearly can also tap the resources of China's technology companies, which are increasingly under its thumb. The Australian Strategic Policy Institute has a project called Mapping China's Tech Giants, and it follows Chinese tech companies, all of them heavily involved in the collection and processing of vast quantities of personal and organizational data—everything from personal social media accounts to smart cities data to biomedical data.[26] China's "military-civil fusion" proclaimed by President Xi Jinping means that any information that exists in any Chinese entity's possession can be used by the PLA, and vice versa. The party controls everything.

One obvious use for all the data is to create profiles of prominent individuals—not just CIA agents, but researchers and business executives as well. If the Chinese government can assemble a portrait of an individual's health, travel experience, and financial position with flows of information from social media, facial-recognition cameras, and other sources, it's easy to see how a rich understanding of that individual could be developed. "The data is used to create or improve profiles," Mandiant analyst Scott Henderson told us. "They can likely punch in a person's name and see where they live, what their dog's name is, and how many kids they have. They think it is important to get the best profile of someone."

Several other factors make China's theft of data incredibly dangerous for national security. Security clearance information allows the Chinese intelligence services to positively identify American military officials and intelligence officers, as·noted. Travel and hotel information allows China to determine normal travel activity for certain types of American officials—what intelligence officers refer to as "pattern of life." And credit information reveals who among the American military and intelligence community could be susceptible to being lured into espionage due to financial distress.

By combining the fruits of many different data streams, Chinese intelligence services have enough information to identify intelligence officers and military officials, understand where and when they travel, and even predict which hotels they will stay in. Chinese intelligence services can then couple this powerful data set with their unfettered access to every database in mainland China and identify Chinese citizens and government employees who travel to the same locations at the same time as American military and intelligence officers. In other words, by applying Big Data analytics to potentially billions of records obtained through hacking U.S. companies and through China's authoritarian legal construct, Chinese intelligence services can render U.S. intelligence operations targeting China all but obsolete.

To be sure, there are technical problems in making full use of all the stolen data. One problem is that some data is "structured," meaning it exists in the form of words or numbers that can be easily analyzed. But other data is "unstructured," meaning it is in the form of pictures or video or voice, with limited identifying information. The U.S. Department of Defense tackled this problem in Iraq when U.S. military forces were seeking to respond to the use of improvised explosive devices (IEDs) that were planted along roads and in villages. The Americans had satellite images and images from cameras located in the war zone, but extracting actionable data required them to make sense of the images. That's what the California-based software company Palantir excelled at. Using high-quality imagery from satellites and drones flying overhead, Palantir's software could identify disturbed earth on roadsides or in ditches along convey routes. The Chinese have either developed or stolen very similar capabilities.

Inevitably, machine translation and artificial intelligence will have to be used before the massive sea of data can truly be tamed. Natural language processing—meaning teaching machines to actually understand the words they are hearing—is one piece of the challenge. Ultimately, these advanced tools could give the Chinese access to American decision making in real time. "China wants to have somebody sitting in a big control room in Beijing with a set of screens in front of them looking at every computer system in the United States on a real-time basis," Dickinson, the lawyer who lived in China for fifteen years and is steeped in Chinese national security culture, told us. "Not just computer systems, but also every Internet of Things system, every cell phone system. They'll use artificial intelligence to filter the information so that it's not just a random blob on the screen. That's their goal. There's no question about it."

In fact, the massive theft of data may be helping to improve China's artificial intelligence capabilities. One of the keys to creating AI algorithms or programs is to train them on large data sets. They learn and improve after consuming massive amounts of data. The Chinese have had an advantage in some respects because of their own large population that is not protected by any meaningful privacy provisions. But now the Chinese are obtaining massive foreign data from applications such as TikTok and Zoom, services such as safe/smart cities, and Huawei's massive telecommunications infrastructure in non-Chinese markets. "This is very difficult work, but there is enormous potential to be had from it," de La Bruyère said. "You have to assume they are developing these capabilities."

There are important implications for the use of artificial intelligence in cyber warfare and cybersecurity. China, with its total access to near-limitless data traversing every network within its borders, may soon be able to train AI-based cyber defense tools using these data sets and develop cybersecurity behavioral models. This capability, coupled with China's Great Firewall, will give the Middle Kingdom's cyber defense teams an incredible advantage in cyber warfare.

Indeed, as one might expect, the Chinese are pouring massive resources into all aspects of data storage and data science to advance these goals. One key: with 1.4 billion people, they are in a strong position to collect huge domestic data sets and to develop enough technical talent to power their Big Data analysis capabilities. The Chinese traditionally believe that education is the key to success and that technology offers China a future advantage; Big Data analytics is critical to advancing China's authoritarian worldview. The Chinese steal data even if they currently don't have use for it or know exactly what to do with it. The assumption is that over time their skills will improve. They are playing the long game. "The CCP collects data in bulk and worries about what to do with it later," Australia's Hoffman has said. "Even if it's not all immediately usable, the Party anticipates better technical ability to exploit the data later on." With China's long-term goal of global supremacy and its devotion to meeting strategic benchmarks, data is truly proving to be the oil on which the Chinese machine runs.

* * *

One question we often hear when discussing all this is: Don't American technology companies do some of the same things that China does? Why are you picking on the Chinese if America's Big Tech companies are intruding into people's lives as well?

It's true that if you do a search on Google for, say, a hotel room in a different city and then log out without taking any action, Google sells that information to hotels or tourist associations in that city, and voila! Pretty soon you will see hotel ads from that city and airline flights popping up on your device. Tech companies can even follow you from one platform to another using third-party cookies. American companies are also seeking to use AI to look for trends in the massive data sets they have acquired. All of this can happen because U.S. privacy laws are lax compared with Europe's—apart from a handful of states that have enacted state-specific privacy laws, California being the most prominent.

The key difference between what the Chinese are doing and what America's Big Tech companies are doing is that the American companies simply wish to make money. It's not about control or influence, other than for pecuniary gain. But Chinese tech companies are different. China views its private sector as another weapon in its arsenal. Chinese companies work hand in hand with the Chinese military and intelligence services to weaponize data to control individuals, companies, and nations. For companies in China, this is not optional. A series of laws compel companies operating in China to provide Chinese intelligence and security services unfettered access to their databases. Where the Fourth Amendment to the U.S. Constitution was crafted to protect individual

The Most Hacked Nation on Earth?

Taiwan is arguably the most hacked nation in the world—certainly when adjusted for the size of its population (23.5 million). China does not consider it a nation but rather a renegade island that must be conquered through whatever means necessary. As a result, Taiwan's government reports twenty to forty thousand cyberattacks from China each month.[27]

To learn more, coauthor Bill Holstein spoke with Howard Jyan, director-general of the Department of Cybersecurity under Taiwan's Executive Yuan (i.e., the cabinet). They spoke on Google Meet, not Zoom, which Taiwan government agencies are barred from using because it is owned by China and is widely seen as an intelligence-gathering tool.

QUESTION. You get twenty to forty thousand attacks each month?

JYAN. That is only on the government side (not including the private sector). All the government agencies are connected through a dedicated government service network. Our team monitors this network. We can collect cyberattacks against the government. We have some ability to ferret them out, to remove those attacks from the network.

Most of the attacks are from the other side (China). The reason we know is not based on IP (internet address) tracing. We analyze the pattern for each different group. They have their own patterns.

The APTs (advanced persistent threats) have defined their own scope. Some of the APTs are targeting Taiwan. Some of the APTs are targeting Tibet. Some of them are targeting Hong Kong. Usually there are three to five APTs attacking Taiwan. Some are focused on foreign affairs. Some are focused on Pacific Ocean affairs. And others are focused on the semiconductor industry.

QUESTION. Are the attacks coming from APTs associated with the People's Liberation Army (PLA) or those associated with the Ministry of State Security (MSS)?

JYAN. In the beginning, all the attacks were either from the PLA or the national security bureau (MSS). In recent years, we have found that they are cooperating more with the private sector and semi-military groups.

QUESTION. How are the attacks made?

JYAN. They have lots of mechanisms and different channels. They use social engineering mechanisms, like emails with malware inside or emails with phishing links. They also have spread and delivered malware, or backdoors, to users' end devices. They have used more pro-active attacks against some critical infrastructure. There are a lot of different ways to do this. Sometimes we can trace an attack back to the original group.

Sometimes if an attack on Taiwan is successful, maybe six months or one year later those attacks will show up in other countries. Sometimes they use Taiwan as a test bed.

Two years ago, Taiwan's CPC Corporation, the state-owned oil and petrochemical company, was attacked by APT41. We found out about it and stopped this attack. We called a meeting to ask internet service providers to come together. We shared information and asked them to improve and enhance their defenses. We stopped a second wave of attacks against the company. We shared that information with the United States. A few months later, the United States charged some members of this hacking group. It's one way we are cooperating.

QUESTION. It's difficult for the U.S. government to inspect or audit the networks of its suppliers. How do you handle that issue?

JYAN. Last year, there was one private-sector company that had malware and a backdoor installed by an APT group. The company had contracts with forty different government agencies. We set up a joint auditing group to ask representatives of the major agencies and auditors to work together. We cleaned up that malware to guarantee that the government agencies were safe. Cybersecurity is not only the responsibility of government agencies. The private sector is part of the protection.

QUESTION. Is it true that mobile phones made by China's Xiaomi have backdoors?

JYAN. Not only that. They also have a vocabulary list. Last year, there was one company I won't identify that checked the Xiaomi mobile phone and found a vocabulary list inside it. After that, we checked the Xiaomi product sold in Taiwan, and we discovered that it's most sophisticated. The vocabulary list is dynamic. . . . It is updated frequently. They are looking for words like "Falun Gong" or "Taiwan independence" and others. They will ferret out the messages that contain those words.

rights, Chinese laws are crafted to protect and advance the agenda of the Chinese Communist Party, *at the expense of* individual rights.

Even in a world filled with cynicism, they are operating with a far more complex and sinister agenda than America's private sector. Chinese companies and spies systematically collect unfathomable troves of data—from genetic and health information to location data to endless facial-recognition scans via TikTok. The chief end goal of collecting this data is not to capture market shares; it's to advance China's ambitions of global hegemony. "The CCP's methods are not that different from what we see in the global advertising industry," said Hoffman. "But instead of trying to sell a product, the CCP is trying to exert authoritarian control. It's using capitalism as a vehicle to access data that can help it disrupt democratic processes and create a more favorable global environment for its power."[28]

China and Russia exercise centralized governmental control of Western data, says Doowan Lee, a strategic adviser to the Institute for Security and Technology and adjunct professor of politics at the University of San Francisco. He is a national security expert who previously taught at the U.S. Naval Postgraduate School. "It boils down to two compounding variables," he told us. "Number one is about commodification of privacy data. Think about what we do online and how it is harvested and packaged into different data payloads and then traded. Data weaponization is possible because companies and business organizations can commoditize what we do online and do it at scale.

"The second variable is the asymmetry of control over commercialized privacy data," he explained. "If you look at China, if you look at Russia, if you look at Iran, the nondemocratic countries, they can impose centralized ownership of the data. That's pernicious. In the West, we have the same commoditization of privacy data, but there is no state ownership of it. This is the main schism between the West and the nondemocratic axis."

We also get asked, how does what the Chinese are doing compare to what America's security apparatus does, including the use of wiretaps? Unlike China, the United States has real, enforceable laws that regulate the government's right to access information about U.S. citizens. For example, the Foreign Intelligence Surveillance Act (FISA), enacted in 1978, requires the U.S. attorney general to report on the use of wiretaps to the House and Senate intelligence committees. The goal of wiretapping is to trace criminal or terrorist activity. There were 376 targets of court-approved wiretaps by the NSA in 2021 according to a report by the Office of the Director of National Intelligence. Some 309 of them were foreigners; 67 were U.S. citizens.[29]

Do some abuses occur? Almost certainly. But there is no comparison in terms of scale—the Chinese have stolen billions of pieces of information about Americans. And the U.S. government must live within a legal framework and face constant scrutiny. There are no legal constraints of any sort on the Chinese government's operations anywhere in the world.

And without constraint, the Chinese Communist Party is collecting and analyzing data on a massive scale to bring to fruition its authoritarian global ambitions.

Stoking the Flames

*How Malign Influence Exacerbates America's Political
Divides and Ethnic Tensions*

INFORMATION IS POWER. IT SHAPES OPINION, AND OPINION SHAPES actions. Russian and Chinese strategists have a master's level understanding of how to use and shape the information space to achieve their objectives—both through their own domestic information ecosystems as well as ours. However, it must be acknowledged at the outset that the United States has not done a good job maintaining the integrity of its information ecosystem. Thousands of newspapers have gone out of business, resulting in "news deserts" in many cities and regions, while others have been purchased by hedge funds determined to milk them for profit. The mainstream media has allowed itself to be polarized into the Fox News universe and the MSNBC universe—or worse. The reason that American politics is so vicious is that no one can agree on basic facts.

We saw this play out in coverage of COVID-19. More than 1 million Americans lost their lives to the disease partly because many of them believed the facts as presented by far-right media echo chambers—that it was a Democratic conspiracy against President Donald Trump, and no masks or vaccinations were needed. Simultaneously, whole cities were overrun by lawless mobs, cheered on by MSNBC commentators and Democratic legislators championing calls to defund law enforcement, whose very job it is to secure those cities.

We spoke with Christopher Hadnagy, who is a leader in the field of social engineering and whom we introduced briefly earlier. His latest book, *Human Hacking: Win Friends, Influence People, and Leave Them Better Off for Having Met You*, was released in January 2021. Early in the COVID-19 pandemic and at the height of the Black Lives Matter protests, Hadnagy's team conducted an experiment. "We took two brand new burner phones," he said. "There was nothing installed on them other than fake Instagram accounts, which we had created." Hadnagy used one phone to query Instagram for the term "Cop helps Black guy." "I wanted a video of a cop helping Black people," he said. On the other phone, he searched for "Cop shoots Black guy." The Instagram feeds resulting from a single search were stunning. "On one phone, it was all cops helping everybody," Hadnagy told us. "They were the friendliest cops on the planet. But on the other phone, I got cops who were dirty and bad and shooting everybody."

Part of the problem is how social media algorithms are designed to keep users in their echo chambers. "The way social media providers make a profit is by making sure you stay connected to them for hours because then ads are fed to you, and when ads are fed, they make money," Hadnagy said. "As a society, I believe we're addicted to social media, and applications like TikTok have proven it. Complete nobodies can become millionaires and celebrities overnight because they did some dance on TikTok for thirty seconds. Teenage girls are putting on wet T-shirts, and all of a sudden they've got a million followers."

"The second half of the explanation," Hadnagy continued, "is that other nation-states see that America is addicted to social media, that we live on it, that many people literally don't have real jobs because they make money running TikTok videos. Nation-states look at that and go, 'Holy crap, we can disrupt pricing, we can disrupt elections, we can disrupt democracy. All we have to do is feed whatever garbage we want into the main pipe where the American people are consuming their 'knowledge' from. Adding just a little bit of kerosene to the flame can ignite massive social disruption. Many people think they know everything because they saw it on social media."

Massive consumption of social media is largely to blame for the complete atomization of every societal issue. Millions of Americans consume news on their handheld devices from websites and online sources that reinforce their particular views and shield them from anything approaching an objective truth. Fully one-half of Americans consume news via social media according to a poll by the Pew Research Center.[1] Like Alice venturing into Wonderland, we are individually being led down our own individualized rabbit holes. And the more ideologically and politically fractured we become as individuals, the more susceptible we become, as a nation, to the perils of foreign influence. According to a 2019 study by cybersecurity firm SafeGuard Cyber, "(nation-)states facing the highest volume of misinformation messaging are prime targets because of existing socio-political tensions."[2]

RUSSIA

In the face of international backlash following Russia's invasion of Ukraine in 2022, Putin borrowed a page from China—which long ago erected its Great Firewall to control its citizens' access to Western media—and shut down all flows of information about his "special military operation" from reaching Russian citizens. Ukrainians who reached out to friends or family in Russia by telephone in the early days of the war were surprised to learn that the Russian populace had no idea that the Russian military was raining destruction on Ukrainian cities and committing war crimes. There are signs that Putin's information blackout may be weakening, but some experts say that the closure of Russia's information ecosystem, combined with the establishment of China's Great Firewall, represents a fracturing of the single global internet that we know today into smaller, self-contained "splinternets."

Efforts by the Russian and Chinese governments "to control content on social media platforms and to impose email censorship (along with extensive user surveillance) are the most visible manifestation of governmental pushback against the open and unregulated nature of the Internet," the National Academies of Sciences, Engineering, and Medicine published in a report on encryption in 2022. "To the extent that this trend intensifies, it could entail the end of the World Wide Web, and the development of the 'splinternet'—with individual countries or blocs of like-minded countries imposing substantive content requirements enabled by technological distinctions at national levels."[3] But this fracturing only represents defensive measures taken by autocratic regimes. On the offensive side, Beijing and Moscow continue to take advantage of America's free market of ideas to inundate the American population with propaganda.

We know with certainty the Russians hacked the Democratic Party's computers and released a steady drip of inside information via WikiLeaks that helped President Trump prevail over Hillary Clinton in the 2016 election. WikiLeaks had a disruptive agenda and operated as a proxy for Russian intelligence services, not from a commitment to any higher truth. Whether those actions impacted the election outcome is still hotly debated. What is not debatable, however, is that it never should have happened—but it did.

Beginning in March 2016, the Russian military intelligence service—the Main Intelligence Directorate of the General Staff of the Armed Forces (GRU)—compromised email accounts of candidate Hillary Clinton's campaign chairman and employees, as well as the computer networks of the Democratic National Committee and the Democratic Congressional Campaign Committee.[4] These cyber operations resulted in the compromise of hundreds of thousands of documents that Russian intelligence services leaked to the public through the fictitious personas "DCLeaks" and "Guccifer 2.0."[5] The most significant aspect of this cyber operation was the public disclosure by WikiLeaks of emails allegedly stolen from the Clinton campaign chairman, John Podesta, hours after the *Washington Post* published a lewd video considered damaging to then-candidate Donald Trump.[6]

This leak of stolen private emails from the Clinton campaign also corresponded with a significant increase in malign influence activities on social media by Russia's Internet Research Agency (IRA).[7] On October 6–7, 2016, at times corresponding to the *Washington Post* publication, IRA operatives posted more than eighteen thousand messages on Twitter, allegedly seeking to diminish the impact of the *Post*'s revelation while simultaneously undermining the Clinton campaign.[8] Using fictitious virtual personas, IRA operatives, posing as Americans, connected with a significant number of Americans to obstruct the political processes of the United States through fraud and deceit.[9]

The Russians appear particularly skilled at playing both sides of America's partisan wars. Hadnagy said he had an associate whose company analyzes threats. "They uncovered social media accounts that literally were owned by the same Russian group but were arguing with each other to create the heat," he told us. "So, you've got one group over here that's saying, 'We should arm all the teachers,' and you have another group there that says, 'All guns should be banned in America.'

"Now you're getting the tribes together and you're creating the catalyst for it. I don't want to give them credit, but it's genius if you own both sides of the argument. You can keep fanning the flames nonstop because if at any time the debate cools down, you can jump back in and fan the flames again. It's great for Russia to see political discord in this country. It hurts our economy, it hurts tax collections, and it hurts faith in the government."

One of the smartest analysts of the Russian disinformation game is arguably Clint Watts, author of the book *Messing with the Enemy: Surviving in a Social Media World of Hackers, Terrorists, Russians, and Fake News*. A West Point graduate and former special agent with the Federal Bureau of Investigation, Watts has spent a career identifying and countering malign influence. He has documented how, in the 1980s, the lead Soviet spy agency, the KGB, used what they called "active measures" to plant bad information around the world, including the false narrative that the U.S. government unleashed the AIDS virus on unsuspecting populations.[10]

The Russian hand in America's 2016 elections was something Watts watched in real time. "Starting in the late summer of 2015 and extending through the fall, Russia undertook the largest, most sophisticated, most targeted hacking campaign in world history, breaking into the email accounts of thousands of American citizens and institutions," he wrote.

Today, he and his colleagues at the Foreign Policy Research Institute have mapped out the entire Russian disinformation ecosystem. At the heart of the system are three intelligence agencies—the FSB, which replaced the Soviet-era KGB but which operates in a very similar manner; the GRU, which is the military's intelligence arm; and the separate SVR, which is a foreign intelligence service that performs some of the functions that the KGB once did. Each of the three agencies uses front news organizations whose anti-Ukrainian and anti-American stories are picked up by English-language websites. The Russian media environment "is built on an infrastructure of influencers, anonymous Telegram channels, and content creators with nebulous ties to the wider ecosystem," Watts said.[11]

In one sense, the Russians may be cleverer than the Chinese because they understand "wedge" issues such as gun control and abortion, and they play both sides. Watts's team showed how, on Ukraine issues, the Russians put out starkly different messaging on social media.

To right-wing English-language audiences, it planted articles saying "Russia: Hunter Biden Connected to Financing of Pentagon Funded Bio-Labs in Nazi-Led Ukraine." At the same time, it planted this headline in left-leaning publications that could be expected to be suspicious of NATO: "Give War a Chance: NATO and Neo-Nazis Want Ukraine Conflict to Go on Forever."

Although it was considered a ransomware attack, one newly emerged Russian hacking group called SiegedSec sought to exploit America's raging abortion debate following the Supreme Court's decision to overturn *Roe v. Wade*. SiegedSec announced that it had hacked the servers of pro-life (antiabortion) state governments in Kentucky and Alabama. "Like many, we are also pro-choice, one shouldn't be denied access to abortion," it wrote in a run-on sentence, possible evidence that a nonnative English speaker wrote it. "Keep Protesting, Keep Yourself Safe, Fuck the Government," it wrote, obviously trying to inflame passions.[12]

The Internet Research Agency is an important part of the Russian ecosystem seeking to exploit America's wedge issues. A criminal complaint filed against it in the Eastern District of Virginia, even after the 2016 election, charged that the agency sought to inflame American divisions on issues such as "immigration, gun control and the Second Amendment, the Confederate flag, race relations, LGBT issues, the Women's March, and the NFL national anthem debate."

The most recent racially motivated revelation came in July 2022 when the Justice Department charged Aleksandr Viktorovich Ionov of spreading propaganda through a U.S. African American group. Ionov remains in Moscow and is hardly at risk of arrest as long as he stays there. But the details of what he did—and what his American allies did—are revealing.

Working with the Russian intelligence agency FSB, Ionov developed a relationship with the Uhuru Movement, which is part of the African People's Socialist Party and has been based in St. Petersburg, Florida. Ionov paid to fly the founder and chairman of the group, Omali Yeshitela, to Moscow in 2015. It's not clear if any money changed hands, but Yeshitela told colleagues upon return to the United States that he wanted the Uhuru Movement to be "an instrument" of the Russian government. Just weeks after the Ukraine invasion, the Uhuru group allowed Ionov to appear on their YouTube livestream where he said, "I would like to address the free people around the world to tell you that Western propaganda is lying when they say that Russia invaded Ukraine." The fact that a domestic U.S. group would seek to enlist Russian support and extend support in return demonstrates how deeply the Russians have penetrated.[13]

It was also disclosed in September 2022 that the Internet Research Agency was behind a major collapse of the Women's March movement years earlier in 2017.[14] The controversy centered on Linda Sarsour, who was one of the prime movers behind the Women's March, a mobilization against President Trump. More than 4 million people around the United States took part in rallies in January 2017.

Within days, the Internet Research Agency launched a massive online campaign to discredit the Women's March and sow the seeds of bitter controversy between white and Black feminists, between Jews and Muslims, and other groups. Here's how the *New York Times*, which broke the story exclusively, told it:

At desks in bland offices in St. Petersburg, using models derived from advertising and public relations, copywriters were testing out social media messages critical of the Women's March movement, adopting the personas of fictional Americans.

They posted as Black women critical of white feminism, conservative women who felt excluded, and men who mocked participants as hairy-legged whiners. But one message performed better with audiences than any other.[15]

It singled out the fact that of four cochairs, Sarsour was a Palestinian American activist whose hijab marked her as a Muslim. One hundred fifty-two different Russian accounts produced material about Sarsour, and public records show that 2,642 tweets were launched, many finding large audiences.

It is the interplay between Russian propaganda outlets and troll farms on the one hand and Fox News, Newsmax, One America News, and similar organizations on the other that is most troubling to us. The coauthors of this book are both radical centrists, dismayed at the antics of those who have divided America so sharply. In this case, even though American conservatives have been fiercely critical of the Soviet Union and now Russia, different individuals, such as Fox News host Tucker Carlson, have made common cause with Russia's disinformation masters. Both Russia Today and Chinese state media broadcast clips of Carlson to support the idea that the United States was developing bioweapons in Ukraine.[16] In effect, these conservative voices are working with one devil to undercut President Biden, whom they regard as an even worse devil.

We reckon that history will show they helped undermine and discredit the very nation they professed to love. "People are asking if the far right in the U.S. is influencing Russia or Russia is influencing the far right, but the truth is that they are influencing each other," said Thomas Rid, a professor at Johns Hopkins University who studies Russian information warfare. "They are pushing the same narratives."[17]

Russians speak openly about their strategy to destroy America from within on public television. Russia's Malek Dudakov, a political scientist specializing in America, said on Russian television in March 2022, "With America, we should be working to amplify the divisions and—in light of our limited abilities—to deepen the polarization of American society."

He continued: "There is a horrific polarization of society in the United States, very serious conflicts between the Democrats and Republicans that keep expanding. You've already mentioned that America is a dying empire—and most empires weren't conquered. They were destroyed from within. The same fate awaits America in the near decade."[18]

All these sorts of messages become more powerful when the Chinese amplify them. Sputnik television alone has reached seventeen agreements with major Chinese media, which shared its articles 2,500 times in 2021 according to Vasily V. Pushkov, the international cooperation director for Rossiya Segodnya, the state company that owns and operates Sputnik.[19]

CHINA

The Chinese use the term "global discourse" to describe the battlefield of opinion. They want to erode the ability of Western media organizations to define that global discourse and replace it with flows of information that, in the words of Xi Jinping, "tell China's story well." It is an incredibly ambitious agenda—one that China shares with Russia, and it is showing signs of success.

The Chinese also learned from Russia's interference in the 2016 election. They are using social media to create an alternative anti-American, anti-Western narrative that some people in the world—in places such as Africa, the Middle East, and Asia—seem to be accepting. China and Russia are also seeking to widen the political and ethnic divides within the United States and between its allies.

One of the best examples of how China is cooperating with Russia to undermine the world's democracies is China's amplification of Russian president Vladimir Putin's justification for his invasion of Ukraine. According to the Russian narrative, the United States and its NATO allies *forced* Putin to invade Ukraine, which was on the verge of invading Russia, the Kremlin claimed. Ukrainian "neo-Nazis" intended to commit "genocide" against the Russian population in Ukraine's eastern regions and in Russia itself. All these accusations were broadcast and posted so thoroughly in China that the Chinese people, as a whole, were persuaded that Putin's war was a just one.

Prior to the Russian invasion of Ukraine, the Chinese Communist Party even created a 101-minute video that compliments Putin for seeking to cleanse Russia of Western-inspired political and cultural toxins. This is the core maxim of authoritarianism: anything that challenges the state is evil and must be eliminated. "The most powerful weapon possessed by the West is . . . the methods they use in ideological struggle," the video's narrator states.

In the worldview shared by Putin and Xi, Mikhail Gorbachev was "not enough of a man" to stand up to his own people, and his weakness in the face of shifting social movements directly resulted in the collapse of the Soviet Union in 1991. Chinese leaders also blame Gorbachev for visiting China in May 1989, which helped fuel student unrest that ultimately led to the brutal crushing of dissent in Tiananmen Square on June 4, 1989. "They have taken only one lesson from [the Soviet collapse], and that is you do not allow any freedom of expression," Sergey Radchenko, a professor at the John Hopkins School of Advanced International Studies, said, "because this kind of freedom inevitably leads to loss of political control and that creates chaos."[20]

Despite American social media platforms banning Russia Today and Sputnik from appearing on their sites after the Russian invasion of Ukraine, Chinese influencers continued to circulate pro-Putin reports on Facebook, where its channels command more than a billion viewers worldwide. "As Western governments collectively encouraged Silicon Valley to restrict the reach of Russia's disinformation ecosystem, China's propaganda system quickly became an alternate vehicle for the Kremlin's false narratives," a report from the Australian Strategic Policy Institute concluded.[21]

Simply because they have more money and people, the Chinese appear to be somewhat bigger players in America's social media and traditional media environment than the Russians at the moment, even if the Russians have been successful in finding common ground with right-wing media personalities such as Fox News's Tucker Carlson. The evidence of what the Chinese are doing is everywhere.

The Central Committee of the Communist Party demonstrated in November 2021 just how seriously the party regards the internet. "The

Central Committee has made it clear that failure in the cyberspace domain will spell disaster for the Party's long-term governance," *China Daily* quoted a Central Committee document as saying. "The Party therefore attaches great importance to the Internet as the main arena, battleground, and frontline of the ideological struggle" against Western values.[22]

The pugnacious former Chinese Foreign Ministry spokesperson Zhao Lijian boasts that he personally has more than a million followers on Twitter (@zlj517). One role Zhao performs, whether consciously or not, is to amplify disinformation that comes from suspected Russian spinmeisters. In March 2020, just after the pandemic started, he retweeted a report from the Canadian Centre for Research on Globalization that concluded the coronavirus had started in the United States. Zhao asked his followers to retweet it further. But the think tank and website (www.globalresearch.ca) are run by Michael Chossudovsky, a former professor at the University of Ottawa, and the website has been cited by the State Department as being "Kremlin aligned." So, a Russian sympathizer created fake news under the rubric of a Canadian think tank, and the Chinese government promoted it.[23]

Chinese government entities, in fact, are flooding global social media with fake accounts used to advance their authoritarian agenda and confuse the world about issues such as its repression of the Uighurs. The *New York Times* obtained documents online from the Shanghai Pudong Public Security Bureau Public Opinion Technology Services, published in Mandarin. The office was looking for private-sector contractors to do its dirty work. The key platforms were Twitter and Facebook—both of which are banned in China, but which the Chinese government is using to penetrate the American information ecosystem. The public opinion specialists in Shanghai were looking for contractors to rapidly create websites that would distribute false information using "bots," which are fully automated accounts operated by a program rather than a person, allowing posts to be published in volumes not possible for human-operated accounts.[24]

The Chinese scheme was observed shortly after the outbreak of the COVID-19 pandemic. To combat true reporting linking the origins of the virus with Wuhan, China, Chinese government influence operators created a fictitious Swiss biologist to malign the United States. "Wilson Edwards" loudly proclaimed that the United States was interfering with the World Health Organization's (WHO) efforts to track down the origins of the coronavirus in Wuhan—even though it was really the Chinese government that was hampering the WHO inquiry. The actors then used more than five hundred Facebook accounts to amplify this message worldwide. The Swiss government, when asked, said a Swiss citizen named Wilson Edwards did not exist. But the fake scientist's accusations had already been quoted in the Chinese media. Facebook took down the accounts—after the fact.

It does not seem to matter that Twitter and Facebook take down fake Chinese government accounts after they have been revealed, because the government simply launches more. They can do so at an astounding rate at least partly because of their automated bots.

"It doesn't matter if an individual account or even thousands of accounts are suspended," Darren Linvill, a professor at Clemson University who studies social media disinformation, said to the *New York Times*. "They create more at an astounding rate, and by the time the account is suspended (which is often very quickly) the account has already done its job."[25] But, as SafeGuard Cyber points out, "information warfare is waged on multiple fronts." Social media platforms are "but one facet of social media operations to influence conversations and perceptions."[26] It has reached the point that the Chinese and Russian information operators can influence Google, YouTube, and Bing search engine rankings of articles and videos on issues that are vital to them.

The Brookings Institution and the Alliance for Securing Democracy reported that China's global news and propaganda infrastructure, including websites located outside of China, can shape how articles on the Uighurs in Xinjiang Province, for example, are ranked and displayed in search engine rankings in the United States and elsewhere. SafeGuard Cyber refers to this practice as "black-hat SEO"—or search engine optimization.[27] The tactic involves the use of bots to promote articles that give favorable impressions of Chinese policies to the first page of search engine results. According to Forbes, 75 percent of web surfers never scroll beyond the first page of results.[28] That means that if the Chinese government can manipulate American search engines through ad buying such that the first page is predominantly pro-China, the vast majority of American internet users will only see what the Chinese Communist Party is feeding them.

More alarmingly, this is not a two-way street. The dominant American search engines are little used in China, with restrictions causing Google to command only 2 percent usage throughout the Middle Kingdom. And because the Chinese government compels its search engines to require that advertisers obtain an internet content provider license from the state in order to advertise, the government has significant control over attempted manipulations of its information space. In other words, Chinese black-hat SEO is a one-way influence effort.

The ways that the Chinese attempted to control and influence coverage of the Winter Olympics in Beijing in February 2022 were particularly revealing. The Chinese government and the International Olympic Committee (IOC) knew that China's critics were going to try to use the games to shine a spotlight on not only China's treatment of its Uighur population, but also on its significant increase in political repression in Hong Kong, as well as its constant military and diplomatic pressure against Taiwan, the Philippines, and other neighboring countries.

The Chinese, in the absence of any meaningful pressure from the IOC, took advantage of the COVID-19 pandemic to impose the strictest controls on Western journalists that were conceivably possible. The journalists were kept in "closed loops," far removed from Chinese society. It was a dramatic shift from the relative openness that the Chinese government tolerated for the 2008 Summer Olympics, which were also held in Beijing.

But China went far beyond controls on foreign journalists. Chinese diplomats hired at least one public relations firm—New Jersey–based Vippi Media—to run a social media campaign led by "influencers" to promote the games. A contract filed in the official registration of foreign agents in Washington, DC, showed that the diplomats paid the firm for at least 3.4 million impressions on TikTok, Instagram, and Twitch, highlighting "touching moments" and "positive outcomes" at the games.

To do that, Vippi Media hired a *Real Housewives of Beverly Hills* TV star of Chinese descent (who also claimed lineage to Confucius), a Paralympic swimmer, and a self-described "brand king," among others, to promote the touching moments on Instagram and TikTok. These influencers had about 5 million people who followed their videos, photos, and other content on everything from travel to sports and from fashion to women's issues. The posts were not properly labeled as ads, as required by TikTok and Instagram. This social media campaign allowed the Chinese "to boost the reach and the resonance of their messaging to make it appear to be authentic, independent content," according to Jessica Brandt, a Brookings Institution expert on foreign interference and disinformation.[29]

Video plays an increasingly important role in China's propaganda efforts online. Western news organizations have clearly and repeatedly documented how the Chinese Communists have subjected the Uighur people to mass detention and sought to eliminate their identity. But the same Shanghai police unit mentioned above purchased services from a video company to make at least twenty videos of "happy" Uighurs for distribution on Twitter. Altogether, these videos appeared thousands of times. Twitter ultimately shut down the accounts, but not until after the Chinese had created a parallel reality that thousands of Americans saw. The Chinese don't necessarily have to convince people. They only need to sow seeds of doubt and confusion.

China's influence also reaches beyond social media into the traditional media space, namely radio and television. A single Chinese state-run firm, China Radio International (CRI), has at least thirty-three radio stations in fourteen countries—including English-language broadcaster WCRW in Washington, DC—to broadcast news favoring the Chinese Communist Party's viewpoint, according to Christopher Paul, a senior social scientist at the RAND Corporation. More than a dozen of CRI's FM radio stations in cities across the United States broadcast subtle pro-Beijing propaganda. If it were blatant propaganda, it could be easily ignored, but subtle propaganda is much more enticing and therefore more insidious.

The Federal Communications Commission (FCC) does monitor foreign ownership of radio stations, but CRI obfuscates its ownership by making purchases through shell companies or by owning several partial stakes that add up to a controlling interest. "While China takes full advantage of the opportunities of the free market, and Chinese firms buy up U.S. media, foreign firms are denied similar access in China," Paul wrote.[30]

It is much the same in television. China Global Television Network America broadcasts overt propaganda that reaches tens of millions of American households via cable television each day. It is part of the international arm of China Central Television, Beijing's main domestic propaganda organ.

That's what America's wide-open system allows—anyone with money can pay to broadcast and publish "content" that millions of Americans see. Unlike China, we have not erected a digital firewall to block foreign content—it would be unconstitutional to do so. Indeed, the Supreme Court has consistently held that the First Amendment protects Americans' right to receive foreign information and ideas.[31] By contrast, China's Great Firewall blocks access to the vast majority of American social media and news outlets in order to control China's domestic information environment.

It appears the Chinese government and Communist Party are attempting to turn their system of internal controls loose on the entire world, the *Washington Post* has reported.[32] This is not some fringe website—it is one of America's most respected newspapers. The *Post* reviewed hundreds of bidding documents, contracts, and company filings, all in Chinese. China's government agencies, military, and police are buying tools that allow them to "mine" Twitter and Facebook to create a database of what is being said about issues that China cares about. They are using Big Data and artificial intelligence methods, such as natural language translation, to do this in real time.

This would allow for the mapping of social and professional networks, as suggested in a previous chapter, but many of these systems include an alarm system that automatically flags "false" statements and reports on China. These tools look for viral trends—meaning stories or statements about China that start circulating and then gain momentum. Ultimately, that seems to give the Chinese the power to launch their own offensives on social media to counteract any negative material. "The ultimate purpose of analysis and prediction is to guide and intervene in public opinion," an analyst at the People's Daily Online Public Opinion Data Center was quoted as saying. "Public data from social network users can be used to analyze the characteristics and preferences of users, and then guide them in a targeted manner." In other words, China is trying to win the global discourse in real time, twenty-four hours a day. The *Washington Post* story escaped broad attention, perhaps because it was published on New Year's Eve in December 2021.

One of China's main propaganda goals is to spotlight the past and current treatment of America's minority and indigenous populations. China's "wolf warrior" diplomats conduct much of this effort, whether in their own names or under assumed names. One can see from the tweets of the Foreign Ministry's Zhao just what the strategy is: "#COVID seems to be racially discriminatory in the #US. Mortality rate among the whites has been much lower than that among American Indians, although average Indian patients were younger."

It's also worth reading Zhao's statement at a press briefing on April 14, 2022. When asked about a report showing that congressional redistricting is hurting Black Americans, he said this:

[The report] shows that African Americans get only 73.9 percent of the American pie of equality white people enjoy. Black people have slipped further behind white people in wealth, health, education, social justice, and civic engagement. This gain exposes the persistent racial discrimination in the U.S., which has seeped into all aspects of social life.

The utopia depicted by [American] words is shattered by reality. The U.S. claims to champion openness and inclusiveness. It declares that life, liberty, and the pursuit of happiness are unalienable [sic] rights all men are endowed with, and that the American dream is out there for all who set out to chase it. . . .

The U.S. government should take a hard look at the country's own human rights issues, earnestly protect the equal and lawful rights of African Americans and other ethnic minorities, and square rhetoric about human rights and equality for the tangible benefits of each and every American people [sic].[33]

We can debate how much truth there is in what he says, but his remarks represent a wholesale assault on the legitimacy of any American government to advance American and international values in the world.

Moreover, the ultimate objective of both China and Russia may be to foment genuine ideological and physical unrest in the United States and elsewhere. According to a Mandiant report, the firm's threat intelligence office discovered a network of hundreds of fake accounts on Twitter, Facebook, and YouTube, as well as dozens of other sites such as Tumblr, Vimeo, TikTok, and Medium. In 2021, Mandiant identified two different threads to this campaign.

One was to embolden Asian Americans concerned about racial discrimination to protest against Chinese nationals whom Beijing considers enemies. In April 2021, for example, thousands of posts in multiple languages called on Asian Americans to stage a rally on April 24 in New York City and "fight back" against these individuals. Significantly, the Chinese campaigners digitally manipulated an image to depict a much more significant gathering to instill fear in its target audience.

The second thread of this campaign sought to bring physical pressure against people who argued that COVID-19 originated in China. But the posts showed a masculine fist smashing small human characters. "Shut Up Your Mouth. Don't Make Fake News About COVID-19," the posts said. The implication was obvious—anyone who said the disease originated in China should be physically assaulted.

The campaign did not seem to work, but the Chinese clearly were experimenting and testing the limits of their abilities. "The attempt to physically mobilize protesters in the U.S. provides early warning that the actors responsible may be starting to explore more direct means of influence and may be indicative of an emerging intent to motivate real-world activity outside of China's territories," Mandiant concluded.[34]

THE ADVERTISING PROBLEM

It is not a secret that America's adversaries use social media to recruit spies—primarily on LinkedIn. LinkedIn, which is owned by Microsoft, is an ideal vehicle for this because it is not blocked in China. The reason is that LinkedIn agreed to censor posts containing sensitive material. So Chinese intelligence agents are able to sit at their desks in Beijing or Shanghai, create fake accounts, and send out friend requests to prominent Americans, attempting to create online relationships that might lead to some form of consulting or employment. It's common for LinkedIn users to click a box on their pages stating that they are "looking for work" and to disclose their security clearances. "We've seen Chinese intelligence services doing this on a mass scale," said William R. Evanina, the former director of the U.S. National Counterintelligence and Security Center, which oversees all activities tracking foreign spies targeting the United States. "Instead of dispatching spies to the U.S. to recruit a single target, it's more efficient to sit behind a computer in China and send out friend requests to thousands of targets using fake profiles."[35]

Sometimes the payoff is huge. A former employee of the CIA and the Defense Intelligence Agency, Kevin Patrick Mallory, was sentenced in 2019 to twenty years in prison for spying for China. The relationship started when he replied to a LinkedIn message from a Chinese intelligence agent posing as a think tank representative.

Malign influence and foreign espionage activities are allowed to persist mainly because large social media companies generate revenue by boasting massive user bases to demand huge advertising fees. But America's Big Tech companies are not only making money *from* Chinese and Russian accounts through advertising—Google, in particular, is also generating advertising revenue *for* those governments, says Gordon Crovitz, a former journalist who became the publisher of the *Wall Street Journal*. He is now co-CEO of NewsGuard, which identifies websites that are sources of disinformation. It has discovered three hundred Russian disinformation sites. It works with U.S. Cyber Command and the Department of State as well as major tech companies such as Microsoft.

NewsGuard, based in New York City, is organized very much like a news organization. It has layers of human editing and review processes before reaching any conclusions about the nature of a website. One of the most important questions it asks is whether a site discloses ownership and control. It's no surprise that disinformation sites try to pretend to be something they are not.

"Of the three hundred disinformation websites in Russia, everybody knows RT, Sputnik and Tass," Crovitz explained to us. "They are government funded. That's just a drop in the bucket. There's Pravda, which is privately owned by a pal of Putin's, and there are these think tanks that are quick to hop on the latest information."

Because the Department of Justice has not enforced the Foreign Agent Registration Act against online news sources the way it did against Nazi propaganda that appeared in print during World War II, "RT has become the single most popular source of news on YouTube in the United States, the United Kingdom [Britain], Germany, and other markets," Crovitz explained. "They did that by creating a fantastic YouTube news channel with videos of hamsters chasing cats, car crashes, natural disasters, and every once in a while, stories about how Vladimir Putin is not such a bad guy. Of course, now it's full of disinformation about the war in Ukraine. They attracted a large audience of people who had no idea that RT stood for Russia Today. To them, it looked like AFP, NBC, or BBC."

NewsGuard analyzes websites that appear in a user's search and attaches red or green icons to them as they are displayed on a user's screen to tell viewers whether they are legitimate or not. It is something like the old-fashioned *Good Housekeeping* seal of approval. Microsoft is alone among the social media players in licensing NewsGuard and making it available to customers of its Edge browser.

The Russian disinformation campaign is well organized, NewsGuard has found. "We recently found a website called Russofile.com, which has very little traffic, but it looks like an aggregator of Russian disinformation that editors of Russian disinformation sites use like it is the Associated Press (the wire service that hundreds of American news organizations rely on) of Russian disinformation. They will pick up a story and rewrite it in their own words to fulfill their mission of spreading Russian disinformation. That was useful for Cyber Command just to know there was such an organized site."

Working with Microsoft, NewsGuard issued a report on how the disinformation about the United States operating a bioweapons lab in Ukraine started out. "We traced the provenance, or origin, of that, along with Microsoft, to a video posted on a YouTube channel back in November before the war," Crovitz said. "As soon as the invasion happened, RT and Sputnik started running stories saying, 'One of the reasons we have to invade Ukraine is because the U.S. is running these bioweapons labs in Ukraine, as reported by this YouTube channel in November.' That YouTube channel is run by an American in Moscow who has previously published other Russian disinformation. That's what we call 'prepositioned disinformation.' It makes it looks more legit because RT and Sputnik are able to say, 'It's already been established, already reported.' They are super sophisticated. We are not."

For brands, NewsGuard tries to help them keep their programmatic advertising off disreputable websites. Programmatic advertising is automatic advertising. According to Crovitz, the way the ad industry has evolved is that a third of all ad spending in the world is done through elaborate computer systems. That's hundreds of billions of dollars.

Advertisers and their ad agencies use consolidators like Google, which is the largest "demand-side platform" in the world, to place their ads on media sites, including social media sites, where certain kinds of individuals are shopping or viewing. Different brands target different demographics. Google serves a large percentage of the three hundred Russian disinformation sites. "Everything is done through computers, so the advertiser has no idea where the ads have been run," Crovitz said. "We did a report that estimates that $2.6 billion a year goes to disinformation sites, including Russian ones. The largest advertiser on Sputnik News was Warren Buffet through GEICO, the insurance company he owns. He never intended for the ads to go there, but it's subsidizing Russian disinformation. It's just a crazy system. As long as Google is allowing Russian disinformation sites to monetize their traffic with ads, they are going to keep getting subsidized by GEICO and every other company you've ever heard of. That's where the ads just end up. It's insane.

"To be fair to the advertisers and ad agencies, this problem has been a known problem for two or three years. There really wasn't a solution to it because until we came along, there wasn't a list of disinformation sites," he explained.

But overall, Crovitz accuses the large social media companies (with the exception of Microsoft, his customer) of being major allies of Russia's Politburo and the Chinese Communist Party. "I refer to them as the useful idiots," he said. "That's what Lenin called the capitalists. The capitalists were going to sell the rope with which they were going to be hanged. The digital platforms not only allow the distribution of disinformation. They allow it to be monetized through advertising. It's a crazy system."

THE FUTURE OF MALIGN INFLUENCE

The technological tools to allow far more pervasive influence operations are beginning to roll out. The Center for Security and Emerging Technology reports that artificial intelligence can now generate text that quantifiably shapes people's opinions.[36] China or Russia could use AI to generate floods of messages on social media that might just persuade viewers to believe something that is completely fictitious. Using deepfakes—artificially generated or altered videos—China or Russia also could distribute fake video segments with every appearance of authenticity. The searing video of George Floyd's death in Minneapolis triggered unrest, violent protests, and further killings in American cities, providing a real-world example of how quickly viral content can turn American cities into war zones. The power to create that level of societal unrest is in the hands of America's adversaries.

The goal of the authoritarian regimes in Moscow and Beijing is to undermine Americans' faith in their own democracy. Regarding all the data that China has been stealing, Taiwan's Howard Jyan said in our interview with him, "they can do lots of things with the data. They can do personal profiling. They can analyze the individual. They can know the social relationships of this individual. They can analyze what you like and what you dislike. Even your political preferences. Based on this, they can then affect your country's election. They can deliver the information through social networking. They can do information warfare against the individual or against the whole society. It is not like a traffic accident you can see. Information warfare disinformation or misinformation could change your perception of your whole country."

This is hardly a fringe concern. Columnist Ezra Klein, writing in the *New York Times*, explains it this way: "Imagine a world in which the United States has a contested presidential election, as it did in 2020. If one candidate was friendlier to Chinese interests, might the Chinese Communist Party insist that ByteDance (the owner of TikTok) give a nudge to content favoring that candidate? Or if it wanted to weaken America rather than shape the outcome, maybe TikTok begins serving up more and more videos with election conspiracy theories, sowing chaos at a moment when the country is near fracture."[37] This is what is at stake.

Let's now turn to how Americans have created systems that are so vulnerable.

CHAPTER 6

Software Meltdown

The Problem with Trust

CHASE CUNNINGHAM IS A HIGHLY EXPERIENCED CYBER WARRIOR. HE spent twenty years in the U.S. Navy, much of it supporting the National Security Agency's cryptographic efforts. After he left the navy, he was "detailed," or sent on assignments, to the CIA, FBI, and Defense Intelligence Agency. "I got to see everything," he says now. Along the way, he earned a PhD in computer science and wrote a book in 2020 titled *Cyber Warfare—Truth, Tactics, and Strategies*. He works as chief strategy officer for cybersecurity firm Ericom Software and has branded himself as "Dr. ZeroTrust."

Based on his expertise, we asked him a series of simple questions starting with this one: Is America's software safe? "No. Unequivocally, no," he immediately replied. "The very nature of the internet and how we build software means that, because it is borderless and boundaryless, there is inherent risk to it."

How did it happen that smart people in America built systems that are so vulnerable? "It's one of those things where the 'nifty cool' factor of the internet outpaced the ability to keep it secure," said Cunningham, who is originally from Texas and hence prefers colorful language. "Like everywhere else, usability trumps security every day, twice on Sunday. In this instance, people figured out that they could do stuff and make money on the internet with software, with the cloud. The rush was to grow the market. No one asked, 'How do we do this correctly and securely with an eye on national security?' The fact that we have an interconnected global society makes things very complicated."

So, who is responsible for the current state of cybersecurity? "I would say all Americans are responsible for it," Cunningham said. "I think the corporate world probably expedited that process, but I think the fact that we are as tied to the internet as we are—especially the generation that's coming behind me, meaning my kids—means it's even more their responsibility than it is a corporate issue."

In this chapter, we will explain why America's software is so vulnerable. It's part of the explanation for how China and Russia have been able to penetrate our computer systems so deeply. The lack of security in our software is not necessarily a design flaw; it is a conscious choice that is made with the development of every new design feature for everything from your Waze app to the controllers that operate the electricity grid. Security exists on a spectrum. On one end of the spectrum is total security, and on the other is total efficiency. To achieve greater efficiencies, we inherently give up security.

The heart of the issue is how software is "built." Dating back to the time when creating the internet was seen as a great and noble undertaking, many volunteers and nonprofit software developers built the plumbing—the foundational code that undergirds the internet and all our computer systems. They posted their software in open-source repositories so others could copy and edit it for their own purposes. Others then used that foundational code to build some of the most complex and "trusted" software we use on a daily basis—often using automated tools that introduced the possibility of error.

In general, humans write software typically using three to five different programming languages, such as Java and Python, for any specific program. Different languages have different strong points and are therefore useful for different types of programming. The code that humans write—that which makes sense to the human mind—is put through a "compiler" that changes it into machine-readable binary code (ones and zeroes) that a computer can read to execute the program. The word "code" covers both what humans write and the machine-readable version of it. There can be millions of lines of code in a software application.

"Algorithms," "programs," and "applications" are not the same thing. In fact, they form a hierarchy. Programmers write specific pieces of logic called algorithms. Algorithms form basic logic gates, such as: "if [X], then [Y]; but if [NOT X], then [Z]." Multiple algorithms work together to run programs. Then it takes many different programs to create an end product that can be used, which is an application, or simply "app."

Software developers routinely borrow code that others have written to create their final products. Only a small percentage of an application of millions of lines of code may be proprietary or unique. Many times, developers find code that has been "published" in public repositories or libraries, such as GitHub. They can also use propriety software available only for their company. For instance, whenever Microsoft updates its email client, Outlook, the software developers do not write a wholly new program. The developers will build upon the code from the previous version. If there is an unknown flaw in the previous version's code, it can be unknowingly copied into the latest version as well.

Malicious actors can take advantage of this system in multiple ways. If a hacker or malicious insider can insert "bad" code into a repository, it can produce many vulnerable programs. This practice is called repository poisoning. Other ways malicious actors can take advantage of this is either by stealing the credentials of a legitimate software developer and publishing a malicious version of his or her code, or by publishing software packages whose names are similar to other legitimate packages. That creates confusion, mistakes, and vulnerabilities.

If a software developer makes a mistake and downloads the wrong software package from one of these repositories, the hacker can gain access to the end user's computer and install additional malware. The hacker can also then move into that end user's entire network. This is one form of what are called "supply-chain attacks." The supply chain that created an end user's software has been compromised, resulting in vulnerable programs or applications.

The entire internet and large swathes of the world's IT systems are based on something called the Linux kernel. It was invented by Finland's Linus Torvalds in 1992 and acts as an intermediary between the hardware of a computing system and the software or applications that are installed on a computer. Considered "open source," Linux has been updated multiple times by the world's community of programmers. No one "owns" the Linux kernel. But the U.S. Department of Defense Advanced Research Projects Agency, or DARPA—successor to the organization that created the internet, ARPA—has now recognized that the Linux kernel could be the source of major vulnerabilities because Huawei has been one of the largest contributors to updating and maintaining it. DARPA, the military's research arm, wants to try to use machine learning to identify risks in the kernel, but it may simply be impossible. "People are realizing now: wait a minute, literally everything we do is underpinned by Linux," said Dave Aitel, a former NSA computer security scientist. "This is a core technology to our society. Not understanding kernel security means we can't secure critical infrastructure."[1]

One of the best, simplest examples of what can go wrong with open-source software is what happened with Apache's Log4j. This is a piece of software that records events such as errors and routine system operations inside software programs. Log4j is used primarily by software developers to track changes in applications being built. It was developed and is maintained by volunteers at something called the Apache Software Foundation.

Software developers have "borrowed" the Log4j code library thousands of times, perhaps hundreds of thousands of times, and incorporated it into their own programs. Rather than going through the time and expense of writing their own logging software, they use Log4j. As a result, Log4j is in millions of computers. It's part of our entire software ecosystem. For example, it's in the online game Minecraft, which is owned by Microsoft, where it is used to log activity such as total memory used and user commands typed into the console. It's also used in cloud and interactive services such as Apple iCloud, Amazon Web Services, and Twitter. Many multimillion- and billion-dollar companies make money from it every day.[2]

The problem started in November 2021 when the cloud computing arm of Alibaba, the Chinese technology giant, spotted a vulnerability in Log4j, dubbed "Log4Shell." (The use of the term "shell" implies that something has been taken over and controlled.) Microsoft soon reported that it had also discovered Log4Shell in Minecraft. By then, the variant had already spread globally. Hackers believed to be Chinese had figured out a way to subvert Log4j that opens the door for malicious activities such as stealing sensitive information, taking control of a system, and even using a system it controls to slip malware into other computers surreptitiously. Log4Shell was like a nuclear bomb exploding in cyber-space—the shockwaves were enormous.[3]

U.S. officials said hundreds of millions of devices were at risk and issued an emergency directive ordering federal agencies to mitigate the threat by Christmas Eve. Jen Easterly, director of the Cybersecurity and Infrastructure Security Agency (CISA), mentioned earlier, called it "one of the most serious flaws" she has ever seen.[4] Even after the Apache Foundation issued a patch, some users continued to download the flawed version. The tech world exploded in anger and frustration.

The *MIT Technology Review* caught up with a man it identified as Volkan Yazici, who is a member of the Log4j project. It did not reveal his location but reported that he was working twenty-two-hour days trying to fix the vulnerability in Log4j. "The team is working around the clock," Yazici said via email. "Log4j maintainers have been working sleeplessly on mitigation measures. . . . Yet nothing is stopping people to bash us for work we aren't paid for, for a feature we all dislike yet needed to keep due to backward compatibility concerns."[5]

Sometimes the volunteers quit because no one is paying them. In 2018, the developer behind an open-source project called ua-parser-js quit. The software was used by Google, Amazon, and Facebook. Someone else took control of the project and added malicious code to it to steal cryptocurrency. The Department of Homeland Security had to issue a warning to users.

"The internet is a house of cards, to be perfectly frank," Cunning-ham told us. "It's all kind of cobbled together and held up by a variety of collaborations between corporate this and open source that and volunteer here and private there and whatever else. If at any one time, any one of those particular entities decided to say, 'Screw it. I've had enough,' and they took their toys and left the sandbox, we'd be in a very bad place. Everything is intersectional. That's the problem with constant connectivity. The more connected you are, the more risk you inherently take on."

There were two other major penetrations of the software supply chain in late 2020 and 2021 that were more complex but help illustrate the vulnerabilities of America's software supply chains—SolarWinds and Microsoft Exchange.

SolarWinds is a Texas-based company that makes the software that allows big companies to manage their sprawling computer systems, which means the software has an overview of how entire systems work. Because it is a trusted brand, companies allow SolarWinds to issue updates of its software that automatically go into their systems. This model of frequent updates to software, like how Tesla updates AutoPilot in its cars, is at the heart of how the software industry works these days.

The problem was that a Russian state-sponsored group affiliated with its Foreign Security Service (SVR), also known as Cozy Bear or APT29 (the same group that hacked the Democratic National Committee), took advantage of a silly mistake. During its reconnaissance of SolarWinds' systems, it found an email server that had not been given a strong enough login or password. The login was "administrator," and the password was "solarwinds123"—which were easy to guess. The chief executive officer would later blame an intern for posting the password on GitHub, the software collaboration site, in a personal account. But blaming an intern rang hollow. The company's IT managers had simply failed to take basic precautions.[6]

Cozy Bear was able to patiently and methodically work its way into the systems of the people who actually write the code that goes out to SolarWinds customers, which carried the product name Orion. They were able to insert their malicious code and trick the compiler into applying a signature to the end product, so that any end user seeing the update being made in his or her system would assume it was an authentic SolarWinds product.

This was more than a simple parlor trick. Adam Meyers led the cyber forensics team for CrowdStrike, the world-renowned security firm that SolarWinds hired to determine just how the SVR got in. Meyers, during an interview with National Public Radio's Dina Temple-Raston, likened the attack to the urban myth of an evil neighbor hiding razorblades in Halloween candy. "Imagine those Reese's peanut butter cups going into the package, and just before the machine comes down and seals the package, some other thing comes in and slides a razor blade into your Reese's peanut butter cup," he said. "Instead of a razor blade, the hackers swapped the files so the package gets sealed and it goes out the door to the store."[7]

Their malicious code spread like wildfire. As noted earlier, more than eighteen thousand high-profile customers, including multiple U.S. government agencies and tech companies such as Microsoft and FireEye, were affected. The White House acknowledged that Cozy Bear carried out the targeted cyberattacks on several U.S. government agencies. At one point, the Russians were able to penetrate some areas of the Department of Defense.

While the government and private industry were still mopping up the SolarWinds mess, a new malevolent campaign broke out in March 2021. Microsoft said that attackers, starting two months earlier in January 2021, had compromised its Exchange server, which provides email service to thousands of customers. They had exploited four software vulnerabilities. Some thirty thousand organizations in the United States were attacked as the hackers gained access to their email accounts using PowerShell to give them control of systems. PowerShell is a Microsoft program that allows for task automation and scripting. Shortly after discovery, Microsoft issued a "patch" so that customers could seek to mitigate the damage.

The attackers seemed to be setting the stage for a broader campaign because many of the targets they chose were smaller, less robust, less modern companies. "Even if these organizations are not the primary target, they can be a conduit to other organizations they are connected to," Gartner analyst Peter Firstbrook told CSO (chief security officer) Online. "If I can hack into your Exchange and your customer is the Defense Department, then I can impersonate you and send phishing messages to the Defense Department. The hackers are setting themselves up with a rich attack infrastructure to go after other higher-value targets."[8]

At first, who did it was unclear. Microsoft initially blamed a hacking group called Hafnium, which had some ties to China's Ministry of State Security. It also said that Chinese entities with whom it had shared some of its security source code may have been responsible. It was not until the summer that the Biden administration and European governments concluded that it was in fact China's Ministry of State Security itself that was involved.

Even though the hackers went through the process of identifying software vulnerabilities, the fact that Microsoft had shared at least some of its source code with the Chinese government and other Chinese entities triggered some suspicions that it was used against the company—and the entire world. "That's something the Chinese government has done a pretty good job on," Cunningham said. "If you want to do business in the giant Chinese market, which everybody does, they tell you that you have to share your source code. They were able to do whatever they wanted with that code. I don't think that's something that should ever shock anyone. It's the cost of doing business in mainland China."

The combination of the SolarWinds and Exchange hacks, followed not long after by the Log4j hack, amounted to a dramatic assault on all American computing systems, despite largely escaping the attention of the broader American public. Over the space of about a year, the software in millions of American computer systems was penetrated. The Russians and Chinese could still be using these positions to invisibly move across networks to even more organizations. Malware allowing for backdoor access was almost certainly installed, meaning that even if the attackers left a particular system, they could return at will. "I would say the likelihood that they are still somewhere in those systems is pretty strong," Cunningham said. "My experience tells me that they probably put in backdoors somewhere to something that would give them access when they wanted it."

Paul E. Black has been a computer scientist at the Commerce Department's National Institute of Standards and Technology (NIST) for twenty-five years, most recently in its Software Quality Group. He possesses a genius-level knowledge of computers. For example, he has experience with Python, C, Perl, Java, Pascal, C+, ML, Lisp, Fortran,

RPG II, Assembler, and Forth programming languages. He also edits a well-known online dictionary of algorithms and data structures. It was with some trepidation that we conducted an interview with him.

To create its list of known vulnerabilities (see https://nvd.nist.gov), NIST functions as a clearinghouse. If a major company or a hospital chain discovers a software vulnerability, it typically will report that to the software vendor, which then shares it with NIST. The institute collects vulnerabilities from many different sources and then sorts them out to eliminate overlaps or repetitions. It gives each vulnerability a name, like CVE-2022–32207. That way, assuming that the software vendor issues a patch or a fix, every company that suffers from a particular vulnerability can know which patch to use. Hundreds of vulnerabilities are discovered each week, and in a year thousands of them are reported.

Making the vulnerabilities known publicly is part of a conscious calculation. "Suppose you're a researcher and you find a problem with PowerPoint software," Black said. "If you keep it completely to yourself, somebody else who is smarter, some larger nation-state that has a lot of resources, will probably be able to discover that same weakness. Just keeping it to yourself isn't going to buy you much. Hopefully, if you talk to the people in charge of the software, they can quickly develop a patch. Hopefully, when the vulnerability is announced to the public, you announce a patch at the same time."

Black was aware of the fact that China's Ministry of State Security was observed accessing NIST's list of vulnerabilities, but still argued that the virtues of going public with the information outweigh the risks of doing so. "I'm sure other nation-state actors are watching those lists very carefully," he said. "But the [expert] community has decided it's better to tell the good guys about the problem. The bad guys are going to find the problem anyway."

But the system does not work smoothly, to put it mildly. Software vendors do not always choose to issue patches to fix their own software. "If you as a user say, 'Oh, I've got a two-year-old version of XYZ running on my computer and someone found it has a problem," Black speculated, "the vendor may say, 'Upgrade to the latest version of the software because we've fixed the problem there. We're not going to go back and dig out the old code and issue a patch. Sorry.' Sometimes the developers say it's too difficult. They may judge that it's inconsequential." Another problem is that it may take weeks or months for a software firm to issue a patch, giving malicious actors plenty of time to exploit a vulnerability.

A relatively low percentage of companies make full use of the patches even if they are issued. "Software tends to be more brittle than we like," Black said. "A patch may break the software. We may be using software to produce locomotives and we put in the patch, and all of a sudden our machine tools don't run anymore. It takes us a week or so to figure out how to adapt something because of how the patch was applied. Companies will often apply a patch to a test machine. Only then do they roll it out to their systems across thousands of computers. It takes time for those patches to be applied."

Then there are companies that don't hear about the discovery of a vulnerability or simply decide they have too many other problems that demand their money and personnel. There is a large number of people "who just don't bother to fix it," Black said. "Patches are not always applied and often not as rapidly as smart people in the tech community think wise."

One of the riddles about known vulnerabilities is how can a developer, who has borrowed code from open-source repositories, know that his or her software is compromised? "As a developer, I may develop a piece of software and not realize there is a problem with it," Black said. A developer may see an imperfection or possible problem but conclude that it would be impossible to break into the software by exploiting it. "Yet some ingenious person may figure out an attack based on that problem," Black explained. "So technically, yes, I released that software with a vulnerability. I was a reasonable developer, but someone else found a vulnerability on down the road."

Black also noted that changes in a company's overall IT system can have a negative impact on software. Software, after all, has to interact with a computer's operating system and its hardware, and these elements often are built into large networks, sometimes with cloud computing. "It's true that software doesn't break, but it's also true that there are so many other things in our ecosystems," he said. "Sometimes a new version of an operating system may invalidate something you have going on in your software. The environment around it can change."

Black likened the attitude of people working with software to their attitude about personal health issues—they accept imperfections. "As a human being, I have possible diseases," Black said. "I may have cancer right now, but I can't go to the doctor once a week. We just don't do that. We do a risk trade-off in our lives. If I'm feeling tired, I might try to get more sleep before checking for some hormonal imbalances. I don't want biopsies of all my major organs each week because I might be developing cancer. Software has some analogous challenges. I wish I had a happier answer. Our systems are riddled with problems."

Another expert view comes from Stephen Soble, who has been involved in U.S.-Chinese relations ever since studying Chinese at the School of Oriental and African Studies in London, at the University of British Columbia in Canada, and then at both Stanford University and National Taiwan University. A graduate of Harvard Law School, he was trained as an attorney who negotiated complicated cross-border business deals, often involving technology.

That led him in the direction of information technology issues. In 2012, he founded a company called Assured Enterprises, based in northern Virginia, that invents and sells security products and provides scanning services to other companies. Like everyone else in the business world, he obviously wishes to sell his services. But at a deeper level, in our experience, he is one of the most profound thinkers on the subjects at the heart of this book. Here are excerpts from an interview:

Q. Our adversaries have learned how to penetrate our software and our clouds. How do we do a better job writing software?

A. First of all, we have to face up to the nature of the problem we have today, and we as a society haven't. Frequently, I talk to chief information security officers, and one of my questions is, "What do you think is the incidence of known vulnerabilities in the shrink-wrapped, off-the-shelf software or the proprietary software that you pay for?" Frequently, the answer is, "When we get it, there are not any holes in it. The vulnerabilities appear later." That's not accurate.

Sometimes we get an answer that, "Well, there are a few (known vulnerabilities), but the reputable software companies patch them pretty quickly." That's not accurate either. The statistics that have been validated by research institutes and not-for-profits show that something on the order of 81 percent of all software sold in the United States contains known vulnerabilities at the time it's released.

Why is this the case? When you engage a software development house and ask them to develop a piece of software, the requirements document they are given tells them about how the software should perform. It may also address the latency, or the time delay, the customer is willing to tolerate between the execution of an instruction and the completion of that instruction.

If you give an engineer a requirements document and it does not say, "You have to eliminate all known vulnerabilities," why would they even try? It's not required.

The requirements rarely say, "You must ship zero known vulnerabilities in your software. And if there are any known vulnerabilities in your software at the time you ship, you are 100 percent liable for the useful life of the software." Rarely is that done. We've seen a couple of contracts where that's done. That's usually when very big corporations with excellent law departments are procuring from a small vendor. The small shop doesn't have the commercial or financial flexibility to figure out how to be 100 percent secure at the time they ship. So they just take the risk and leave it to their insurance companies (if something goes wrong).

We know small software developers that have gone out of business because of this. They had vulnerabilities and were caught, and their insurance was inadequate. The whole premise of how we transact business is that security is an afterthought. Security is not in the requirements we mandate of each other.

Q. Why do companies knowingly tolerate the existence of holes in their software?

A. The problem with risks and vulnerabilities is that no two risks, no two vulnerabilities, are necessarily alike. In the risk and vulnerability world, we talk about low vulnerabilities, then medium, high, and critical vulnerabilities. If you use the word "high" or "critical," everyone is going to get concerned. But the question is, what do you do about the mediums and lows? Do you just ignore them because you don't have money or time to deal with them, or are you are taking a thoughtful look and saying, 'Given the risks we face and given the type of data that is being protected, yes, we can afford to resolve the low risk and we can fix some of the medium risks that can open up access to another area of our company. Maybe those are the ones we need to ferret out and close along with the high risks and critical risks."

Q. In the most recent Chinese hack of telecommunications providers, they attacked older, legacy equipment. What do we do about this?

A. Timely question. Over time, virtually any software can and will develop known vulnerabilities. The longer the piece of equipment and the software have been in use, the more likely they are to have developed known vulnerabilities. What we're talking about is that there are software protocols that go down to the binaries, to the 0s and 1s, that make up the code that over time can be exploited.

How do hackers learn how to exploit them? Sometimes it's hit or miss. They get lucky. Sometimes the hackers are truly brilliant in their ability to find a way of exploiting a code sequence. Sometimes it's as simple as going to a U.S. company that sells perfectly legal penetration test kits (which some companies buy to test their own systems) and using those tools to discover vulnerabilities that are buried in a target company's software. In a sense, we, the technology world, make it easy for hackers to succeed. The ways for the hackers to find these holes is too easy. The system is not geared to protect data and to prevent breaches.

Q. It appears that the vast majority of American computing systems have been penetrated in some way. What do you think?

A. I don't think there is any serious argument about this. Our system taken as a whole is not secure. Frankly, if the Chinese or Russian government has sufficient reason to want to get some particular information from a particular source and they are willing to throw time, money, personnel, and equipment at it, they will probably get it. It's just a matter of time. It's not a matter of whether it's so secure that they won't get it. This applies to our critical infrastructure, our data storage, many financial institutions, and the vast majority of our small and medium-sized businesses, including those in the defense industrial base. We are not as secure as we need to be.

* * *

Software is not the only challenge facing Americans. As connection speeds continue to increase, off-site data storage is easier to achieve and increasingly more affordable for businesses and individuals alike. However, much like challenges to software, off-site data storage—commonly known as the "cloud"—can, at times, be nothing more than a digital Potemkin village.

CHAPTER 7

Someone Else's Server

The Vulnerabilities of Cloud Computing

IN THE BEGINNING OF THE INFORMATION TECHNOLOGY ERA, COMPANIES hired vendors to build their IT systems on the companies' own premises. At first, mainframe computers dominated these systems, and employees tapped into company resources like printers and file servers through local area networks. Few employees had access to the internet, and nobody logged into the company network from home or from the road.

As with the first ransomware attack described in chapter 2, to compromise a network, an attacker generally needed to trick an employee into inserting a floppy disk with a malicious payload into their work computer. With few exceptions, such as the Morris worm,[1] early cyberattacks generally only affected the targeted organization and did not spread to others. These networks were relatively easy to defend precisely because they had limited access to the wider internet. In other words, they had clear perimeters.

A network perimeter is a logical boundary between a company's internal network and the outside world. Think of it like a medieval castle: tall spires, impenetrable walls, a drawbridge over a deep moat, the works. Anyone leaving the castle over the drawbridge to reach the outside is frisked and interrogated by castle guards to ensure no one is smuggling out secret keys or diagrams of the castle. Anyone seeking entrance to the castle is similarly stopped, checked for credentials, and frisked for contraband. If a band of marauders tries to rush over the drawbridge and overrun the castle guards, the portcullis drops and boiling oil is poured through the murder holes, cutting them down before they breach the walls. The townspeople work and live inside the castle. So long as their only interaction with the outside world is by passing through the castle guards, they can carry on about their business with very little risk (so long as no one on the inside is a threat).

Then, in the modern-day version of the analogy, along came the mass adoption of the internet on laptops, tablets, and smart phones. Employees began interacting with clients and customers using their company's systems from anywhere in the world. Suddenly, the castle's townspeople can harvest crops from the fertile fields and hunt the forests outside the castle walls. They can engage in trade with neighboring castles. They can interact directly with the outside world. So, the townspeople begin coming and going at will—through windows, tunneling under the walls, and right over the drawbridge en masse. The castle's defenses were not built for this. Suddenly the castle's perimeter is no longer its stone walls.

In the modern world, this change came abruptly not only because of mobile devices but also because companies built computer systems that were public facing, developed global supply chains, and allowed employees to access social media and bring their own devices to work. The COVID-19 pandemic, with its emphasis on working from home, completed the picture—the network perimeter has effectively evaporated.

"For most of the past 30-plus years, the overarching plan to secure networks and digital infrastructure was one that was predicated on the concept of perimeter-based security," Chase Cunningham, the cyber operations specialist we introduced in the previous chapter, wrote in his 2020 book, *Cyber Warfare—Truth, Tactics, and Strategies*. "Most organizations across the globe subscribed to the concept that if the walls were high enough and the outward boundaries of the network were hard enough, then the enemy would not be able to 'get in.' Entire global architectures have been built and deployed to leverage that concept and billions of dollars have been spent to engage in 'defense in depth' and the 'castle and moat' methodology of security. It has all been for naught."[2]

He continued: "The perimeter-based model of security has categorically failed to keep pace with the evolution of the Internet, the proliferation of devices and accesses, and the explosion of cloud computing and an increasingly mobile and bring-your-own-device (BYOD) workforce. There is no perimeter anymore. The moment a user can take home a laptop, log in from a home PC, or use a mobile device or app to access a component of the network, that defensible perimeter is essentially cut to pieces."

To rein in this rapidly expanding attack surface, many companies have looked to cloud computing to both regain command of their cybersecurity and to capture economic efficiencies. Technology companies such as IBM, Microsoft, Amazon Web Services, Oracle, and Google have been able to persuade many companies that it would be safer and cheaper for the tech giants to manage their servers and software applications off-premises. The vendors argued that they are specialists in both IT and cybersecurity and have the size and flexibility to deliver services at scale. Therefore, they could also do a better job protecting the systems for less money than the companies would have to spend if they did it all by themselves.

It has been one of the biggest trends in the technology field of recent years. Cloud providers have earned billions of dollars providing these services to their "tenant" companies. Amazon, Microsoft, and Google accounted for 65 percent of the $53 billion in global cloud-service spending in the first quarter of 2022 according to Synergy Research Group. That's a staggering amount of money for a *single quarter*.[3] Major consulting firms such as Accenture and Deloitte help sell these services, and the technology media has been laudatory. President Biden's Executive Order on Improving the Nation's Cybersecurity even directs that executive branch agencies must "accelerate movement to secure cloud services."[4] There is, in effect, a powerful lobby for cloud computing.

For Americans to understand how vulnerable their cloud computing systems have become, we turned to a technology executive who wished to remain anonymous due to the potential impact on her company. We will call her "Jane." She asked that her real name not be used because her comments might paint a target on her company's back. Jane is the chief technology officer of a well-known company and has been an information technology professional for more than thirty-five years—even before AOL started proclaiming, "You've got mail!" According to Jane, to understand the true nature of the threat facing our networks, we must first understand what the cloud is.

At its most basic level, the cloud is simply someone else's server. Rather than companies spending money to manage systems and applications on their own premises, cloud providers take on this role remotely and offer it as a service. But the cloud is not monolithic; organizations can tap cloud providers for a multitude of services. They can buy software-as-a-service, or SaaS, meaning they don't buy their own software but rely on software maintained by the vendor, as well as others. Or they can simply store data in the cloud.

For the different types of services, there are also different types of clouds: public, private, and hybrid. A public cloud shares resources across multiple different customers, or "tenants." Think of this like operating a store in the mall. Each tenant store operates independently and pays rent to the mall for the space it occupies. For this rent payment, the tenant store has all its services, such as water, electricity, heating and air-conditioning, janitorial services, and physical security managed for it by the mall.

But, importantly, none of these services are provisioned only to a single tenant store; they are shared. This is how a public cloud functions. A cloud provider offers its services to its tenants over the public internet, and its tenants share finite resources that are provisioned to each from a single pool based on their needs. Importantly, this means that data from multiple organizations that is stored in a public cloud can all reside on the same physical server at the cloud provider's data center.

While data from multiple tenants is logically separated—that is, there are technical safeguards in place that prevent one tenant from accessing or modifying another tenant's data—vulnerabilities exist. And because resources are shared, tenants can experience outages and significant lag times during periods of peak usage. Think of what would happen to the water pressure if every tenant in the mall simultaneously turned on their faucets.

A private cloud, by contrast, is akin to operating that same store in a stand-alone building on Main Street. Now, the tenant's rent still includes all the same services as it would have had in the mall, but instead of sharing those resources with all the other mall tenants and being beholden to the mall's hours of operation, a single tenant has control over the resources. That is, everything from the heating and air-conditioning system on the roof to the armed security guard standing outside the door. Private clouds allow tenants to benefit from the efficiencies of using cloud services while maintaining control over such important issues as data privacy and cybersecurity.

The downside to a private cloud is the higher price. For this reason, a company might use a private cloud for some of its functions but push others to the public cloud, which is what a hybrid cloud model represents. "Let's say I want to control my research and development systems," Jane explains, "and I want to control my human resources and finance systems. So, I'm going to create my own little private cloud internally to do that, but maybe I'll push email and desktop software to the cloud because I don't care as much about it from a security perspective. I'll keep what I regard as the crown jewels." Only users within the company's "ecosystem" can get access to the private cloud.

One reason a company might want to retain control of its crown jewels is that public clouds can get busy and response times slow down. "Let's say I'm the weather service," Jane says. "I probably don't want to put my tornado alert system on the public cloud because I don't know how busy the cloud will be when the next storm hits. I want to put that on a private cloud that I own and have built to a certain capacity. Financial institutions might make a similar calculation. You don't want to have a broker trying to execute a transaction and you have a problem in the cloud that can slow you down. You want to be able to handle the transactions in a system that has been specifically designed to handle them."

What all this means is that a company's data is moving from system to system, sometimes across multiple cloud providers, and may not be adequately protected. And there are so many points of access. Where is the network perimeter? If attackers can get into any piece of this chain and use fake or stolen credentials, they can move freely throughout much of the system, unless it has been properly segmented and protected.

The issue of whether each "tenant" customer is segmented and protected inside a public cloud is critical. Researchers at Wiz, a cloud security startup firm, hacked into a widely used database service in Microsoft Azure's public cloud in August 2021.[5] They reported gaining access to the databases of thousands of tenants and reported the vulnerability to Microsoft. The company quickly fixed the problem, avoiding a possible crisis.

Wiz went on to report that it found five vulnerabilities that suggested "cross-tenant vulnerabilities," meaning that if an attacker could penetrate one tenant company, it could also penetrate others using the same technique in one fell swoop. To understand this, let's return to our mall analogy. Each store in the mall is segmented. Three walls separate each store from its neighbors, and customers can only enter one store at a time. Moreover, at closing time, the entrance to each store is protected by a metal rolling security door that lowers from the ceiling and locks into the floor.

This model is meant to ensure that only authorized personnel can access each store. A cross-tenant flaw is one that creates a universal key to these security doors, effectively allowing the employees of any one store to open the security door of any other store. A cross-tenant flaw is "the most severe vulnerability that could be found in a cloud service provider," said Shir Tamari, head of research at Wiz. Where a cross-tenant flaw exists, a hacker only needs to compromise one of the tenants to access all data housed in that public cloud environment.

Microsoft, which pays companies that find bugs in its software, issued a statement in response to Wiz's discovery about its cloud offering. "Security is foundational for Azure," it said. "Customers trust Microsoft's multi-layered security . . . with cybersecurity experts actively monitoring to protect organizations' data."

Jane isn't convinced. She uses the analogy of a house to explain the potential problems with cloud computing. "Let's say we have blocked everything up," she explains. "The doors are locked and there are security alarms on all the windows, but we have an eight-year-old child who needs to come and go. So, we've given him a key to the front door. As an adversary, I can easily take the key away from the kid or make a copy without the kid realizing it, and then I have easy access to the house. A number of people believe that simply because they are using a brand-name cloud, they have security. What they don't realize is that, in a lot of cases, the most vulnerable piece of that architecture is their own access point—the eight-year-old, in other words. It's their desktop or laptop they use to access the cloud. It's much easier for an adversary to go into your home computer and steal your password than it is to penetrate the cloud. The cloud is only as secure as its weakest link in the ecosystem, and for most clouds that's the user."

If adversaries can get the key to the front door, so to speak, they do not have to go through firewalls (which attempt to keep unwanted users out of systems) or special systems meant to detect intrusions. They are seen as legitimate users.

Jane continues with another house analogy to explain a second challenge: what if an adversary organization pays to join a cloud? "Let's say you have a room you rent to someone, and that person starts to steal everything in your house. That's very much what we see happening in the cloud. Anyone can get access to the cloud. You just have to subscribe to a provider's services. Cloud providers worry a lot about whether they are going to have a hacker come in and subscribe to their services. When that happens, the adversaries are inside the perimeter of the protection systems of the cloud, trying to break into different rooms in the house. The cloud providers have always been concerned about this."

A final challenge to the cloud is all the different types of software in use. As demonstrated in the previous chapter, the supply chain involved in producing software has been an important infiltration target for both the Chinese and the Russians. "Let's say a resident of the house has brought in a very large box with a hacker hiding inside it," Jane explains. What happens? "It pops out at night and attacks other residents of the house. We see it in software that has been inserted into different applications that might give someone a backdoor into the house."

Jane adds: "The guys who have put so much thought into their cloud architecture are getting defeated because they have not fully secured the interior of the cloud from internal attacks by professional security people configuring applications and devices on the resources they lease from the cloud."

Although cloud service providers promise security, they do not provide a warranty and are not on the hook for damages if there is a breach. "No one gives you a cybersecurity insurance policy when you sign onto the cloud," Jane explains. "You have to buy your own insurance externally. If I get breached or someone else gets breached, it's a very difficult situation," because it is rarely clear who is legally responsible or whose insurance carrier bears what burden. And the cost for litigating such disputes can be high.

The Chinese, in particular, have amassed considerable cloud computing expertise. In July 2021, the NSA, CISA, and the FBI published a joint cybersecurity advisory warning against Chinese state-sponsored cyber threats: "Chinese state-sponsored cyber actors consistently scan target networks for critical and high vulnerabilities within days of the vulnerability's public disclosure," it said.[6] The advisory went on to describe common Chinese hacker tactics, which include targeting "services in hybrid cloud environments to gain access to cloud resources."

Once inside a cloud computing system, the Chinese have demonstrated great ability to "play hopscotch" or "hop" from one company's systems to another, as APT10 did, which lends credence to the possibility that "cross-tenant vulnerabilities" exist and are being exploited by our adversaries.[7]

The Department of Justice said Chinese APT10 hackers got into the systems of companies in an astonishingly wide range of fields: aviation, satellite and maritime technology, industrial factory automation, automotive supplies, laboratory instruments, banking and finance, telecommunications and consumer electronics, computer processor technology, information technology services, packaging, consulting, medical equipment, health care, biotechnology, pharmaceutical manufacturing, mining, and oil and gas exploration and production. Precisely how they did it has never been publicly revealed, but they clearly exploited some form of weakness.

By consolidating data into the hands of a few large cloud providers, we have created highly attractive targets. All it takes is a single point of failure for a malicious actor to penetrate the systems of multiple companies. It is a new front on the cyber battlefield.

Was the marketing pitch for cloud computing providing better security all hype? Not entirely. "For most organizations, their core business is not IT or security," Jane says. "Going to the cloud is going to be a quantum leap in security. But that doesn't make it foolproof, nor adequate."

Stop to consider the cumulative effect of software supply-chain and cloud computing vulnerabilities. "Here's the sad state of the environment today," Jane said. "IT and cybersecurity are not the core business for a lot of organizations. They see paying for those things as a tax on them. They see those types of expenditures and organizations as bottom feeders. Cybersecurity providers are taking directly from their profits."

The government alone cannot fix the problem. "Our country is not set up to have the federal government go in and secure people's critical infrastructure," she added. "All they can do is to try to create policies." The Europeans have started imposing financially significant fines on U.S. tech giants that cannot adequately protect the data of European customers. China has completely clamped down on its technology companies. But in the United States, there are few significant criminal penalties or personal fines for executives who knowingly fail to address cybersecurity issues.

The threat extends beyond the loss of data or intellectual property. The real threat is disruption of critical infrastructure. "[The Chinese] are not going to be like some other organizations that try to steal money," Jane adds. "That's not their purpose. Their purpose is to put software in these systems to hide for a rainy day when they can activate it. From the perspective of an asymmetric war, I think the Chinese, the Russians, and the Iranians, to some extent, are willing to be very patient. . . . They are jealously guarding their hidden access points."

Cunningham's take is that "China nationally and strategically plays the long game. They're willing to wait. They are kind of like the sea snake that's willing lie on the floor of the ocean and just let their adversaries pick at them as they continue to move toward their target. They'll do it for fifty years. They see this as a big-time national initiative, and they will use any and every opportunity to continue to leapfrog the competition until they are the dominant global superpower, which I would say I think they kind of are now," Chase told us.

Russia is a different kind of threat. "The Russians have fallen into a quagmire lately with this physical conflict [in Ukraine]," he said, "but before that they were doing a really good job of using the internet and corporate America's networks to basically fund their activities." These activities spanned multiple types of actors, including those from spy agencies, the Russian military, and criminal organizations. "They had set up an infrastructure that was enabling [ransomware attacks], and then they also were smart enough to make sure they had plausible deniability. But nothing occurs in Russia without someone having oversight."

Jane also puts the Chinese ahead of the Russians in their offensive cyber capabilities. "The Chinese have a large number of people," Jane says. The ability of the Chinese to focus large amounts of resources and apply pressure to our weak points is substantial. "It's part of their doctrine of asymmetric warfare," she said. "Our adversary has been telling us exactly what they are going to do, but we haven't listened. If an adversary really wanted to disrupt our critical infrastructure, I think it would be well within their capability to do that. There are so many places where we have so many systems that can be attacked—our water, our power, our self-driving cars."

Herein lies the problem. On one hand, Chinese and Russian hackers are dedicated to giving their countries an unfair advantage by attacking the U.S. private sector, and on the other, at least some U.S. executives and their boards have willfully ignored the threat in favor of maximizing corporate profits. "The 9/11 of cyberattacks has not occurred yet, so you are not seeing the response from industry," Jane said. If corporate America is waiting for that type of existential moment to act, it is making a potentially fatal mistake.

It is imperative that corporate leaders understand that, while their organizations can outsource data storage and IT services, they cannot outsource responsibility. The cloud is not a panacea of security—far from it. "Every computer system on the planet, in some form or fashion, has got some level of compromised activity for something. It's the very nature of operating in a digital environment," Cunningham said. Companies need to take an active role in securing their cloud access points and in training their employees on proper cloud cybersecurity hygiene.

Vulnerabilities are a fact of life. Americans could never possibly put the proverbial genie back in the bottle. But Cunningham believes that we as a nation are "doing a better job of accepting the reality of the monster we've created. We are dealing with the risks that are inherent to the nature of the way we operate and then applying controls and technologies that keep us ahead of the curve of malevolence."

Unfortunately, this is not a traditional battle where we will ever be able to claim victory. "At the end of the day," Cunningham concluded, "this is about staying a step ahead of the zombie horde."

CHAPTER 8

Stealing the War

Cyber Threats to America's Defense Supply Chain

The greatest long-term threat to our nation's information and intellectual property, and to our economic vitality, is the counterintelligence and economic espionage threat from China.

—FBI DIRECTOR CHRISTOPHER WRAY

AS A WAR FIGHTER WHOSE STORIED CAREER SPANNED MORE THAN forty years, U.S. Air Force general Herbert "Hawk" Carlisle led combat aviators flying some of the most advanced weapon systems on the planet. Before retiring, Carlisle rose to the pinnacle of any air force officer's career: commanding general of Air Combat Command. As commander, Carlisle was responsible for overseeing, delivering, and maintaining all U.S. Air Force combat assets, including more than 135,000 airmen deploying worldwide. "I felt secure knowing that the tireless efforts of organizations across the U.S. defense industrial base provided our armed forces with cutting-edge technology critical to maintaining a tactical advantage over any adversary," Carlisle wrote in the foreword to a Department of Defense report on threats to the U.S. military's supply chain.

Then he added ominously: "However, our military superiority is under direct attack from our most sophisticated adversaries—nations whose cyber actors continuously target the very industry that powers the U.S. military's technological advantage."[1]

After retiring from the air force, Carlisle served as the president of the National Defense Industrial Association—an organization that works to meet military and national security requirements through the innovative prowess of the American private sector. The defense industrial base is comprised of more than three hundred thousand companies that serve as the industrial backbone for the U.S. military. These organizations include major corporations such as Lockheed Martin, Boeing, and Northrop Grumman, as well as all the smaller companies and manufacturers within their supply chains.

The defense industrial base—or DIB, as its name is commonly shortened to—provides the Department of Defense its research and development, manufacturing, and advancements in weapon systems and components critical to sustaining a technologically advanced military that operates worldwide. This vast and complex sector is the sine qua non of America's ability to field, maintain, and advance its military year after year.

However, in 2022, for the first time in history, the National Defense Industrial Association gave the health of the industrial base "below a passing grade." In addition to economic strains resulting from the COVID-19 pandemic, the defense industry "faces sustained and increasing threats of intellectual property theft, economic espionage, and ransomware hacks among other security breaches," the association wrote in its annual report.[2] "Data breaches, intellectual property theft, and state-sponsored industrial espionage in both private companies and university labs are on an unrelenting rise."[3]

Given Carlisle's intimate understanding of the technological imperatives of sustaining America's war-fighting edge, this report should be read as an SOS for U.S. national security. For the first time, the U.S. military can literally see that it could be fighting a Chinese adversary that is armed with weapons developed from stolen American technology, such as its new *Fujian* aircraft carrier that bears a remarkable resemblance to America's *Gerald R. Ford* class of carriers, among many, *many* others.

Carlisle is not the only senior military officer raising the alarm. In June 2022, Major General Cameron Holt—the deputy assistant secretary of the air force for acquisition—gave a keynote address at the

Government Contracting Pricing Summit during which he painted a grim picture of the state of U.S. defense contracting. The Chinese military, Holt said, is able to acquire weapons "five to six times" faster than the U.S. Department of Defense. "In purchasing power parity, they spend about one dollar to our 20 dollars to get to the same capability."[4]

At the close of the twentieth century, the United States enjoyed unrivaled military and economic dominance. But it was the Gulf War, beginning in 1990, in which the United States and its allies effortlessly toppled the Iraqi forces that served as a wake-up call for China. The first conflict of the nascent digital era demonstrated to Chinese strategists the critical role of information technology, including cyberspace, satellites, and advanced communications. Chinese leaders watched with dismay as the American military routed and dismantled the Iraqi army in what is considered one of the most one-sided conflicts in the history of modern warfare.

Going into the first Gulf War, Iraq's military was ranked fourth in the world—having ballooned to more than one million troops, who had been trained on weapons financed by the West to fight its bloody eight-year war with Iran. The Chinese military, though larger in number, paled in technological comparison to the forces commanded by Saddam Hussein. In the early 1990s, China's air force was comprised of few fighter jets, mostly limited to its J-7—an indigenously produced replica of the Russian 1960s-era MiG-21. Iraq's air force, by contrast, was comprised of far more advanced fighters, like the Russian MiG-29—which was comparable, at the time, to the U.S. Air Force's F-16—and supported by advanced antiaircraft missile defense systems. But even these advanced weapon systems proved wholly ineffective against American technology. This was underscored by Iraq's total inability to detect the presence of the U.S. Air Force's "invisible" F-117 Nighthawk stealth fighters, whose bombing campaign in the opening salvo cleared the way for wave after wave of American aerial bombers.

On the ground, Iraqi forces fared no better. The Iraqi T-72 tanks that faced U.S. forces were considerably superior to China's indigenously produced main battle tanks and were supported by advanced short-range ballistic missiles. However, the ability of American forces to combine ground maneuvers with airpower left entire Iraqi armored divisions without support of any kind. Due to the early effectiveness of American "smart" munitions—such as radar and GPS-guided bombs—many Iraqi missile operators turned off their electronics for fear of being detected and targeted. The net effect was Iraqi missile forces launching what amounted to long-range unguided missiles against an American force moving with lightning speed and using precision munitions against Iraqi positions. For Chinese military commanders, dismay turned to horror as they watched General Norman Schwarzkopf's "left hook," wherein 1,900 American tanks annihilated the numerically superior Iraqi tank corps, leaving 4,000 armored vehicles as smoking heaps of twisted metal in the desert.

"The Chinese looked at Iraq and saw an army similarly equipped as theirs with old Soviet weaponry, and they saw how quickly the Iraqis were taken apart," Mandiant analyst Scott Henderson told us. He was with the U.S. Army at the time specializing in China. "A lot of the ease of victory had to do with the information advantage. The Chinese looked at that as a warning to them, but also an opportunity. They decided they needed to leapfrog us. The Chinese realized they did not have to compete with us plane for plane and tank for tank. They could envision how they could get to a level playing field with us using technology rather than building traditional weapons."

The People's Liberation Army (PLA) studied the Gulf War for years. In 1999, two senior colonels in the PLA, Qiao Liang and Wang Xiangsui, published a book titled *Unrestricted Warfare*.[5] It was published by the PLA's own publishing house, implying that the army's leadership endorsed it. In it, the authors argued that hacking into American websites, targeting financial institutions, using the American media, and conducting urban warfare should all be part of a conflict with the United States. Qiao was quoted in an interview as saying that "the first rule of unrestricted warfare is that there are no rules, with nothing forbidden."

China's subsequent campaign of aggressive technology modernization has enabled a sprint to near parity with the United States. Crucial to this achievement has been China's centralized economic control. China makes no secret of its intentions. The government announces openly the technologies it wants to develop. It did so in its "Made in China 2025" plan and also has done so in its various five-year plans. The Chinese government encourages its state-owned enterprises and once private-sector companies (over many of which the Communist Party has reasserted control) to become national champions in these technologies. The Chinese military and intelligence services then provide the companies with advanced research and development obtained through malicious cyber activities, intellectual property theft, and predatory investment practices. This has allowed Chinese manufacturing and technology sectors to bypass many phases of research and development—saving an enormous amount of money. China can more rapidly commercialize an idea that is stolen from an American research lab because the government is sitting on $3.1 trillion in foreign exchange reserves. It can generously fund any technology it deems strategic. By contrast, in the American system, with its focus on short-term profits, the best ideas often face years of development and regulatory burdens before they can be successfully commercialized.

Advanced technologies flow to the People's Liberation Army because of the "military-civil fusion" that President Xi Jinping has declared, and they pose a direct threat to U.S. forces, as the PLA demonstrated in August 2022 by encircling Taiwan and launching at least eleven ballistic missiles. The United States is ultimately waging a government-centric campaign against an adversary that has mobilized its entire society. America's military is not just confronting another military—it is confronting what Dwight D. Eisenhower would have called a "defense-industrial complex" that melds the military with intelligence services, universities, research labs, corporations, and indeed an entire nation.

The stated goal of China's strategy of military-civil fusion is to transform the PLA into the world's most technologically advanced military by 2049, the one hundredth anniversary of Mao Zedong's creation of communist-ruled China. It does not tolerate the quaint distinctions Americans make between their government and the private sector.

Chinese entities have attacked the Pentagon's secrets from a dizzying variety of directions, and the U.S. Navy has been a favorite target because of its highly visible role in defending Taiwan and the South China Sea.

China's APT10 group, it was revealed in December 2018, had stolen the names and personal information of one hundred thousand navy personnel. That, combined with the breach of the Office of Personnel Management in the 2014–2015 time frame, could mean the Chinese have the personal information for nearly every service member in the navy.

All the information stolen in 2018 was in a cloud computing system maintained by private-sector companies—which is another Pentagon vulnerability. As mentioned earlier, the Department of Defense does not have the power to audit the computing systems of the different levels of its supply chain or even to insist that third-party auditors conduct forensic inspections to identify possible Chinese penetrations. Smaller suppliers do not tend to spend sufficiently on IT security, rendering them much more vulnerable than top-tier suppliers. The inability of the Pentagon to better monitor its own supply chain also means that it cannot catch the Chinese creating backdoors into critical military technologies to enable cyberattacks against U.S. ships, aircraft, and communications systems during a hot war.

There are also concerns that China could be using TikTok to observe the movements and living quarters of military members on bases throughout the world. The Department of Defense has banned the use of TikTok on official military-issued phones, but service members have personal devices and regularly use TikTok to communicate with one another and with their families according to public testimony by Brendan Carr, the FCC commissioner cited in chapter 4, who has emerged as a leading TikTok critic. "U.S. service members around the world have participated in a viral TikTok trend where they upload video and audio of their barracks," Carr said. "Hundreds of video tours have been posted from not only multiple U.S. installations but as far afield as the United Kingdom, South Korea, Japan, Italy, Germany, and Afghanistan."

If the Chinese government has access to that data, as is widely presumed, it could obtain details about the barracks' locations and be aware of troop movements. The Department of Defense is seeking to discourage the use of TikTok on personal devices but has not yet been completely successful.[6]

Yet another possible avenue of attack is the Huawei telecommunications equipment that has been installed in regional telephone networks in the American West near U.S. military bases or launch sites for missiles. The FCC's Carr said that cell phone towers around Montana's Malmstrom Air Force Base, which oversees missile fields, use Huawei's technology. That might allow Huawei to track troop movements or to interfere with the launch of an intercontinental ballistic missile, he said. Nebraska and Wyoming also have systems that use Huawei's technology, and they also host American military installations. It was entirely appropriate for the U.S. government to ban the sale of new Huawei equipment in the United States, but the problem is what to do with what is already installed. The FCC has issued a "rip and replace" order to those rural telephone networks, but the deadline does not kick in until 2023 and many thorny issues remain before Huawei's gear can be fully removed.[7]

These are all crucial weaknesses when dealing with China. The extent of Chinese cyber espionage is far more significant—and dangerous— than politicians, media outlets, and corporate leaders would like to admit.

But it is the assault on the defense industrial base that may be the single most important line of attack. "In order to obtain the capabilities needed to support . . . advanced technologies, China relies on both legal and illicit means, including foreign direct and venture investments, open-source collection, human collectors, espionage, cyber operations, and the evasion of U.S. export-control restrictions to acquire intellectual property and critical technologies," a Defense task force reported in its 2018 response to an official inquiry by President Trump.[8]

This creates an asymmetric threat to the United States and its allies. Western nations function on theories of capitalism and free market competition. China, by contrast, is an autocratic regime operating a command economy. Everything and everyone in China exists to benefit the state. Just as China recognizes no distinction between business and government interests, it also does not distinguish between traditional espionage and using government resources to target Western companies and steal technologies for the benefit of its own industries. Where the United States has prohibitions on using government resources to conduct espionage to provide an advantage to any particular company or organization, China makes this common practice.

The fruits of this espionage-fueled modernization have plainly manifested themselves in China's march toward maritime superiority. Since the early 1990s, China has been transforming its navy into an advanced modern force capable of contending with the U.S. Navy. According to the Department of Defense, China's current fleet comprises the largest navy in the world, with 355 vessels—from ballistic-missile submarines to surface combatants to oceangoing amphibious landing ships.[9] And in June 2022, the Chinese navy launched its first so-called indigenously produced aircraft "supercarrier." Named for China's Fujian Province, this new supercarrier forms the cornerstone of China's modern blue-water naval force being built with the stated goal of supplanting the U.S. Navy's presence in East Asia by 2035.

Since World War II, the hallmark of global military dominance has been the ability to project power anywhere in the world. To military strategists, this is largely measured in the ability of a nation to deploy and sustain carrier battle groups. In 2022, the United States had eleven carrier strike groups—six on the East Coast, four on the West Coast, and one stationed in Japan. Each U.S. aircraft carrier is over one thousand feet in length and carries a complement of sixty to seventy aircraft and more than five thousand crew members. To illustrate the comparison with other blue-water navies—those capable of deploying vessels outside of their territorial waters, China has three carriers; the United Kingdom has two; and Russia, France, and India each have one. Importantly, each of these aircraft carriers—with the exception of *Fujian*—is only a fraction of the size of American supercarriers. Indeed, many of these carriers more closely resemble the U.S. Navy's amphibious landing ships used primarily to launch and recover helicopters.

Fujian is different. Though the Chinese navy has been conducting carrier operations for more than a decade, until now their two seaworthy carriers were small carriers that used ski-jump-like devices to launch planes. They were based on a 1980s-era Russian *Kuznetsov*-class carrier. The newly launched *Fujian* is billed as being entirely "Made in China." However, a close inspection reveals that this nearly one-thousand-foot supercarrier is based on the design and technology of the American *Gerald R. Ford*–class aircraft carrier. Readily apparent from Chinese propaganda photos are the housings for *Fujian's* four electromagnetic catapults, capable of launching her entire complement of advanced aircraft in under an hour. Truly a floating forward airbase, *Fujian* will enable China to project naval power worldwide.

The acquisition of technology and expertise necessary to indigenously build, launch, and logistically sustain a carrier battle group in a span of twenty years is simply stunning. Jim Fanell, a retired U.S. Navy captain who served as the director of intelligence for the U.S. Navy's Pacific Fleet, has been a leading voice about the threats of Chinese industrial espionage for more than a decade. Fanell points to many aspects of *Fujian* that are the result of Chinese intellectual property theft, most notably the electromagnetic aircraft launch system. "Given [China's] past espionage activities surrounding its first aircraft carrier, there is no question that the PRC has once again stolen [military] technology from the U.S. Navy. Anyone who suggests otherwise is only providing cover for the PRC's espionage programs."[10]

While the eighty-thousand-ton carrier is the most visible piece of copied military hardware, China's technology theft is evident across its military. In 2017, Director of National Intelligence Dan Coats testified to Congress the U.S. intelligence community's assessment that Chinese hackers had stolen data on advanced U.S. airframes, including the F-35 Joint Strike Fighter and the F-22 Raptor fighter jet.[11] Today, the fruits of this theft can be seen flying above Shanghai in the Shenyang J-31 and Chengdu J-20. These fifth-generation fighters are a far cry from the Cold War–era knockoffs the Chinese flew at the turn of the century—and the similarities with their American counterparts are beyond mere outward appearance. In 2000, nearly every fighter in China's inventory was limited to engaging targets within visual range. China's navy and air force were incapable of engaging targets over the horizon. Today, as a product of cyber espionage, the air-to-air missiles and precision-guided munitions in China's fifth-generation fighters can outreach American and allied weapons.

Another carbon copy of American military technology can be found in military transports. Taking off and landing from the commercial terminal at Charleston International Airport in South Carolina provides a rare glimpse into the scope of both the complexity and prowess of U.S. military logistics. Stretching almost the entire length of one runway sit two seemingly endless columns of gray C-17 Globemaster III heavy freight aircraft. Operated by the U.S. Air Force and Air National Guard, these four-engine behemoths are responsible for rapidly deploying personnel and equipment in and out of combat zones throughout the world. Distinctive in both size and shape, the C-17 forms the backbone of the U.S. military's heavy airlift capability.

In 2006, a Boeing aerospace engineer named Dongfan Chung stole the C-17 designs and handed them over to the Chinese government. In 2011, Chung was sentenced to twenty-four years and five months in prison.[12] That same year, China's Xi'an Aircraft Industrial Corporation began work on China's copy of the C-17: the Chinese Y-20. According to the *China Daily*, the Y-20 is capable of flying over nine thousand miles without refueling and can carry over two hundred tons.

But Chung's traditional espionage on behalf of the Chinese government was not China's only source of sensitive military technology on the C-17. In 2013, the Defense Science Board reported that more than fifty Defense Department system designs and technologies had been compromised by Chinese hackers.[13] Prominently listed in that report was the C-17, as well as the F-22 and F-35 fifth-generation fighter jets and the electromagnetic aircraft launch system recently unveiled on the *Fujian*.

In 2014, the FBI arrested a Chinese national and permanent resident of Canada for his part in a six-year conspiracy that allowed Chinese hackers access to the networks of Boeing. In his 2016 guilty plea, Su Bin admitted to having enabled the hackers to steal sensitive military information—including information on the development of the C-17, as well as the F-22 and F-35 stealth fighters—and export it to China. Beginning in 2008, Su identified for the hackers individuals within Boeing with access to sensitive information China sought who would be lucrative targets for exploitation. After one of the Chinese hackers "gained access to information residing on computers of U.S. companies, he e-mailed [Su] directory file listings and folders showing the data [the hacker] had been able to access," Su's 2016 plea agreement reads. Su admitted that he had directed the Chinese hackers "as to which files and folders [they] should steal." Su and the Chinese hackers "did this specifically with respect to data related to certain aircraft programs or technology." Su would then translate the information from English to Mandarin on behalf of the hackers.[14]

For his part in the conspiracy, Su was sentenced in 2016 to just four years in federal prison. While the Justice Department touted Su's guilty plea as a strong message that "stealing from the United States and our companies has a significant cost," no criminal penalties were ever imposed against the Chinese hackers with whom Su conspired. In total, the scheme yielded the Chinese government and its defense industry 630,000 files totaling sixty-five gigabytes of sensitive information pertaining to the C-17 and 220 megabytes of flight-test data pertaining to the F-22 and F-35.[15]

However, shortly before the FBI arrested Su in Canada in 2014, the U.S. Department of Justice had scored its first indictment of a different set of Chinese hackers. In May 2014, the U.S. Attorney's Office for the Western District of Pennsylvania presented its case to a grand jury seeking an indictment of five Chinese military hackers for espionage and hacking into the networks of six U.S. companies. "From at least in or about 2006," the indictment reads, "members of the People's Liberation Army . . . conspired together and with each other to hack into the computers of commercial entities . . . to steal information from those entities that would be useful to their competitors in China, including state-owned enterprises."[16] Finding sufficient evidence to charge the Chinese hackers, the grand jury returned thirty-one counts ranging from economic espionage, to computer fraud and abuse, to aggravated identity theft.[17]

The six charged hackers were all part of the PLA's Unit 61398, which has been described in previous chapters. But these six were just the tip of the iceberg. According to the groundbreaking 2013 Mandiant report revealing the activities of Unit 61398, between 2006 and 2013 the unit stole "hundreds of terabytes of data from at least 141 organizations."[18] To sustain such a large team of hackers, the on-keyboard operators "would need to be directly supported by linguists, open-source researchers, malware authors, industry experts who translate task requests from requestors to the operators, and people who then transmit stolen information to the requestors."

In other words, the Chinese military's Unit 61398 is a very well-funded and organized element with the full backing of the state whose mission was to steal intellectual property from the U.S. defense industry. In addition to the Justice Department's indictment, Mandiant's incredibly detailed 2013 report made clear that "the Communist Party of China is tasking the Chinese People's Liberation Army to commit systematic cyber espionage and data theft against organizations around the world."[19] In total, Mandiant revealed that Unit 61398 was responsible for more than one hundred intrusions into U.S. entities across twenty different sectors.

* * *

Following the establishment in 2015 of the Strategic Support Force within the PLA, grouping all the military's cyber and information warfare forces together, there appeared to be a lull in Chinese state-sponsored hacking against the American defense industrial base. But the reprieve was short lived. While the Strategic Support Force cyber operators refocused their efforts on Chinese war-fighting capabilities in cyberspace, China's Ministry of State Security (MSS) quickly took over as the lead organization for commercial cyber espionage. In doing so, the MSS began to use contractors to target the American defense industrial base. For example, in 2017, the Justice Department indicted three owners and employees of the Guangzhou Bo Yu Information Technology Company Limited—known more commonly as Boyusec. Following the indictment, multiple security researchers confirmed that Boyusec was an MSS contractor and that two of the indicted individuals had direct ties to Chinese intelligence cyber operations.[20]

What received little attention at the time is a startling revelation: the MSS was crowd-sourcing its commercial cyber espionage targeting the

LIVING THROUGH A HACK BY UNIT 61398

The chief information officer of a subcontractor for multiple defense companies, including Boeing and Lockheed Martin, spoke with coauthor Bill Holstein on the condition of anonymity. The cybersecurity firm, FireEye, made the introduction. This account first appeared in *Chief Executive* magazine in 2016. Here's his story.

"I was out on the golf course on a Saturday in May 2013 when my CEO called," the CIO recalled. "This was everyone's worst nightmare. He told me he was having trouble with the company's email system and asked me to check it out. I looked at email on my phone and, sure enough, we had problems. It was the canary in the coal mine because our email server had its own private network to the internet. That network was being saturated with data leaving the building.

"We didn't know what was going on for a couple of days until we looked at where the traffic was going. All of it was going to one location in Shanghai, and we didn't have any customers or operations there. The information being targeted was export-control documents we had filed with the U.S. government to export equipment to the UK, India, and Spain. But it seemed like the real target was the U.S. Navy because what we were exporting was similar to what we make for the navy. Whoever was doing this wanted to take an easy route to help their own navy.

"With help from FireEye, we discovered they had been on our systems for two months before we found them. The forensics work showed that they did a lot of poking around and knew what they were looking for. They had set up a process for getting the data out by compressing the files so they could be exfiltrated.

"We stopped them manually in mid-exfiltration, and they couldn't get back in. Which meant they did not have time to clean up and cover their tracks. We could see all the trails they had left. Our whole directory of emails and passwords had been compromised. They had taken a lot of documents and RFPs [requests for proposals], but they had not yet taken our drawings, which are the secret sauce. If they had gone for the drawings first, it would have been better for them.

"The Mandiant people at FireEye told us that the attack was similar to other attacks by a unit of the People's Liberation Army called simply Unit 61398. They had been tracking these guys and knew their patterns. This unit represented what they called an Advanced Persistent Threat (APT). We had a firewall and virus protection. But realistically, if someone is good and they want to target you, they are going to get in. There is no way to stop it. The key question is: how fast can you limit it?"

U.S. defense sector. This arrangement effectively allows for a disaggregated—and near limitless—pool of hackers operating from anywhere in the world to use common advanced tools to target and exploit companies in the American defense industrial base. For network defenders, this shift in tactics poses a significant challenge.

This challenge is due in large part to the cybersecurity models currently most prevalently in use. The current cybersecurity construct is predicated upon knowing what "bad" looks like. Antivirus and malware detection software is primarily based on signatures, or identifiable features, of malicious activity. It works like this: when hackers breach a network, they leave signatures, which are like digital fingerprints. These fingerprints can include anything from the email address used to send a spear-phishing email, to the spoofed IP address the hacker's traffic appears to be coming from, to the malware the hacker deploys to compromise the network.

Once a breach occurs and is detected, digital forensic analysts parse through audit logs to identify these fingerprints and then use them to create signatures to detect similar activity in the future. These signatures are fed into intrusion detection systems and shared with the larger cybersecurity community to inoculate other networks. So, the next time that email or IP address communicates with a network, the traffic will automatically be blocked. Similarly, the next time that specific malware is deployed against a network, the intrusion detection system or antivirus software will identify it as "bad" and either block the traffic or quarantine the file.

Think of it this way—if there is a wanted sign depicting the face of a bank robber posted on the door of a bank, all a security guard needs to do is to watch out for that bank robber and not let him into the bank. Simple, right? Deny access to the known bad guys so that the bank can carry on its business with the presumed "good" clients. But what happens when a white-haired grandmother with a walker, a twelve-year-old boy with a jar of quarters, and a teenage girl chewing bubble gum all walk into the bank? The guard looks at each, sees that they don't match the known "bad," and holds the door open.

The problem with Chinese intelligence services crowd-sourcing commercial cyber espionage is a significant increase in the breadth of signatures that companies now have to identify to defend their networks. If an individual hacker modifies the malware or uses a different IP address to launch his attack, the system does not recognize the traffic or activity as a known "bad." In the same way, while the cybersecurity community maintains long lists of signatures to identify bad actors, it is exceedingly difficult to identify the "bad" when the signatures are constantly changing. By contracting out for cyber espionage, the Chinese government is able to diversify the fingerprints targeting specific sectors to increase effectiveness, target a substantially larger number of companies, and focus its professional military hackers on developing tools and access for destructive cyberattacks and cyber warfare.

Around the same time the Justice Department indicted Boyusec, a different Chinese hacking group was quietly penetrating the network of another defense contractor—one with far greater implications for the U.S. military. Due to the sensitivity of the program, the government redacted the victim company's name and affiliation in all official correspondence, except to verify that the company was a defense contractor working on sensitive programs for the U.S. Naval Undersea Warfare Center. In the end, the Chinese hackers stole more than six hundred gigabytes of data from the contractor's system.[21]

Charged with developing next-generation submarine technologies and weapon systems, the Naval Undersea Warfare Center represents a strategic asset for U.S. national security. Occupying the northern third of the Newport Naval Station in Newport, Rhode Island, the Naval Undersea Warfare Center is the navy's focal point for all research, development, testing, and evaluation of undersea warfare capabilities—everything from autonomous submersibles to small modular nuclear reactors to next-generation sonar. Heavily reliant on universities and other private-sector partners to meet the unique technical requirements of undersea warfare, the center has an unclassified budget of over $1 billion. And contractors working on these types of projects are precisely the target Chinese hackers supporting the advancement of the Chinese navy were looking for.

The unnamed contractor was secretly developing a supersonic antiship missile capable of being launched from submarines. "Sea Dragon"—as the secret program was named—was scheduled for initial deployment on U.S. submarines in 2020. Considered a "game changer" by military experts, submarine-launched supersonic and hypersonic antiship missiles are incredibly difficult to shoot down and nearly impossible to evade. But in January and February of 2018, as tensions between the Chinese and U.S. navies in the South China Sea continued to rise, Chinese hackers penetrated the contractor's network and stole the plans for the Sea Dragon, along with details about hundreds of other mechanical and software systems.

While the full extent of the impact to national security caused by this compromise remains classified, the apparent damage is irrevocable. In 2019, in the wake of the Sea Dragon breach, the U.S. Navy published an internal cybersecurity review detailing the extent of Chinese cyber commercial espionage targeting military technologies. The navy's "dependency upon the defense industrial base presents another large and lucrative source of exploitation for those looking to diminish US military advantage," the report reads. "Key DIB companies, primes (prime contractors), and their suppliers, have been breached and their [intellectual property] stolen and exploited. These critical supply chains have been compromised in ways and to an extent yet to be fully understood."[22]

China's astonishing rollout of its nuclear capability, as evidenced by its building of thousands of missile silos, was also based at least in part on stolen American technology. That pattern of espionage at the Department of Energy's Sandia and Los Alamos laboratories in New Mexico may have been in progress for a quarter of a century. It was first detected in the late 1990s—and was even the subject of a congressional commission—but top U.S. officials in both Republican and Democratic administrations were eager to expand the U.S. relationship with China and chose to ignore the warning signs.[23] As a result, the United States now faces two nuclear powerhouses—Russia and China.

The espionage and theft of intellectual property has been consistent over time. Chinese commercial espionage has become so prolific that in 2020, FBI Director Christopher Wray announced that the FBI had "a thousand investigations involving China's theft of U.S.-based technology." America's long-term military advantage is being eroded by years of intellectual property theft from the defense industrial base. China is not merely stealing sensitive military information; it is also using it as a springboard to launch its next generation of weapon systems. What's more, Chinese penetration of defense industrial base networks represents a significant threat to the integrity and reliability of U.S. military technology.

FICTION . . . OR FUTURE?

Imagine, for a moment, that the United States is leading a coalition to halt a Chinese incursion into Taiwan.

The U.S. Seventh Fleet, headquartered at the former Imperial Japanese naval base in Yokosuka, has dispatched the USS *Gerald R. Ford* carrier strike group with its full complement of over sixty aircraft, as well as three *Arleigh Burke*–class destroyers, a *Ticonderoga*-class cruiser, and a *Virginia*-class fast-attack submarine to the Taiwan Strait. While transiting the East China Sea, *Ford's* airborne early-warning aircraft gets a radar hit on the Chinese *Fujian* aircraft carrier steaming east to intercept the *Ford*—staying just out of range of *Virginia's* Sea Dragon antiship missiles. Immediately, the strike group sets general quarters, manning every battle station.

Ford's F-35s are the first to get airborne. As soon as a division of eight are airborne, *Ford*'s combat information center alerts the pilots to inbound enemy aircraft. Chinese J-20s from the *Fujian* form an attack profile over the horizon. Intelligence indicates that the J-20s can carry a hypersonic air-launched variant of the Sea Dragon antiship missile. Under the rules of engagement, the American F-35s are permitted to engage to protect the strike group. Flying at nearly twice the speed of sound, the F-35s close with the J-20s. The American pilots get radar locks on their targets well before they can see them.

Over the radio, the flight lead calls out, "Fox 3," and squeezes the trigger. The AIM-120 advanced medium-range air-to-air missile (AMRAAM)—the most advanced air-to-air weapon in the navy's inventory—fails to fire. The lead's specialized helmet allows him to look through his cockpit at the F-35s flying in close formation around him. Expecting to see the contrails of eight AMRAAMs marking the paths of missiles screaming toward their Chinese targets, the pilot sees nothing.

"Fox 2," he barks into his headset. Nothing. Exasperated, he yells, "Fox 1!" Each pilot frantically presses the weapon release button again and again with no result.

A few miles ahead of the F-35s, the formation of J-20s drops down to one hundred feet in altitude and launches their hypersonic antiship cruise missiles at the strike group. Out of the fourteen Chinese missiles launched, seven find their targets. Four missiles strike at the waterline of two destroyers, sinking them almost immediately. Two others explode inside the hangar bays of the *Ford*, damaging all aircraft within and destroying the elevators used to lift them to the flight deck. The final missile strikes the bow of the cruiser. As the smoke settles, the carrier and cruiser are both disabled, and the two destroyers slip beneath the waves into the darkness.

The J-20s then turn their sights on the F-35s. With no working weapon systems and no carrier on which to land, the fighters point their noses east and make a last-ditch effort to outrun the J-20s to the Marine Corps air station on the Japanese island of Okinawa.

What happened? Several years prior, Chinese hackers compromised a small subcontractor using a spear-phishing email. As it turns out, the subcontractor—an offshoot of CalTech—manufactures a small micro-controller for the F-35's missile launch system for Lockheed Martin. This well-financed start-up, which had recently won the bid to subcontract on the navy's newest fighter, finished compiling its computer-aided design—or CAD—files for the chips just before a long weekend. Over the weekend, Chinese hackers modified the CAD drawings to include a small—almost imperceptible radio frequency receiver. The hackers made no other modifications to the network and deleted all log files, hiding any trace of their activity.

The microcontrollers then were incorporated into the infinitely complex F-35 and passed every test the navy had with flying colors.

Those receivers lay dormant. But when the *Ford* strike group crossed into the East China Sea, the Chinese used their electronic warfare capability to transmit a signal that acted as a kill switch for the microcontrollers. Knowing the range of the U.S. submarine's Sea Dragon missiles, the Chinese strike group intentionally stayed outside of striking distance of any American weapon but *Ford*'s aircraft. With no indication that anything was amiss, the F-35 pilots launched to face China's most advanced strike fighters—armed with ship-killing weapons developed from data stolen from the United States—with no functioning air-to-air combat weapons.

This could be the face of the next war, which could be unimaginable in scope—even if nuclear options can be avoided. It is widely assumed that if the fighting were to escalate beyond a single incident, the major powers would seek to disrupt the critical civilian infrastructures of their foes' banking, food, electricity, and gasoline systems in a new version of the Cold War's mutually assured destruction (MAD).

As China's most renowned military strategist Sun Tzu famously wrote, "Victorious warriors win first, then go to war, while defeated warriors go to war first, then seek to win." In the battle to establish next-generation military technological dominance, China is winning. Let there be no doubt, without a significant change of course and a whole-of-nation effort to secure our critical technologies, China will win the next war before we ever fire a shot. The United States is leaving itself essentially unable to defend against a much larger, more focused, and more cohesive adversary.

Part II

The Response

What Must Be Done

Retreat from Globalization

Easing Corporate America's Addiction to China

CORPORATE AMERICA'S ADDICTION TO CHINA DID NOT HAPPEN OVER-night. It has taken decades for an estimated seventy thousand American companies to establish their massive presences throughout the main-land.[1] For many years, their presence in China was seen as in keeping with broader American goals of encouraging a measure of political liber-alization and economic reform. The concept of globalization—indeed, a near religion—has held that business was just business.

The Chinese, being long-term strategists, understand the appeal of their vast market. They have been watching the behavior of foreigners trying to get rich in China since the days of the British Empire—when a nineteenth-century British merchant reputedly exclaimed, "If only we could add an inch to the shirttail of every Chinaman, we could keep the mills of Lancashire running forever!" The gleam in foreigners' eyes has never disappeared.

It has been only in the past decade, since Xi Jinping took power, that the Chinese have drawn in American and other foreign companies so deeply, allowing them to make sufficiently large profits, that they have begun using those companies as geopolitical tools. The Chinese have been astute in recognizing that business is more than business; it carries strategic implications.

American companies have fought hard to comply with the rules and wishes of the Communist Party while also adhering to U.S. laws and maintaining an appeal to the American consumer base. This balancing act has become increasingly difficult, as World Wrestling Entertainment superstar and actor John Cena found after "mistakenly" referring to Taiwan as a sovereign nation. Cena's effusive apology to the people of China—in Mandarin—to prevent his films from being banned in China both turned off American consumers and served as fodder for late-night television hosts for weeks. But American professional sports and Hollywood self-censor themselves as a matter of practice to ensure Chinese viewership and avoid the ire of the Communist Party.[2]

On the corporate side, American companies have been obliged to redraw their airline route maps and hotel maps to delete Taiwan as a separate country and to treat it as part of China. Apple routinely deletes apps from its App Store that it fears will anger Beijing. Moreover, China has consciously lured in major Wall Street firms recently with sweet deals because it believes, correctly, that they possess political clout in Washington. Incredibly, the Chinese government sought to persuade American business groups to lobby against a $52 billion piece of legislation aimed at helping the United States maintain its lead in semiconductors.[3] That bill morphed into the CHIPS and Science Act.

Few people in the world understand what American CEOs are thinking about their China operations better than James McGregor, who lived and did business in China for thirty years. He is chairman of APCO Worldwide, Greater China, and served as president of the American Chamber of Commerce of China before retreating to the United States at the onset of COVID-19 more than two years ago. Some things have changed since then—China has suffered COVID lockdowns and supply-chain disruptions, and Beijing has reimposed party and governmental control of its once-thriving technology companies. But the heart of McGregor's analysis still resonates.

"The formula with China is that you can't *not* be there," he told us. "Nobody says it's going to be a lot of fun. You have to be there, it used to be, because the market was so big and growing. China now represents a third of global growth, surpassing Japan, Europe, and America collectively. It's adding hundreds of millions of people to its middle class. It's looked at as a 'market for the decades' at the same time that the United

States and Europe have kind of topped out. People now are focused on how to be in the China market and have a robust business there and not screw up their entire global future."

Now that relations between the United States and China have deteriorated over a host of issues, what are American CEOs thinking about continuing to operate in China? "I think most American company CEOs are patriotic people who care about the United States," he said. "But every economic incentive they have is about not being tied to any country. Our system is all about free market results, not about how much business you do in America or what you do for America. Globalization untethered them from having a strong business incentive to put America first in their business plans. If your market in China is bigger than it is in the United States, which is the case for many major U.S. multinationals, and the China market is much more of a future market than others, Xi Jinping may be more important to you than Joe Biden from a business standpoint." He added pointedly, "Meanwhile in China, there is not a single noodle shop that doesn't have to make sure whatever they are doing keeps the Chinese government happy."

One of the key challenges in contemplating how American companies might be persuaded to ease back on the volume and level of technology they sell in China is that competitors from other countries would seize the opportunity to increase their own sales. "If American companies retreat from China, the Koreans and Japanese and Germans and God knows who else will then usurp American companies," McGregor said. "That's the problem. If you're not in China doing business, your competitors will be in there. And the Chinese market is so robust and fast moving that you will find yourself no longer being a global leader."

But isn't there a way to prevent semiconductors designed by Qualcomm in the United States and manufactured in Taiwan from ending up in the hands of the People's Liberation Army (PLA), which uses them in its jet fighters and missiles? "Everything is 'dual use' now," McGregor explained. "Dual use" means a product or component can be intended for either civilian or military purposes. "It used to be that if you were trying to keep technology away from a country's military, it was very clear that a particular technology was going to guide a missile," McGregor said. "But it would be almost impossible to prevent the PLA from buying chips. The chips go into a big sales system (an internal Chinese distribution system) and make their way from there. It's not like the Taiwanese are selling directly to the PLA. To prevent their chips from ending up in the hands of the PLA, they would have to quit selling to China. If you quit selling to China, you're out of business."

It's obviously a quandary of historic proportions. But McGregor has some hope. "The actions of China in the past decade and past couple of years have alienated China from so much of the developed world. If we all could come together and figure something out. . . . Are we going to be in the position of Germany today? Germany is looking back on its decisions to rely on gas and coal from Russia. The result was that Putin felt he could do what he wanted. What happens in ten years if China invades Taiwan and the U.S. economy and its advanced manufacturing companies are so tied into China that the Chinese are able to prevent any kind of U.S. response? That kind of calculation is happening in Washington today."

What would "figure something out" mean? We will devote the rest of this chapter to precisely that question. American and other foreign companies need to be able to retain critical distance from Beijing—they need to be able to stand up to its demands and resist supporting its authoritarian surveillance state. We will first concentrate on what that means in the realm of semiconductors, because it is arguably the single most important industry in China's relations with the world. Passage of the CHIPS and Science Act, with $52 billion in subsidies to semiconductor makers, is a major development in that competitive landscape, as are the sweeping restrictions on semiconductor sales to China for U.S. companies or companies using U.S. technology. As some pundits have argued, taken together these steps may be the most ambitious piece of industrial policy in fifty years.

Then we'll turn to the argument about whether Apple and other American companies can successfully "reshore" any meaningful percentage of their production now in China. Clearly, some CEOs have made a mistake by relying too heavily on suppliers in China without creating alternative suppliers in other countries. A final piece of the equation is a new American law that has just taken effect barring the import of goods from China made with forced labor in Xinjiang or elsewhere on the mainland. It could have much more sweeping consequences than previously foreseen.

China bought $430 billion worth of semiconductors from manufacturers worldwide in 2021, more than it spent on imported petroleum.[4] China manufactures some chips on its own but, until recently at least, they are not the most sophisticated. Foreigners still possess a commanding lead in many different aspects of designing and making the most advanced chips, namely the ones whose circuits are only three to five nanometers in width, which have applications in artificial intelligence and facial-recognition systems.

China recognizes that semiconductors are the number-one "choke point" that the techno-democracies possess over it.[5] The Center for Security and Emerging Technology (CSET) at Georgetown University in Washington, a relatively new but important think tank because of its concentration on China-related technology issues, issued a report in May 2022 based on a series of stories that a Chinese scientific newspaper published in 2018. Written in Chinese and appearing in a relatively obscure newspaper, the articles had completely escaped attention in the West. In the articles, the Chinese science writers identified semiconductors as their country's number-one vulnerability. Then, in the same month, CSET issued a report titled "Preserving the Chokepoints."[6] They were not trying to be funny or ironic; think tanks lack humor. In the maritime context, choke points are strategic waterways of economic and naval significance—such as the Suez Canal in Egypt, the Bosporus Strait at the mouth of the Black Sea, and the Strait of Malacca connecting the South China Sea to the Indian Ocean.

It's obvious that private-sector companies from different countries, who see one another as fierce competitors, will not be able to agree on a strategy to limit the volume of their sales or limit the level of technology they sell in China. They cannot cure their addiction by themselves. Governments will have to be involved, which is hotly controversial, but which we argue is also essential. It's also obvious that the United States alone cannot maintain the techno-democracies' lead in semiconductors.

The effort must involve other allied nations—another controversial concept, but one we again argue is critically important. We need to retreat from unfettered globalization that benefits our adversaries, while embracing and enhancing globalization when it comes to our relations with like-minded nations.

Free market economists and theoreticians will scoff at this idea, but there are few national security imperatives greater than forging a global technology strategy with semiconductors at its core. China has clearly articulated what its strategy is in key technologies and devoted enormous resources to them, in addition to targeting the techno-democracies for the theft of those technologies. But we have refrained from defining a strategy because it goes against our traditional notions of capitalism.[7] The United States believes that private-sector companies have the sole responsibility for charting their technological paths, with no regard for U.S. national security or well-being. Unfortunately, that's a losing strategy in countering the ambitions of the techno-giant that China has become.

It bears taking a brief detour to explain semiconductors and the complexity of manufacturing them.

What are semiconductors? Semiconductors are the tiny conductive components inside a computer that enable the efficient flow of electricity across a circuit. At the most basic level, modern computers operate as an incredibly complex system of switches and circuits. The ones and zeroes of binary code—the machine-readable language that tells a computer what to do—dictate how electrons flow through a circuit. Put enough of these signals together, and the computer performs the desired process. In other words, if you don't have semiconductors, you don't have computers.

What are they made of? The vast majority are based on circular silicon wafers. There has been some experimentation with different materials, but for now, silicon continues to dominate. Many individual semiconductors are printed on each silicon wafer.

How are they made? Humans, often using advanced software called electronic design automation (EDA) tools, design the circuits. The techno-democracies have so far possessed a lock on designing the most advanced chips. After they have been designed, powerful light, guided by mirrors and lenses, etches those circuit designs onto the chips.

How do the chips come off the silicon wafers? They don't come off. The wafers are diced into individual semiconductors. The chips also have to be tested and packaged on circuit boards. Even if a chip is fabricated (manufactured) in the United States, much of that testing and packaging activity takes place in East Asia—partly because that's where most of the world's electronic products are assembled. Labor there also is cheaper.

Why does everyone seem to be trying to make smaller and smaller circuits? The narrower the circuits, the more functionality can be crammed onto a single semiconductor. More tiny transistors and other components can be added. The chip becomes more powerful and can store more data.

Just how small are these circuits? As noted, the most sophisticated chips have circuits that are only three to five nanometers wide, much thinner than a human hair.

Why, in general, haven't the Chinese been able to catch up? There is an incredibly intricate supply chain of machines, software, chemicals, lenses, and mirrors. The Chinese have not been able to develop the best automated design software. And they lack human capital. It takes years of experience to learn how to perform all the steps involved in designing and making the most advanced semiconductors.

A possible exception to this pattern has been the recent news that China's main vehicle for semiconductor manufacturing, the state-owned Semiconductor Manufacturing International Corporation, known as SMIC, has produced or obtained a chip with circuits of only seven nanometers in width. But the chip could have been stolen from Taiwan or based on Taiwanese designs.[8]

Where the Chinese have clearly been making gains is in the manufacturing of lower-end chips and circuit boards. American companies may design the chips and build the equipment to produce them, but the physical production of many chips has shifted to China and Taiwan.

This is a huge, complicated subject, so let's start by concentrating on two different sets of actors in different parts of the semiconductor supply chain. The first are companies that make the equipment used to make semiconductors. They are in the United States, Europe (primarily Holland and Germany), and Japan. Then there are the companies that use that equipment to actually make semiconductors. Those companies are primarily in South Korea (Samsung Electronics), Taiwan (Taiwan Semiconductor Manufacturing Company, or TSMC), Japan (which has multiple chip makers), and the United States (Intel, Nvidia, Xilinx, and others—Qualcomm designs chips but does not manufacture them).

Manufacturing Equipment. The single most advanced piece of equipment is made by a company called ASML Holding in Holland and uses extreme ultraviolet (EUV) light to create tiny circuitry. The machine is astonishingly complex and includes components from the United States, Japan, and Germany—the Germans are masters of making precision mirrors and lenses. It took decades to develop the use of EUV. The key is that EUV light has tiny wavelengths, so it can create smaller circuitry than other forms of light. The machine costs more than $150 million, and shipping it to customers requires forty shipping containers, twenty trucks, and three Boeing 747s.[9] ASML is the only company in the world that can make one of these EUV machines.

The United States has enjoyed some success in persuading the Europeans to cooperate in halting the export of this equipment to China. The Chinese were able to order one of these machines and sign a contract, but the United States persuaded the Europeans and Japanese that selling the equipment to China was not in their self-interest. The Trump administration first succeeded in blocking the sale in 2019, and the Biden administration has maintained the same policy stance.[10] Trying to expand upon that success, the Biden administration is also seeking to persuade ASML and Japan's Nikon not to sell equipment from the previous generation of ultraviolet light technology called deep ultraviolet lithography (DUV).[11]

For its part, Germany is blocking the sale of a wafer fabrication company to China. In November 2022, the government of Chancellor Olaf Scholz said it was halting the sale of Elmos Semiconductor's wafer fabrication subsidiary to Silex Microsystems, a Swedish company wholly owned by a Chinese company.[12]

All that is promising. Another key test is whether Britain will reverse the Chinese acquisition of Newport Wafer Fab, a plant in Wales that transforms logs of silicon into circular wafers that eventually get cut into chips. That is obviously a crucial step in the manufacturing of chips. Nexperia, a Dutch subsidiary of Wingtech Technology, made the acquisition in 2021. Wingtech is based near Shanghai, and about 22 percent of its ownership can be traced back to the Chinese government. For all intents and purposes, Wingtech and Nexperia are serving the interests of China's party-state.

After the American government objected to the sale, Britain's business secretary, Kwasi Kwarteng, triggered a national security review of the sale. A final decision has not yet been made. But it's another signal that cooperating with European allies to prevent China from obtaining advanced semiconductor manufacturing equipment is possible.

Note that two different types of action were taken or contemplated—blocking exports of manufacturing equipment and the other reversing or forbidding a Chinese acquisition of a non-Chinese company. Any strategy to thwart China's semiconductor ambitions would have to involve multicountry export controls, as well as reviews of Chinese acquisitions of the sort that the Committee on Foreign Investment in the United States (CFIUS) conducts. It has to be a coherent, unified strategy or the Chinese will pick it apart. To his credit, on September 15, 2022, President Biden issued an executive order that bolsters CFIUS and specifically expands its charter to review and potentially block any acquisition that threatens U.S. technological leadership.[13]

One possible challenge to any global, synchronized effort to prevent the Chinese from reaching parity with today's chip leaders is presented by American makers of the equipment themselves, CSET argues in its "Preserving the Chokeholds" report. China is the largest market for American manufacturers of such equipment, and they want to avoid export controls. The largest U.S. company in this industry, Applied Materials, says that half of its manufacturing already takes place in Singapore. One reason for moving offshore is to obtain easier access to customers in East Asia, where most of the world's electronic products are assembled, and to obtain access to technical talent and labor.

But another reason may be that these manufacturers want to be in position to sell machines to China whose American content has been designed out. This would be the ultimate statement of "statelessness"—American companies relocate to Southeast Asia and make equipment that has no American components so they can continue selling to China.

CSET recommended that the U.S. government take this possibility very seriously.[14]

East Asia and Finished Chips. Devising a strategy in East Asia to moderate the sale of advanced chips to China could be more difficult than any initiative in Europe because of geopolitics and ancient animosities. East Asia has a much longer written history than Europe does, but it has lagged far behind the Europeans in creating a regional trading bloc such as the European Union—it simply has not been able to create one—much less the equivalent of NATO. And East Asia is where several large chip-making companies are located. Some 90 percent of the most advanced chips are manufactured in Taiwan, for example.

Yet another recent CSET report, titled "Silicon Twist: Managing the Chinese Military's Access to AI Chips," concluded that the People's Liberation Army is obtaining American-designed chips that are helping it improve its artificial intelligence capabilities, which looms large in the future of warfare.[15] They are manufactured by TSMC and Samsung and are sold to intermediary companies with nondescript names such as Beijing Lanfun Qifu Technology Co. and Beijing Hengsheng Technology Co., which then build them into larger systems or sell them as they are to the PLA.

The United States seems to be groping for a winning strategy. It proposed a semiconductor industry alliance with Japan, South Korea, and Taiwan called the Chip 4 Alliance, but the Japanese counterproposed a bilateral alliance involving only the United States and Japan. There is a great deal of historical animosity between Japan and Korea, primarily because, most recently, the Japanese occupied the Korean Peninsula from 1910 to 1945, committed significant atrocities against the Korean people, and sought to eradicate the Korean language and any sense of Korean nationality. Getting these two U.S. allies to cooperate is difficult on many issues.

Another impediment is that neither Japan nor South Korea would want to join a formal industry association that includes Taiwan because that would surely anger Beijing, which would then retaliate against Japan and South Korea. Each has extensive sales on the mainland. Such is the fear that China's neighbors feel. China has explicitly warned South Korea not to follow the U.S. lead and said that it should not be blamed if it takes "countermeasures" against South Korea.[16] The matter is compounded because two South Korean chip companies operate factories in China.

The Biden administration recently started talks on creating a fourteen-nation Indo-Pacific Economic Framework, which would exclude Taiwan.[17] The United States also has nurtured "the Quad," consisting of India, Japan, Australia, and the United States—but once again excluding Taiwan. Neither would be an effective vehicle to manage a semiconductor strategy.

Attempting to patch together some type of cooperation, the Biden administration in June 2022 launched an initiative to deepen economic engagement with Taiwan called the "U.S.–Taiwan Initiative on 21st-Century Trade." Items on the agenda include coordination of export controls and measures to secure semiconductor supply chains. If the United States can informally combine the Taiwan initiative with its other regional alliances, it might set the stage to be able to moderate and better control the semiconductors sold to China. Chinese companies "all rely on the Taiwanese chip maker for custom-built AI-powered chips that power everything from computer vision to cloud servers and autonomous driving to fifth-generation, or 5G, mobile technology base stations," Taiwan-based analyst Liam Gibson wrote. "Besides TSMC, only Samsung Electronics and Intel can manufacture these kinds of chips. If all three stop shipping chips to China, China's fourth industrial revolution will grind to a standstill."[18] We coauthors do not advocate halting sales, merely doing a better job of controlling the level of technology and ultimate use.

Once again, the globalization mind-set of American business leaders threatens any such effort because U.S. venture-capital firms, chip industry giants such as Intel, and other private investors are investing to help China's semiconductor industry move up the technology ladder, the *Wall Street Journal* reported. These investors took part in fifty-eight investment deals in China's semiconductor industry from 2017 through 2020, double the number of deals from the previous four years. The *Journal* based its report on research by the New York–based China research firm Rhodium Group. One particularly sensitive deal involved Intel investing in

Primarius Technologies Co., which specializes in chip design tools where U.S. companies currently hold leadership.

The Biden administration is aware of these investments and sought authorization from Congress, as part of the CHIPS and Science legislation, to screen American investments in China in semiconductors, quantum computing, artificial intelligence, critical minerals and materials, and high-capacity batteries.[19] But that measure was stripped out of the bill as part of the compromises that were necessary to enact it.

Instead, the government is relying on actions by the executive branch. In the summer of 2022, the Biden administration made it clear that it would not approve shipments of equipment capable of making chips with circuits smaller than fourteen nanometers[20] and cracked down on the sale of equipment used to make less sophisticated memory chips.[21] It also announced new restrictions on the electronic design automation (EDA) software tools that are so essential in designing the most sophisticated chips.[22]

Then, in early October, the Department of Commerce announced the most sweeping export controls on the sale of semiconductors and chip-making equipment in a decade. Employing the same "foreign direct product" rule that President Trump used to target Huawei, Commerce also banned any sale by companies throughout the world if their products are made with U.S. technology, software, or machinery.[23]

One problem with the American strategy so far is that it has been sporadic and not comprehensive in nature. No one knows yet for certain whether the Commerce Department will be able to build the expertise and capabilities to truly enforce the new rules or whether it will wink at some questionable export requests and allow them to proceed. The Department of Commerce has taken other actions against Chinese state-owned enterprises and companies on its "entities list" that have been suspected of selling to the Chinese army or its surveillance state in Xinjiang Province. It has also banned sales to the Semiconductor Manufacturing International Corp., China's primary chip vehicle.

Nor does anyone yet know whether fellow techno-democracies and the private sector in general will accept the direction set by the Biden administration. What is needed is a consistent, coordinated campaign across multiple fronts with multiple allied countries. "This effort will demand employing regulatory tools like export controls, investment security mechanisms, and restrictions on data and capital flows, as well as interventions in the market such as the restoration of industrial and manufacturing bases independent of Beijing and standards organizations not co-opted by the CCP (Chinese Communist Party)," wrote Matt Turpin, a visiting fellow at the Hoover Institution. "The question remains: can democratic governments, along with their companies and citizens, build the next generation's digital operating system to protect global norms, prosperity, and security—even as the CCP seeks to undermine them?"[24]

Any such coordinated strategy would challenge the Washington bureaucracy because different agencies have different responsibilities—the Commerce Department manages export controls, and its ranks would have to be dramatically expanded to handle the volume of work (there are currently more than five hundred Chinese companies on the entities list, and the department's links to the intelligence community would have to be enhanced). The Treasury Department has complete overview of the foreign investment screening mechanism CFIUS, which is already a multiagency coalition. And the Treasury Department and the Securities and Exchange Commission monitor monetary and investment flows. Strong leadership would have to be exercised from the White House.

There are still other pieces of the chip equation. The United States is going to benefit from major announcements of new chip plants in Ohio, Texas, and Arizona. Intel said in January 2022 it would spend at least $20 billion to build two new chip factories near Columbus, Ohio; Taiwan's TSMC began construction of a $12 billion semiconductor complex near Phoenix; and Samsung Electronics chose Taylor, Texas—near Austin—for a $17 billion factory.[25] In a related move, Micron Technology, the Idaho-based maker of memory chips, announced a $40 billion expansion of its current headquarters and investments in memory chips.[26]

This much investment by the world's leading chip makers could be transformative if the United States takes full advantage of it and overcomes the typical political sniping. Efforts by the Obama administration to jump-start the solar panel and electric vehicle industries were torn apart by partisan wrangling, ultimately resulting in the bankruptcy of Solyndra and A123 Systems.

The CHIPS and Science Act, which also includes $24 billion in advanced manufacturing tax credits, was critically important in luring the latest chip investments. Some of that funding also could be used to encourage the reshoring of the cutting, testing, and packaging of chips from Asia, which has become a more important part of the semiconductor supply chain.[27] Altogether, the new law will provide $280 billion in funding for a range of high-tech research and investment projects, including space and 5G wireless communications.

A key component of reestablishing a healthy semiconductor industry on U.S. soil is training the people to operate these plants, a responsibility that would fall to universities but perhaps even more directly to community colleges, technical colleges, and vocational schools. America's manufacturing infrastructure and talent pool have been allowed to dissipate. Workforce development is one area where America has consistently failed, but the CHIPS act will make more money available to build a labor pipeline.

And where will all these chips be used? If the American goal is to create a vibrant semiconductor industry on U.S. soil, then at least some of the customers for those chips ought to also be in the United States, which suggests that the consumer electronics, computer, and smart phone industries could start to be reestablished here. The United States allowed all that type of manufacturing to go offshore, much of it to China. As long as those products are made in China, the Chinese will be able to penetrate them.

Any such global semiconductor strategy would have to be coordinated in a highly secure manner because Chinese hackers have demonstrated the ability to penetrate computer systems and monitor unprotected communications of the United States and its allies. The Chinese government certainly would find a way to punish any company it suspects of cooperating in what it would undoubtedly view as a sinophobic global conspiracy. Indeed, the Foreign Ministry's Zhao Lijian, whom we mentioned in chapter 5, has already called the effort to prevent the sale of DUV manufacturing equipment "classic technological terrorism."[28] Any successful strategy would also require that the techno-democracies continue to harden their protections against Chinese espionage, both by human and digital means. It would be a hollow victory to develop next-generation technologies only to have them stolen.

A global semiconductor strategy might establish the template for how global techno-democracies can cure their companies' addictions to China while keeping them financially viable. It presumably could be done even for technologies where the United States and allies currently lag behind China, such as 5G wireless communications. Sweden's Ericsson and Finland's Nokia, whose governments are now joining NATO, possess some key technological strengths in 5G. These tech powerhouses should be included in a coordinated strategy among the techno-democracies to leapfrog China's Huawei. None of these strategies should be carried out by a go-it-alone America. Welcome to the new globalization.

THE APPLE SYNDROME—HELD HOSTAGE?

Of all major American companies, perhaps Apple is the most deeply entrenched in China—so much so that it must adhere to the Chinese government's policies on censorship, data processing, and other issues. So much so that only recently has it chosen to start diversifying its near-total dependence on China as its global manufacturer. A handful of suppliers have started building plants in Vietnam and India, raising the prospect that Apple might start shifting its production.[29] The COVID lockdown of the Apple plant in Zhengzhou and the escape of many workers from inside the complex made the headlines and put a crimp in Apple's ability to produce its new iPhone 14.[30]

But so far, Apple remains hooked on China. Only 3.1 percent of Apple's global manufacturing base in 2021 was in India. More than 90 percent of Apple products such as iPhones, iPads, and MacBook laptops were made in China by contractors.[31]

It's worth pausing to reflect on the deep presence Apple has achieved, with Chinese help, and how it has had to make compromises with Beijing as a result. The *New York Times*, in an excellent article in May 2021, laid it out in a comprehensive fashion.[32]

Current CEO Tim Cook started Apple's move into China two decades ago when he was chief of operations. Hon Hai Industries, also known as FoxConn, was the Taiwanese company that Apple tapped to operate its factories in China. The Taiwanese speak Mandarin Chinese and know how to run disciplined factories. Various levels of the Chinese government built roads, utility services, dormitories, and all the physical infrastructure that Apple would need. All of Apple's parts suppliers are located near FoxConn plants. It is a massive manufacturing platform involving 3 million workers. The vast majority of Apple's products are made in this fashion.

Over time, the Chinese government's demands on Apple have increased. Apple was already censoring its App Store in China, effectively making it part of the Chinese government's censorship machine. It had deleted thousands of apps in recent years, including foreign news outlets, gay dating services, and even the Dalai Lama.

Perhaps the toughest showdown came recently after China passed a law that all data about all Chinese citizens had to reside inside China's borders. To comply, Apple decided to build a quarter-mile-long data center in Guiyang, deep in China's interior. In short order, the Chinese government insisted on managing the facility. Chinese state employees physically manage the computers that store the data, and the encryption keys used to unlock that data are stored on-site—at the Chinese government's insistence. "Apple's compromises have made it nearly impossible for the company to stop the Chinese government from gaining access to the emails, photos, documents, contacts, and locations of millions of Chinese residents," the *Times* concluded. Apple, meanwhile, proudly proclaims that it is committed to protecting the privacy of all its users.

Despite these claims about protecting privacy, multiple reports have suggested that the Chinese government has been able to penetrate iPhones once they are in use. It was Alphabet, the parent company of Google, that in 2019 discovered that security flaws in the iPhone had led to a "sustained effort to hack the users of iPhones in certain communities over a period of at least two years." It was widely reported that the targets were Uighurs living or traveling outside of China. Apple responded by saying that the attack was "narrowly focused" and hit fewer than a dozen Uighur websites.[33]

Is it possible that the Chinese government has learned how to penetrate Apple's systems in China and perhaps the world? If the government controls each player in the company's supply chain and controls its data center, the opportunities for mischief would abound.

Multiple experts have called on Apple to diversify its manufacturing footprint more quickly. At one point early in the Trump administration, the CEO of FoxConn announced a $10 billion liquid crystal display factory in Wisconsin. Then–House Speaker Paul Ryan, who was from Wisconsin, took part in a ceremonial ground breaking with President Trump. It would have been an important step in recreating a consumer products industry in the United States, but it never happened. Why not? It may have been that Apple calculated—with FoxConn—that the costs of diversifying did not justify doing so. It may have concluded that the surest way to continue increasing quarterly earnings was to maintain the existing footprint.

It also could have been that Apple was scared of what might happen if it started to diversify. This is only speculation, but it is grounded in the experience of the lawyers at the Seattle-based law firm Harris Bricken, who have deep expertise in China.[34] They recommend that companies interested in "reshoring" production back to the United States or elsewhere get all the details lined up before advising their Chinese partner or manufacturer because they've observed the following things happening after foreign companies inform their Chinese partners that they are leaving:

- The Chinese partner keeps all the foreign company's tooling and molds, the heart of its intellectual property. The obvious threat is that the Chinese partner will begin making the product themselves and compete against the foreign company that was once its partner.
- The Chinese have registered the foreign company's brand names and logos in countries such as Thailand so the foreign company

cannot make its own brand-name products or have them made in that country.

- The Chinese partner tells the Chinese government about the dispute, and the foreign company discovers that its components are being seized at the Chinese border for allegedly violating someone else's trademark or design patent.

- The Chinese partner says it will not ship any more product effective immediately because the foreign manufacturer is late on payment and owes it hundreds of thousands of dollars, which is untrue. But it triggers action by the Chinese government against the foreign firm.

In effect, the Chinese have learned how to essentially hold some foreign firms hostage. "Manufacturing in China has become much riskier, but leaving China has become much riskier as well," Harris Bricken said.

Harry Moser is an old-school manufacturing guy with deep family roots at the old Singer sewing machine factory in Elizabeth, New Jersey, within eyesight of Lower Manhattan's skyscrapers. "My grandfather was a foreman and ran a department," Moser explained to us. "Dad was an assistant superintendent and ran about a third of the factory. It was the largest factory of any kind in the world—2.5 million square feet with five thousand employees. I drove past there twenty years ago. Nothing is made there anymore. I have found nothing made in the United States by Singer anymore. It was all wiped out by imports." That was the result of the wave of globalization that shifted much U.S. production to East Asia, Mexico, and other cheaper labor locations.

For his part, Moser made a career selling machine tools and equipment as the globalization push proceeded. "But it was made more difficult by industry after industry, company after company, going under before I could sell them anything," he said. "I concluded something had to be done." That led to his founding the Reshoring Initiative, a nonprofit that has pioneered the case for bringing back at least some American manufacturing to the United States, which is called "reshoring" or "onshoring."

One of Moser's key concepts is called the total cost of ownership (TCO) formula. He argues that many CEO's made decisions to set up or expand manufacturing in China because its labor costs were so much lower than in the United States. But there are other factors, such as logistics and "coordination costs"—such as having to send engineers and other supervisors to China on lengthy assignments—that CEOs have not factored into their cost calculations. When they understand their total costs, in Moser's view, they will shift their thinking on about 20 percent of what they now import.

There are signs that is happening. The Reshoring Initiative estimated in August 2022 that American companies reshoring production, combined with new investment decisions by non-American companies, would create nearly 350,000 jobs in 2022. About two-thirds of those new jobs will be the result of reshoring. "What started as a trickle in 2010 has become a torrent today," the Reshoring Initiative said.[35]

What are you hearing from manufacturing companies these days? "I hear fear," Moser said, speaking from his summer home in Maine. "I have had a surge of companies come to me in the last three to four months, and it's clear that somebody high up in the company told them, 'Get the work out of China.' The thing they're concerned about could be the delays like the mess out there now [associated with COVID lockdowns and port delays]. But underlying it is the risk of decoupling in which China gets so pissed off at us or there is an incident over Taiwan, and suddenly nothing comes out of China."

He notes that the Chinese government has vowed reprisals if Congress passes the CHIPS and Science bill, which it did.[36] No retaliation has happened yet, at least not publicly, but the mere threat implies that the government could choose to interrupt or halt the shipment of parts from China to U.S. factories that assemble them into products. "Most or many U.S. companies are so dependent on China that it would be existential for many of them [if China were to interrupt the flow of goods or parts]," Moser said. "If it happened to any one company, that company could find other suppliers. But if it happened to ten thousand U.S. companies all at the same time, it would be a disaster. There simply are not enough suppliers here. I'm convinced that corporate leaders are starting to recognize the substantial risk they face in being dependent on China."

Moser says he is telling corporate leaders to use his total cost of ownership formula to calculate what pieces of their production chain can be brought back to the United States without hurting their profitability. "That turns out to be 20 to 30 percent of what they are getting over there," he said. "At least get started and bring back the things you can without hurting your profitability."

The real problem is not any disruption facing major retailers that source goods made by Chinese-owned factories in China. "It's easier for Walmart," Moser explained. "If they've been getting shirts in China, they can get shirts out of Bangladesh. But if you have a component coming in from China to go into a refrigerator you're assembling here and it's cast in China or made by injection molding, and you can't get the part and you can't get your tooling out if something goes wrong, you've got a mess."

Moser is encouraged by what he sees as reinvigoration of the semiconductor industry in the United States, but he warns that the new plants that have been announced are just a first step. "Most every major country is building or increasing semiconductor manufacturing," he said. "In five or seven years, there will be an excess of chip capacity. When that happens, it will be all about competing on price—and U.S. chips will be more expensive because of wage rates and regulations and other problems. It's going to cost more to make a chip here than in China or Taiwan. If the government just works on the chip foundries but does not develop the consumer electronics industry, then we'll go from being dependent on Taiwan and China for chips to being dependent on China to buy our chips to build the infotainment systems and servers and medical devices to ship back to us. We don't want that."

"We say," he continued, "that if you want chip foundries to succeed, you have to have a rising tide that lifts all the boats. You bring back a broad range of electronic assembly and automate it so that most of the chips that are made here are consumed here in the country."

It will require a major shift in American thinking to fully realize the gains, Moser argues. It will require shifting some resources from encouraging young people to get four-year liberal arts degrees toward spending more on engineers and manufacturing apprentices. "We have an excess of liberal arts graduates," he said. "Many of them are working for Starbucks." He would cut tuition for engineering students and offer government loans to apprentices so the required wage rates paid by the employers could be low enough that the employers would not have lost money if the apprentice is hired away by another company.

Moser's views reflect a recognition that manufacturing is strategic. No nation can defend its prosperity and national security by relying on another manufacturing platform located twelve time zones away across the Pacific Ocean, particularly if the Chinese government is prepared to manipulate supply chains to its advantage. One critical industry where the Chinese could exert tremendous pressure on American manufacturers is that of rare earths, which are used in electric car batteries, weapon systems, and a wide variety of high-tech goods. China controls an estimated 80 to 90 percent of these materials. If America is to once again think strategically about its manufacturing base, this would be one crucial gap to address.

A last piece of the U.S.-Chinese manufacturing puzzle is how rigorously a new American law will be enforced.[37] The law, which took effect in June 2022, bars Chinese-made products from entering the United States if they have any links to Xinjiang Province, where the forced assimilation of Uighurs is underway. The law puts the burden of proof on importers into the United States—they have to produce evidence that their supply chains do not run through Xinjiang or involve slavery or coercive practices.

That is exquisitely difficult because an American company could have dozens of suppliers in China, and each of them could have dozens of sub-suppliers, who might contract their work out to other entities. American companies can hire auditors to study their supply chains in China, but if those auditors are Chinese, they are not necessarily going to reveal that cotton products or solar panels may have been made in Xinjiang. Other products from Xinjiang include food products such as tomato paste, hops, walnuts, and peppers and industrial products such as rayon and beryllium.

The experts say that that rigorous enforcement of the law could affect 1 million businesses globally. "The public is not prepared for what's going to happen," said Alan Bersin, former commissioner of U.S. Customs and Border Protection. "The impact of this on the global economy, and on the U.S. economy, is measured in the many billions of dollars, not in the millions of dollars." And it could result in American CEOs further rethinking their Chinese supply chains. Clearly, the era of unbridled manufacturing expansion in China is coming to an end.

SUMMARY OF RECOMMENDATIONS IN CHAPTER 9

- The U.S. government should use the CHIPs and Science Act to revive the manufacturing of semiconductors on U.S soil. It will be important to follow through to foster and encourage the development of related industries that can purchase and use the chips. That should be accompanied by efforts to train the people who will be necessary to operate the new plants being built by Intel, Samsung Electronics, and Taiwan Semiconductor Manufacturing Corp. Doing that will require governmental encouragement for "reshoring" as a whole so that U.S. companies can maintain critical distance from Beijing's demands. This would be a "rebalancing" not a "decoupling."

- Government should undertake a comprehensive strategy to maintain the U.S. lead in the design of advanced chips through an alliance with the "techno-democracies," and it should use similar strategies to regain lost ground in technologies such as 5G and rare earths where the Chinese have established leadership positions.

- These coalitions or alliances should collectively ban the export of critical technologies, place bans on investing in Chinese companies in those areas, and establish tough reviews of Chinese acquisition of technology assets outside of China. They also should cooperate to protect key technologies from Chinese espionage and intellectual property theft.

CHAPTER 10

Social Disorder

Reining in Social Media and Big Tech

On October 29, 1969, two refrigerator-sized mainframe computers exchanged the first communication over the internet. "LO"—two simple letters were beamed more than three hundred miles from the University of California, Los Angeles, to the Stanford Research Institute. As if by biblical proclamation, "LO" ushered in a new era—one where unimaginable troves of information are available with the click of a mouse, where ideas and thoughts can be shared and critiqued by a global audience, where untold economic opportunities abound for even the most remote peoples.

However, "LO" was not a biblical proclamation at all. The first word that crossed the wires of the early internet was supposed to be "LOGIN," but the network crashed after the operator had typed a mere two characters.

Despite these early sputters, the internet roared to life. From global commerce to critical infrastructure processes to basic human interaction—life in the developed world has come to be unimaginable without access to the internet. However, as we increasingly live, work, and play in an online world, the significant influence the internet exerts over our perception of the world around us—and our very sense of self—has bred new existential threats.

As we documented in the first part of this book, we now have fake think tanks and fake experts issuing opinions that receive wide distribution on social media. We have fake social media profiles, including untold thousands that are "bots," or robots managed by programs that make them appear to be authentic—they "like" articles and automatically connect with all accounts recommended by a social media platform. Entire "farms" of these bots can be used to give an influencer a significant following. This technique can be used by anyone from high schoolers in California to foreign spy agencies. And we have seen just how vulnerable social media influencers are to outright bribery, which is what China did with influencers to enhance the "touching" moments of the 2022 Winter Olympics in Beijing.

It speaks volumes that Elon Musk sought to renege on his acquisition of Twitter because the company would not or—more likely—*could* not tell him how many of its registered users were real people. For social media giants like Twitter and Facebook, this poses a direct threat to their business models. Advertisers pay astronomical fees to target individual consumers through these platforms. If a platform's user base is substantially comprised of bots, advertisers would be much less likely to pay a tech giant's asking price. For the rest of us, this portends something far more ominous: If social media giants cannot distinguish between real and fake accounts, how can we protect our information space from a hostile takeover by our adversaries? How can we identify our adversaries' attempts to hijack legitimate social movements to undermine our democracy?

Fixing all this is truly a Herculean task. Let's talk first about what our goals as a society should be: We want to force or persuade social media companies to start exercising more responsibility for the content they host.

We don't want to force Facebook, Instagram, Apple, Google, Microsoft, Twitter, and others into bankruptcy. These are American companies, arguably built on American ideals, but definitely subject to American laws. We need viable social media and technology companies—as well as traditional mainstream news organizations—that are strong enough to secure the American information ecosystem and, by default, the information ecosystems of all democracies. At the end of the day, the information wars against China and Russia cannot be won without the help of our social media giants. As China props up its national champions to extend its authoritarian ideals and its surveillance state, we too need national champions that embrace democratic principles and individual rights to enable those ideals to flourish throughout the world. The power of ideas and information has never been more tangible.

There are a variety of policy strategies the government can use to either force or persuade Big Tech to play as part of Team America, but we will concentrate on just two: social media policy and antitrust policy.

Social Media Policy

The issue is not whether the social media platforms are tilting to one side of the political spectrum or another. That is a red herring. The sheer number of platforms and users guarantees that all manner of ideological and personal convictions can be voiced and are being voiced. The real issue is accountability.

One way to start adding a bit of accountability would be to gradually urge more platforms to verify the real identities of their users. Asking users to voluntarily register with their driver's license numbers or verifiable telephone numbers would start to alter the nature of the internet. Today, platforms allow anyone to create profiles using false names. This ease of anonymity enables hate speech, bullying, and outrageous political accusations to be made because users believe they can't be identified. It also enables our adversaries to operate on American social media with impunity—as observed during the 2016 U.S. presidential election.

While there are significant risks associated with anonymous and pseudonymous speech, the *right* to anonymity is an important freedom that our founders relied on in creating our founding documents. In publishing *The Federalist Papers*, Alexander Hamilton, James Madison, and John Jay used pseudonyms to defend the Constitution to the public. Indeed, activism and the freedom to express support for or displeasure with the government and our social norms has been critical to the development of our democracy. "Whoever would overthrow the liberty of a nation must begin by subduing the freeness of speech," Benjamin Franklin famously wrote under the pseudonym Silence Dogood. Today, this right to anonymity continues to be of immense importance.

In July 2022, following the highly contentious *Dobbs v. Jackson Women's Health Organization* Supreme Court ruling, which overturned *Roe v. Wade*, a group identifying itself as "ShutDownDC" offered up to $250 to service industry workers in Washington, DC, who reported sightings of conservative Supreme Court justices in public. "DC Service Industry Workers . . . If you see Kavanaugh, Alito, Thomas, Gorsuch, Coney Barrett or Roberts DM us with the details!" ShutDownDC posted on Twitter. "We'll Venmo you $50 for a confirmed sighting and $200 if they're still there 30 mins after your message." When Twitter was asked about removing the group, Twitter representatives responded that ShutDownDC's actions did not violate Twitter's terms of service, which comport with the Constitution.

The First Amendment of the Bill of Rights protects the right to anonymous free speech. Ironically, the Supreme Court—the institution currently being targeted by anonymous speech—upheld that very right in a seminal ruling in 1995. The Court held, "Anonymity is a shield from the tyranny of the majority. . . . It thus exemplifies the purpose behind the Bill of Rights and of the First Amendment in particular: to protect unpopular individuals from retaliation . . . at the hand of an intolerant society."[1] Whether one agrees or disagrees with the Supreme Court's decision on abortion is of far less importance than the *right* to express that sentiment. Alarmingly, however—as Musk's recent foray has revealed—Twitter is unable to determine whether groups like ShutDownDC are, in fact, an organic American movement or a Russian influence campaign engineered in St. Petersburg.

The challenge in protecting the right to anonymous speech while safeguarding our nation against our adversaries' malign influence campaigns requires that we achieve a delicate balance. There would rightly be howls of outrage at any proposal that mandates verification of user identities. The chilling effect on freedom of speech and expression, as well as the right to privacy, would be significant. Grindr—the gay dating application—offers a prime example. Grindr requires an email address and a phone number to sign up, but it does not require any further proof of identity. While Grindr has an incentive to prevent bot activity on its platform, it has an equally strong incentive to protect its users' privacy.

How many Grindr users would cease using it if they were required to "out" themselves? By that same token, how many conservative professors would be confident in voicing their strong opposition to gay marriage or abortion rights on anonymous message boards if they could be identified in a liberal-dominated university?

At the same time, our adversaries use the openness of the internet and our social media platforms against us. They target our electorate, they foment political unrest, and they seek to exacerbate societal rifts to divide us internally. This approach follows Sun Tzu's ancient teachings: "Form a single united body, while the enemy must split up into fractions. Hence there will be a whole pitted against separate parts of a whole." To create a bulwark against influence campaigns aimed at dividing us, we need to be able to discern real users from fake, humans from bots, and foreign actors from Americans.

To be clear, we do not advocate for a solution that impinges upon Americans' right to anonymous speech. That would be autocratic. For instance, China requires its citizens to use their national identification numbers—which are akin to Social Security numbers and are used to give citizens a social credit score—to register for WeChat accounts. While this makes the Chinese government incredibly effective at identifying and preventing foreign influence, it also chills speech on the platform because users know that anything written is reviewable by China's feared Ministry of Public Security. This is a defining feature of authoritarianism.

To achieve the right level of accountability on America's social media platforms, we turn to Section 230 of the Communications Decency Act.[2] Often called the internet's most important law, Section 230 provides social media platforms a liability shield both for the actions of third parties on the platforms and for actions taken by the platform when it removes objectionable content "in good faith."

The Communications Decency Act was enacted in 1996 when the vast majority of people had no idea what the internet would become. It was before Google, before Twitter, before Facebook—and before Xi Jinping and Vladimir Putin. Section 230 was enacted as part of an omnibus law aimed at limiting indecent material on the internet. The section was specifically added to protect then-nascent internet platforms with user-generated content from massive litigation. Although the vast majority of the Communications Decency Act was repealed as an unconstitutional restriction on free speech, Section 230 remains intact in its original form.

In his 2019 "biography" of Section 230, Jeff Kosseff appropriately adopted the title *The Twenty-Six Words That Created the Internet*.[3] Section 230 is remarkably short for something of such importance. Those twenty-six words are: "No provider or user of an interactive computer service shall be treated as the publisher or speaker of any information provided by another information content provider." In other words, so long as an interactive service provider does not moderate user-generated content in bad faith, they are absolved of virtually all liability.

Now, more than twenty-five years later, one of the biggest technological revolutions in human history has washed over us. We have a quarter of a century of experience to start making judgments about what is working and what is not. The Electronic Frontier Foundation, a San Francisco–based digital rights nonprofit that opposes major changes to Section 230, explains what it sees as the law's impact: "This legal and policy framework has allowed for YouTube and Vimeo users to upload their own videos, Amazon and Yelp to offer countless user reviews, Craigslist to host classified ads, and Facebook and Twitter to offer social networking to hundreds of millions of Internet users," it says. "Given the sheer size of user-generated websites (for example, Facebook alone has more than 1 billion users, and YouTube users upload 100 hours of video every minute), it would be *infeasible* for online intermediaries to prevent objectionable content from cropping up on their site. Rather than face potential liability for their users' actions, most would likely not host any user content at all or would need to protect themselves by being actively engaged in *censoring* what we say, what we see, and what we do online"[4] (emphases added).

We disagree. Social media platforms are already in the business of moderating objectionable material on their sites. For example, child pornography cannot be shared via Instagram—not because it is a federal crime, but rather because it violates Instagram's terms of service. The law requires that social media platforms report instances of child pornography and exploitation to the National Center for Missing and Exploited Children when they have *actual knowledge* of such instances. While Instagram, and its parent company, Meta, could bury their heads in the sand, the platform has instead developed algorithms that are able to identify objectionable material. Why would a social media platform voluntarily subject itself to moderation and federal reporting requirements? It's a business decision—Meta determined that the dollar value associated with attracting and retaining users and advertisers through a restriction on child pornography was greater than the cost of moderation and potential legal liability for having *actual knowledge*.

Other areas of regulation have similarly resulted in platform self-regulation. For instance, Craigslist—the classified advertisement website—shut down its widely used "personals" section in 2018 when Congress passed the Senate's Stop Enabling Sex Traffickers Act (SESTA) and the House of Representatives' Fight Online Sex Trafficking Act (FOSTA). SESTA/FOSTA does not explicitly strip Section 230 protections, but it creates such substantial ambiguities about liability as to pose an unreasonable business risk for some platforms. "Any tool or service can be misused," Craigslist wrote in a statement following its decision to shutter its personals section in the wake of the new law. "We can't take such risk without jeopardizing all our other services, so we are regretfully taking craigslist personals offline."

Substantial revisions of Section 230 would undoubtedly harm a significant number of large U.S. social media platforms, which is the reason they have lobbied so hard against any such action. And those same business interests, paradoxically, need to be harnessed to guard against inauthentic and malicious activities. That's the central contradiction that must be managed.

A possible compromise on Section 230, rather than simply eliminating it, would be to amend it so that it achieves the original goal of requiring social media companies to "take reasonable steps" to protect their users from any harm. "Back in the 1990s," Gordon Crovitz of NewsGuard explained to us, "the issue was how could AOL and the early portals keep pornography off their sites without being liable for everything on their platform? Section 230 solved that problem by granting them blanket immunity. Twenty-five years later, it turns out there's a downside to blanket immunity—which is that we've got a whole industry of companies like Facebook and Google that were literally founded to be immune. If you tell an industry you're not going to be held liable for any known harms on your platform, we shouldn't be surprised that they behave irresponsibly. We've *told them* they don't have to be responsible."

One option would be a simple modification of Section 230 that would leave the interpretation of the statute to the courts. If, for instance, language requiring the platforms to take "reasonable steps" to protect users were to be inserted into Section 230, the term "reasonable" would obviously be subject to interpretation and would no doubt require litigation, paving the way for the courts to establish norms based on tort law or contract law. "That's what our common law does all day long," Crovitz said. "Chemical companies have to take reasonable steps not to have chemical spills. We tell oil shippers they have to take reasonable steps not to spill oil. That's how our system works. That's okay."

The challenge with this approach, however, is that by not clearly defining the reasonable steps a social media platform is required to take, there invariably will be different outcomes in different legal jurisdictions, and the goal of identifying inauthentic and malicious activity might not be achieved. The goal in crafting such requirements should be to simultaneously protect our national security interests while limiting legal exposure for social media platforms. For American social media platforms to serve as an effective bulwark of democratic ideals against Chinese and Russian platforms' autocratic censorship and surveillance, they must remain competitive in the global marketplace. For these reasons, we advocate that the statute be amended to include narrow requirements social media platforms would have to meet to avail themselves of Section 230 protections.

One such narrow requirement could be the implementation of a method by which users can readily discern authentic accounts from fraudulent personas. Section 230 could be amended to require that social media platforms provide a mechanism for users to elect to be validated. In this way, users who wish to remain anonymous are free to do so without penalty, but legitimate news sources and users have the option to authenticate their accounts to boost their credibility.

Although it's not clear whether Musk will continue these policies, Twitter has offered this service to its users whose accounts are "authentic, notable, and active." This policy restricts the coveted Twitter blue checkmark to those accounts that are "associated with a prominently recognized individual or brand" and "active with a record of adherence to the Twitter Rules." To authenticate these accounts, Twitter requires eligible individuals to verify their identities by providing a photo of a valid official government-issued identification document.[5] The way we know that @elonmusk is the real account of the founder of Tesla and SpaceX is because a blue checkmark follows his name. This is also how we know that, despite the display name of "Elon Musk" and accompanying profile picture of the billionaire, @King_Langabi is not the real Elon Musk.[6]

Twitter does not offer this service to its wider user base, and any law requiring such strict authentication would likely have a chilling effect on speech and run afoul of the First Amendment. However, if Section 230 protections were predicated on social media platforms making such authentication available to all users, it would be up to individuals to voluntarily decide whether they wished to remain anonymous. Were individual users able to distinguish between the accounts, posts, and direct messages of authenticated users versus unverified accounts, market forces would likely lead to a preference for the former. In this way, social media providers could better arm their users to spot inauthentic or malicious activities while preserving the right to anonymity.

Another possible compromise would be for the social media giants to embrace "middleware" tools such as NewsGuard's services that would give users more control over what they see. That would be similar to what Britain enacted in 2022 in its Online Safety Bill. Companies there should be held liable unless they "can show that they are taking reasonable steps to protect the online safety of their users," Crovitz said. "That has to be done by the design of the products."

According to Crovitz, between 10 and 15 percent of Facebook, Twitter, and YouTube users rely primarily on disinformation sources for their news. "Platforms have to open up their products so consumers can check a box, saying 'I don't want ads about gambling,' or they can check a box, saying 'I don't want to see anything that's bad for the kids.'" That would give individual users more control over how they interact with social media and allow them to independently regulate their information feeds.

As of this writing, perhaps the best single piece of legislation pending in Washington is the Safeguarding against Fraud, Exploitation, Threats, Extremism and Consumer Harms (SAFE TECH) Act. It is cosponsored by Senators Mark Warner, Mazie Hirono, and Amy Klobuchar—all Democrats. It is not the ultimate solution, but it takes steps in the right direction by allowing social media platforms to be held accountable for cyber stalking, targeted harassment, and discrimination. "When Section 230 was enacted in 1996, the Internet looked very different than it does today," Senator Warner said in introducing the bill.[7] "A law meant to encourage service providers to develop tools and policies to support effective moderation has instead conferred sweeping immunity on online providers even when they do nothing to address foreseeable, obvious and repeated misuse of their products and services to cause harm."

One further step that should be taken would be to require Facebook and other platforms that accept advertisements or content from foreign governments to clearly label that material. As mentioned earlier, the Chinese government spent $10 billion on ads on Facebook in 2021. No agency of the American government would be able to advertise on Chinese media, yet Facebook is giving the Chinese government a megaphone to propagate misinformation into the United States—despite the fact that its own service is blocked in China. This creates an imbalance in the information space that puts the United States at a significant disadvantage.

"The Foreign Agent Registration Act (FARA) should be enforced on the internet, just like it was in print," Crovitz argues. "FARA was passed in 1937 to counter Nazi propaganda. It said, 'If you are a book or magazine distributor distributing Nazi books and Nazi magazines, you have to have a giant label that says you are distributing propaganda for a foreign government.' That continued on through the Soviet era and the Cold War. But it stopped with the internet. The Justice Department did not enforce it against the digital distributors the same way they did against book and magazine distributors. The platforms lobbied the department. It just didn't happen." It's an idea whose time has returned. The law is already on the books. The only thing that's needed is enforcement.

There are lessons to be learned from the European Union as well. The EU has taken a leadership position on social media issues, as it has on antitrust and privacy. The EU in early 2022 enacted the Digital Services Act that will force internet services to combat misinformation, disclose how their services amplify divisive content, and stop targeting ads on the basis of a person's ethnicity, religion, or sexual orientation.[8]

Frances Haugen, the data scientist who leaked twenty thousand pages about Facebook policies to the Securities and Exchange Commission, described the new law this way: "It is a broad and comprehensive set of rules and standards, not unlike food safety standards for cleanliness and allergen labeling," she said. "But what is also remarkable about it is that it focuses on oversight of the design and establishment of *systems*—like how algorithms behave—rather than determining what is good or bad speech." In other words, the law seeks to improve social media without interfering with freedom of speech.[9] The Europeans have been able to take a series of actions to rein in the influence of the social media giants partly because those companies do not possess the same lobbying clout in European capitals that they do in Washington.

There are additional layers to this problem, and undoubtedly additional challenges will emerge. For instance, even if social media platforms offered authentication to verify the identities of their users and the platforms disclosed foreign advertising proceeds, there would still exist a threat of a foreign adversary co-opting authentic users and influencers. Influencers on platforms such as Instagram and Facebook have exploded in popularity because consumers prefer to hear about products and services from people who are their own age or from people they aspire to become more like. The problem is that the world of influencers is ephemeral. Trends can come and go with stunning speed.

"So, you've been an influencer for a year," Chris Hadnagy, the social engineering expert, explained to us. "You're taking the fame that has become a drug for you. But all of a sudden someone else with a new dance comes along and your numbers start to tank. China comes to you (most likely through an intermediary) and says, 'You don't want to lose your status. We can help keep you in the running, and we'll give you a million dollars to do it.' They don't say, 'Help us disrupt this democracy.' Instead, their suggestion is to talk about certain issues. The influencer says, 'I can go on and talk about Black Lives Matter, no problem. I can talk about gun violence, no problem.'"

The Federal Trade Commission (FTC), which is responsible for truth in advertising, is ratcheting up pressure on influencers to fully disclose any advertising relationships they may have. The goal is not to prevent them from having advertisers, only to make sure they fully and clearly disclose who the advertisers are. Unfortunately, the relationships the FTC requires influencers to report are limited to commercial brands. If influencers are paid to advocate for or against social issues such as promoting the Winter Olympics in Beijing, reporting is not required. This is a shortcoming that exists in the reach of both the FTC's regulatory jurisdiction and the legal requirements to register as a foreign agent.

To protect against this attack vector, the Justice Department's National Security Division should establish a task force to investigate violations of FARA by social media influencers. To bolster the Justice Department's efforts, Congress should amend FARA to make influencers strictly liable for violations. This would shift the burden of discovering the foreign principals behind advertising funds to the influencers and would allow the Justice Department to hold them strictly liable for any violation—whether they push foreign influence wittingly or unwittingly.

We should also address the risks of foreign social media in wide use across the United States. Chinese social media poses the most significant risk to Americans for reasons discussed in chapter 5. At home, the Chinese Communist Party leverages the idea of internet sovereignty "to prohibit internet users from viewing foreign social media and propagating 'heretical or superstitious ideas' online," according to Georgetown University's Initiative for U.S.–China Dialogue on Global Issues.[10] In other words, American social media platforms are blocked in China to prevent the flow of democratic ideals that would undermine the Communist Party. However, the Chinese government encourages (and underwrites) the expansion of Chinese social media platforms into the United States.

To correct this imbalance, the United States should ban social media companies with direct ties to China from the American market, effective immediately. One of the most concerning platforms is TikTok—particularly in light of BuzzFeed's June 2022 revelations that TikTok's American data security personnel have no idea where the data from American users can be found.[11] "Everything is seen in China," a TikTok executive was quoted as saying. TikTok is playing an elaborate game of charades by arguing that it can move the data of its U.S. users to the cloud computing infrastructure of Oracle Corp., but that does not mean Chinese entities cannot access it. China can still see everything.[12]

Banning Chinese platforms could be achieved with a single presidential executive order on national security grounds. Less than a year after the Trump administration issued an executive order banning TikTok and WeChat, the Biden administration repealed that order. Clearly, a more lasting approach is needed. Congress, under its constitutional power to "regulate Commerce with foreign nations," could also ban the use of Chinese social media applications within the United States due to the substantial threat to national security.[13] When Congress acts under its enumerated powers, so long as it does not encroach upon another constitutional provision, its power to regulate is absolute.

Make no mistake, these platforms—including TikTok and Zoom, among others—are Chinese entities with Chinese-written applications whose data is available to the Chinese intelligence and security services. Rarely in history has a nation allowed an adversary to penetrate its communications and entertainment ecosystem so completely. Chinese social media platforms are not benign alternatives to American platforms; they are tools of the Chinese government used for espionage, surveillance, and oppression. American-owned, American-managed companies would seek to fill any void in the market left by the departure of Chinese platforms.

Deciding what to do with WeChat is more difficult. This is the online platform owned by Tencent, one of China's biggest tech companies, which is subject to the demands of the Chinese government. It is used by millions of members of the Chinese diaspora living outside of China to communicate with loved ones back home and vice versa. The 360,000

Chinese students at American universities, for example, rely on it to communicate with friends and family—as well as Chinese government officials. We have had Chinese friends implore us not to advocate for the complete prohibition of the use of WeChat in the United States. But the reality is that Chinese authorities are using WeChat as a tool to monitor Chinese citizens in the United States and elsewhere to identify both dissenters and potential spies. WeChat also serves as a platform for Chinese intelligence services to communicate with their agents abroad. If the use of WeChat in the United States could somehow be segmented from WeChat in China so that communications among family and friends can continue without the Chinese government monitoring it and exploiting it, that would be worthy of consideration. But we remain skeptical that a firewall could be reliably established.

ANTITRUST POLICY

There is a stunning similarity between today's Big Tech CEOs and the Rockefellers, Mellons, Morgans, Carnegies, and Vanderbilts who dominated the American economy in the late 1800s. Those business magnates were quick to recognize the profound changes transforming the American economy in the form of steel, coal, railroads, oil, and big banks. They dominated those critical sectors, often buying out their competitors. If we own a railroad and someone else owns a second railroad, we are competing against one another on price. But if we buy that other railroad, competition is reduced, if not eliminated, and we can raise prices. The "robber barons" became hugely wealthy and thought of themselves as superior to government. The Interstate Commerce Commission was created in 1887, and the Sherman Antitrust Act was enacted in 1890.

But the Sherman Act wasn't tapped until President Teddy Roosevelt and his trustbusters invoked it in 1904 to break up Northern Securities Co., which was controlled by J. P. Morgan and which dominated railroads from Chicago to the American West.

In today's terms, Bill Gates, Steve Jobs and Tim Cook, Larry Page and Sergey Brin, Mark Zuckerberg, Jeff Bezos, and others have dominated computers and smart phones, software and the internet, online retailing, and more, becoming incredibly wealthy. Their clout in the

American economy and politics has become outsized. As in the late 1800s, there needs to be a rebalancing. The problem is that today's monopolists are engaged in a different pattern of activity that our anti-trust laws were not written specifically to address. The outcomes of their actions (such as acquisitions of smaller companies) often have no bearing on price. They may actually result in more services being provided for "free"—in exchange for precious data.

This problem has also been brewing for roughly twenty-five years, ever since the Clinton administration in 1998 launched an antitrust law-suit against Microsoft for "choking off the air supply" of Netscape, a story that coauthor Bill Holstein covered for *U.S. News & World Report*. At the time, Microsoft's Windows operating system did not have a browser that would allow users to connect to the internet. Netscape had one. Micro-soft figured out a way to "bundle" a browser with Windows, and that was enough to cripple Netscape. Microsoft had the resources to contest the antitrust lawsuit by the Department of Justice until the administration of George W. Bush took power in 2001 and the government's ideology shifted away from antitrust enforcement. Not only does Big Tech have the power to resist new legislation—it has the power to use the courts to resist governmental action for years.

One problem today is that not many in Congress understand the power of the platforms that have been created, such as Google's search engine, Apple's App Store, Amazon's online superstore, or Facebook's platform. It was a moment of stunning clarity in 2018 when, in another of a seemingly unending parade of congressional hearings, Senator Orrin Hatch asked Mark Zuckerberg a question that revealed his complete absence of knowledge about the Facebook model.

"So, how do you sustain a business model in which users don't pay for your service?" Hatch asked.

"Senator, we run ads," Zuckerberg replied, barely able to contain a smirk.

One of the primary areas of concern about the power of tech giants today is that they create "platforms" that take on huge importance because of their amplifying "network effects." Amazon's online shopping site has become so powerful that it shapes American commerce. Should

Amazon be allowed to promote the goods and services of companies it owns, or does it have a responsibility to maintain a level playing field for all retailers, including the ones it does not own? Does Apple have the right to charge a hefty fee to the third-party makers of games that sell on its App Store, or has the App Store become, in effect, a public utility that should treat all providers evenly? Does Google have the right to advance articles and ads that benefit its interests when people do Google searches, or should it be a neutral arbiter?

"I think we've seen time and time again that when you have a company that has captured control over a key artery of commerce, that control can be used unlawfully," Lina Khan, chair of the Federal Trade Commission, said in an interview.[14] "That was partly what animated the passage of the antitrust laws where Congress recognized that the dominance of railroads and their control over key arteries of commerce was really allowing these small number of companies to pick winners and losers in our economy to shape the trajectory of innovation." Note her use of the term "key artery of commerce." Her suit to break up Facebook appears to be advancing in U.S. courts. It seeks to reverse Facebook's acquisition of Instagram and WhatsApp. A bill cosponsored by Senator Amy Klobuchar (D-MN) has also been introduced in Congress that would prohibit the tech giants from using their platforms to promote their own goods and services over those of others, but it faces scant prospect of passage because of intense lobbying against it. Tech companies poured tens of millions of dollars into lobbying against it, and the chief executives of Google, Amazon, and Apple all personally lobbied against the bill.[15]

The Europeans have a freer hand to act. The European Digital Markets Act, another major piece of legislation Europe has enacted, specifies that companies that become "gatekeepers" reaching a specified number of customers and possessing a specified amount of sales and market capitalization would be required to make their services interoperable with smaller providers and cannot exploit their own platforms at the expense of others. It also bars them from buying smaller companies if it can be proven that such moves would limit competition. It should be examined as a possible model for the United States.

Let us repeat that the goal of improved antitrust policy and enforcement should not be to force breakups but rather to moderate Big Tech's behavior by having clear sets of rules. Antitrust policy becomes a lever used to bring Big Tech into greater congruity with American interests.

Each of these social media and antitrust policy approaches should be coordinated with the Europeans, who have expressed interest in the idea of trans-Atlantic coordination. If any of that happened, governments would have much more powerful tools than any single government currently possesses. Japan should be drawn in as well, creating a global policy framework. That's ultimately what it might take to significantly alter Big Tech's behavior.

As with so many of the latest technologies, Americans have been eager to exploit the fun, positive, and valuable aspects of the internet. But we have utterly failed over the course of twenty-five years to address the negative consequences of allowing technology powerhouses to reach such positions of dominance. "Inertia is too kind of a word to describe what's happened in the United States; there's been a lack of will, courage and understanding of the problem and the technologies," said Jeffrey Chester, executive director of the Center for Digital Democracy, a public interest group. "And consumers are left with no protections here and lots of confusion."[16]

Learning how to limit the power of Big Tech and how to work with social media platforms to regulate inauthentic activities is part of the even broader challenge of redefining the relationship between the U.S. government and the private sector as a whole, a theme that also runs through the next three chapters.

Summary of Recommendations in Chapter 10

- Section 230 of the 1996 Decency in Communications Act must be altered. There are several possible ways. One would be to insert that social media providers have to take "reasonable steps" to protect users. Another would be to require social media platforms to allow users to authenticate their identities. A final would involve the use of "middleware" that gives users more control over the content presented to them. One or more of these initiatives should be taken.

- The SAFE TECH Act, which would hold social media platforms accountable for cyber stalking, targeted harassment, and discrimination, should be enacted.
- The Justice Department should enforce a 1937 law requiring that foreign government advertising on social media be prominently labeled as such.
- TikTok and Zoom should be banned, either by the president through executive order or by Congress through legislation. Ways should be explored to create a firewall between American use of WeChat and the use of that service in China.
- Antitrust laws written in the nineteenth century should be updated to create clear rules for how technology companies manage their platforms. Europe's new laws offer insights. Cooperation with Europe, and Japan, to create common policy frameworks could be effective.

CHAPTER 11

Re-Architecting Security

What the Private Sector Must Do

CONTROL OVER THE INTERNET IS AN ELUSIVE CONCEPT. IN THE EARLY days of ARPANET—the U.S. government–funded precursor to the modern internet—one man was arguably in control. Jon Postel, a computer scientist who helped create the Stanford Research Institute's Network Information Center, was responsible for issuing and maintaining network addresses for ARPANET. The network addresses, which are critical for directing the flow of web traffic, are unique numerical identifiers that allow packets of information to go to the correct recipient. In his role as internet numbers coordinator, Postel was the central authority for the operation of ARPANET.

As the commercial internet was born in the early 1990s, Postel continued to issue addresses and manage the global domain name system through an entity called the Internet Assigned Numbers Authority (IANA). In 1997, however, the Clinton administration and the U.S. Department of Commerce asserted their control over the domain name system.

In response, Postel personally emailed the operators of eight out of the twelve organizations that control the address books for the internet and asked that they reconfigure their systems to pull addresses from a computer Postel controlled at IANA rather than one controlled by the U.S. government. In one fell swoop, Postel hijacked the internet and wrested it away from the federal government.

Shortly after Postel's death from a heart condition, the federal government created the Internet Corporation for Assigned Names and Numbers, a nonprofit organization more commonly referred to by its acronym ICANN to manage the domain name system under contract with the Department of Commerce. Though the government began transitioning many of IANA's responsibilities to ICANN, the Commerce Department maintained veto power over all ICANN decisions. In other words, the U.S. government maintained effective control of the flow of traffic across the internet.

That changed, however, in 2016. Under pressure from the international community following the Edward Snowden revelations about the extent of the NSA's internet surveillance, Congress passed legislation that fully transferred control of the internet to ICANN. It functions as a multi-stakeholder organization with a government advisory committee comprised of representatives from 111 nation-states.

It would be tempting to argue that the United States should start closing off its internet-based communications and computing networks—in cooperation with fellow techno-democracies—to protect them from China, Russia, Iran, and North Korea. Despite ICANN maintenance of the domain name system, these four key adversaries have begun exerting their own control over their domestic digital spaces, closing off large portions to access by outsiders while continuing to maintain unfettered access to networks in the West. Surely that's an unfair advantage. Surely we should devise a way to keep them out.

But creating such a complete "splinternet" would be a mistake. While authoritarian regimes throughout the world seek to control access to information and, by proxy, their own people, the founding principle of the internet was to establish an open forum for the exchange of ideas. Trying to shut down the authoritarian world's access to our internet would leave billions of people behind their own digital iron curtains or, in regions without access to the internet, completely cut off from the flow of information and cut out of the stream of commerce. It would lock the United States into perhaps an even longer period of confrontation with the authoritarian axis than it already faces. As former *Washington Post* chief Katharine Graham once said, "democracy depends on information circulating freely in society." To counter the rise of autocracies, it is far preferable to extend the reach of American platforms and open information.

That's the argument made by Doowan Lee, the San Francisco–based national security expert and founder of VAST-OSINT, which provides automated solutions for detecting the origins of misinformation. "Do we abandon everyone who is living behind these firewalls?" he asked us in a video interview. "Sometimes we are so self-centered. About 99 percent of the time, we are concerned about how we protect our data from foreign actors. But we forget that out of seven billion people on the planet, four or five billion don't have access to the open internet. Unless we break down that barrier, we cannot prevail. Eighty percent of the world would end up adopting Chinese standards of data ownership no matter what we do in the United States, Europe, Asia, and Africa. That's not going to work.

"How do we push unadulterated, unmolested information into Iran, China, Russia, and Venezuela?" Lee continued. "Did we win the Cold War because we put massive pressure on the Soviet bloc? No, it imploded on its own because of the information environment. There are now a small number of companies trying to build low-orbit satellites. This conversation has to focus not just on protecting our own information but also on breaking down the authoritarian barriers to flows of information."

Achieving such a strategy will be difficult and will involve many different moving pieces. It will require accelerating efforts to build an internet that is not as reliant on a patchwork of volunteers and nonprofit foundations maintaining open-source software, as Google says it is trying to do. It will require improving the way that software developers write software throughout the whole development cycle. Furthermore, a successful strategy will require a major shift in thinking at the top of American companies, both management and boards of directors, to elevate the role of cybersecurity in how they build and maintain their computing and communications systems.

It will probably take a full decade for America to secure its computing systems. The pattern of penetration is so deep because of the malware and backdoors that have already been inserted into thousands of U.S.

systems. The private sector could take some steps in the right direction. But ultimately the private sector does not presently have the right set of incentives to fully clean up its act. Government will have to use a mix of sticks and carrots to change the cost-benefit calculus that takes place at the top of the corporate world. This gap between the private sector and government, which in some ways is a key to American prosperity, is also our Achilles' heel. Neither China nor Russia recognizes such a distinction. That is the very nature of authoritarian regimes—all actors exist to serve the interests of the party in power.

The first part of the new American strategy is to go on offense. Star-Link, part of Elon Musk's SpaceX, is the most visible of the companies building small satellites to supplement existing networks of satellites that are circling the globe. The Chinese Communist Party watched with trepidation what Musk did with StarLink's satellites when the Russians invaded Ukraine. Although the Russians succeeded in knocking out Viasat's satellite internet services, Musk's constellation of small satellites 350 miles above the battlefield prevented Russia from controlling the information flow in and out of Ukraine.[1] Time after time, StarLink successfully thwarted Russian cyberattacks targeting its network, going toe-to-toe with—and beating—one of the world's foremost cyber powers. So far, four hundred thousand people around the world have subscribed to StarLink's internet service. Other competitors are entering the game. Viasat and Amazon are launching or expanding their own low Earth orbit satellite services. Both hope to launch thousands of satellites. Taken together, what these three companies are seeking to do would have outsized geopolitical consequences.

Since 1998, the Chinese Communist Party has relied on the Great Firewall to censor and monitor the digital lives of its 1.4 billion citizens. The Great Firewall is a massive system used to block IP addresses, tamper with and redirect traffic, and filter content deemed by the party to be "offensive." Now imagine for a moment that thousands of shoebox-sized satellites are orbiting 350 miles above the earth and outside of the Communist Party's reach. Anyone who could obtain a small twelve-inch antenna would have high-speed communications even in the absence of base stations and other equipment normally required to support internet access. This would effectively render the Great Firewall null and void, granting the Chinese people unfettered access to the internet. For an authoritarian regime relying on total control of its population to remain in power, this is a nightmare scenario. For the United States, few technologies offer such a substantial counterweight to China's ever-expanding technological reach. The U.S. government should consider subsidizing the spread of these satellites because of their strategic value.

This strategy meshes very well with the White House's announcement in late April 2022 that it would work with fifty-five other nations to push rules for the internet that are underpinned by democratic values. The announcement received very little attention in the United States, but the Chinese were clearly listening. Not long afterward, they announced they were creating the World Internet Conference, with a Chinese official in charge of seeking to create an internet that was favorable to Chinese interests.

While we promote exporting a democratically oriented internet, we have to address the challenges to ensuring that our domestic cyber terrain is defensible. Google has announced that it will spend $10 billion over five years to advance cybersecurity by improving the security of the third-party foundations whose work supports the communications of the internet; securing the software supply chain to prevent attacks like the one that hit SolarWinds; and expanding the zero-trust security model, in which no person, device, or network enjoys inherent trust. It is easy to be suspicious that this is just a public relations move aimed at mollifying policy makers in Washington, but Google does have the scale to make an impact. "We don't just plug security holes," Kent Walker, president of global affairs for Google and parent company Alphabet, said on the company blog.[2] "We work to eliminate entire classes of threats for consumers and businesses whose work depends on our services." A year after that announcement, the company declined to comment on how much money has been spent and to what effect.

The needs are indeed broad and wide ranging. More of the repositories and libraries of open-source software need to take part in validating their software and then issuing online certificates of authenticity. Software development houses must overcome the temptation to rush software to market with known vulnerabilities merely because it meets performance specifications—it is far better to get it right from the beginning.

The eight-hundred-pound gorilla in the room is fixing the way the private sector produces software, which is at the heart of so many network penetrations. Increasingly, the concepts of isolation and micro-segmentation apply to software development. For many years, most software applications have been called "monoliths" by industry insiders, meaning there is one giant body of code for everything. That makes it difficult to see how different pieces of the puzzle interact with one another or to build in controls. More recently, developers have started switching to a microservices architecture. The idea is that a microservice should only serve a single purpose and operate on its own data. This practice creates its own potential problems, but it is clearly more secure than the old monoliths.

We asked NIST's Paul Black what it would take to start making dramatic progress on the integrity of America's software. He said software developers "could start tomorrow. The knowledge and skills are available. There are too many times when a senior manager pressures a software writer, saying, 'We've got to get this out [to market], we've got to get this out,' in contradiction of their best practices. Imagine if an architect designed a bridge but wouldn't release his designs until he or she figured out the likely stresses and strains on the bridge. But then along comes a superior who says, 'No, we don't have time. We have to get the design out by January. We don't have time for those computations.' As a society, we'd be outraged. Yet we as a community do that all the time in software."

Because of the intense competition in the software industry, Black argues it will take a sea change in attitudes before the industry reforms. "We get rid of doctors who do not practice well, who engage in malpractice," he said. "When was the last time you heard about a programmer being drummed out of the profession because they did not take sufficient care? Unfortunately, we in the software community don't hold ourselves to sufficiently high standards."

Black likens the scale of the challenge to what faced the auto industry as the OPEC oil embargo struck in the mid-1970s. "Automobiles had terrible gas mileage before the gas crisis of 1976," he said. "Cars leaked oil and got twelve miles to a gallon. As a society, we started to expect better. Today we expect that if we buy a car, it won't have problems. It will be able to run forty or fifty thousand miles just adding oil and gas. If we as a society said, 'No, we won't accept bad software,' things would get better. But now the refrain is, 'All software has bugs.' It's a mind-set that's hard to change."

He agrees that one lever government has is writing its contracts to purchase IT products from the private sector with clear sets of expectations about how a software program will perform over time. That would imply getting rid of, or at least limiting, the indemnities currently allowed. To a limited degree, this has begun to take shape. In September 2022, the U.S. Office of Management and Budget (OMB) released a memorandum requiring federal agencies to obtain attestation from software developers affirming that each developer follows secure development practices before the agency runs third-party software on government networks.[3] While self-attestation is an important first step, the federal government should reinforce secure software development practices by enshrining the OMB requirement in the Federal Acquisition Regulation (FAR) and the Defense Federal Acquisition Regulation Supplement (DFARS) as mandatory contractual clauses. Because of the purchasing power of the federal government, this would have a substantial spillover effect for the commercial sector.

Another important step in injecting more responsibility and accountability into the software development process would be to institute a licensing system for software engineers. They are the only kind of engineer in America who does not require a license. "Anyone anywhere can write software, and you don't even have to have a background in coding or security," Chase Cunningham, the cyber warrior we introduced in chapter 6, told us. He is deliberately provocative. "If you wake up tomorrow morning and decide you have a great idea for identifying dog crap on your daily walk, you can go off and build a GPS-enabled application to put on your phone to stop yourself from stepping in dog poo. You also could ship that out to a million users and do it all within thirty-six hours." The government should not be in the business of licensing software developers, but it could encourage the creation of an industry-wide institute or licensing mechanism.

Black also supports the idea that software developers should be licensed but says that ultimately it will require an all-of-society approach to make America's software more secure. "It's important for everybody to say, 'We want more secure software,' and to not produce or put up with poor software," Black said. "It's important not to insist that 'I want the software right now,' regardless of how it was produced."

Software developers should also consider whether the utility of including administrative applications in all software packages is outweighed by the risks of these apps being targeted by hackers. For example, one of the most useful applications offered as part of Microsoft's Windows operating system is PowerShell. Network administrators and security teams use PowerShell extensively to automate tasks, improve forensic analysis, and assist with incident response both in servers on premises and in Microsoft's cloud platform. However, the same utility that makes PowerShell such an important tool for administrators also provides hackers with the ability to leverage this tool to gain access to and control a victim's network.

This type of threat is called "living off the land," wherein hackers utilize legitimate software and programs running on the target system. One way it works is like this: an attacker will target an employee of a company or organization through LinkedIn. The attacker will make overtures about a job offer and ask the employee for an email address where the attacker can send a "standard" nondisclosure agreement. The employee, excited at the prospect of a job offer, provides his email address, and the attacker sends the agreement via email during business hours. Attached to the email is a .pdf, which, unbeknownst to the employee, has malicious code embedded in it. Once the employee opens the .pdf, the file executes a script in PowerShell on the employee's computer that gives the attacker access to the employee's device. From there, the attacker can move laterally throughout the network, obtain higher-level privileges, and carry out whatever malicious activity the attacker wishes—all without tripping intrusion detection systems.

Attackers use PowerShell for a variety of reasons. The first is its ubiquity. Since Microsoft introduced Windows XP, PowerShell has been a feature included on every Windows operating system. And in 2016 Microsoft released the source code for PowerShell to be an open-source, cross-platform framework capable of being run on Linux-based computers as well. The second reason, as described above, is camouflage. Because PowerShell is a legitimate tool used widely by system administrators and cybersecurity teams, an attacker's activity can go undetected because it appears to be consistent with normal administrator activities. Finally, attackers use PowerShell because it is an incredibly capable tool. By targeting a single program, an attacker can remotely access a considerable number of applications critical to the functioning of a network.

There are many ways for individuals to better secure PowerShell: ensure that you are running the most updated version, enable logging, and set the execution policy to "restricted," to name a few. But, as a society, we need to ask a more basic question. Should programs like PowerShell be installed on every computer running Windows? In 2021, cybersecurity firm McAfee reported that threats leveraging PowerShell rose by 208 percent in the final three months of 2020. As the threat landscape continues to evolve, software companies should begin looking at ways to administer their services more responsibly. In the case of PowerShell, perhaps Microsoft should include that application in its suite of tools as an exception rather than the rule.

Blaming developers for America's software mess is not entirely fair. Ultimately, it is the decision making at top levels of the corporate world that will be most important in securing our systems. Stephen Soble, the CEO of Assured Enterprises whom we introduced in chapter 6, is at the forefront of arguing that companies, led by their boards of directors, must organize themselves to protect their data rather than playing an elaborate blame game after a breach has occurred. While many companies have hired chief information security officers (CISOs), one knee-jerk reaction after a breach is to simply fire the CISO. Being a CISO has become one of the most hazardous burnout jobs in corporate America. Directors and officers also increasingly retain outside counsel and cybersecurity experts and rely on insurance to help them "mitigate" losses after a breach. But as cyber insurance costs skyrocket, mitigation is proving to be less cost efficient.

Soble argues that managers and directors must place more emphasis on the protection of their data. Like other cyber experts, he assumes that old-fashioned network perimeters cannot be defended. He envisions a different approach to addressing cybersecurity issues through corporate leadership.

"The issue is the board of directors, the audit committee, their understanding of their responsibility, and their personal liability for security and for their company's data security," Soble said. "It is not very difficult to educate the board of directors about what they should be doing and why. It's also not difficult to provide the information to the board so that they don't have to be technical."

The key to getting through to directors and officers is to demystify cybersecurity. "They don't have to listen to the CIO and the CISO cross swords about some technical issue," Soble continued. "What they want to know is, how do we define the risk we have today? How do we quantify it? How do we manage it?" Cybersecurity professionals need to be able to articulate to corporate leaders how the organization can put itself in the best security position, within commercially reasonable limits, to maximize profits and limit risks. Directors and officers understand fiduciary responsibility in other areas—cybersecurity should be no different.

At a basic level, many directors and officers do not know how much risk their organizations face. Clients often tell Soble, "We don't really know how much risk we have. We don't really know what we need to know." Or they voice the refrain: "No one knows how to do this. We're not any worse off than anyone else. We're all in the dark."

Other common responses Soble hears from IT administrators are, "Everyone gets hacked," or "It's the cost of doing business," or "There's nothing you can do about it." But accepting those answers is defeatist. "All these excuses that get thrown around all the time are intended to cover up the fact that we have not organized ourselves to protect the data and prevent data breaches," Soble said. The focus needs to shift to front-end protection.

Boards of directors need to understand what their personal liabilities are in the event of a data breach. "They have to understand that when you calculate the losses caused by a data breach, you are calculating a whole array of costs," Soble said. This includes other costs, such as regulatory penalties, attorney's fees, and litigation costs. Beyond fees and costs, directors and officers also must consider the reputational risk, increased insurance premiums in the event of a breach, and decreases in valuation for publicly traded companies.

Presently, companies believe they should spend just enough on cybersecurity to avoid liability in a negligence suit. If the industry standard is to spend 1 percent of a company's operating costs on cybersecurity, directors and officers who spend 1 percent are unlikely to face a suit so long as they meet that threshold and hire a brand-name cybersecurity firm. As Soble puts it, "People said, 'Let's hire a SWAT team, an external company. Let's put them on retainer. Their employees will come and fix our situation. If we get a good company, they'll keep us on the straight and narrow.'"

There seems to be broad agreement within the cybersecurity community that the way that many companies and their boards approach security is seriously flawed. "There is some degree of truth to the argument that some companies don't really want to know how to defend their systems," said a cyber expert who requested anonymity. "In general, most will at least design and do a preliminary audit that protects them against a compromise due to gross incompetence." If "gross incompetence" can be proven in court, it increases a company's insurance exposure.

"In reality, security auditing and secure development practices generally receive minimal funding," she added. "Security is layered, and there must be a balance between implementation and maintenance cost versus the value of the target you are protecting. For most, it's cheaper to deal with a breach than it is to implement better security practices. It will frankly probably take some sort of legal reform that imposes monetary penalties before this gets better."

As she suggests, what the government might be able to do is shift the economics of the corporate decision-making process by requiring companies to report data breaches above a certain size to the government, which means they would become publicly known. The Securities and Exchange Commission has no cyber enforcement powers, but it does have the power to require publicly traded companies to disclose risks that are "material," a word accountants and auditors love to argue about. The SEC is in the process of requiring companies to disclose "material" cybersecurity incidents, meaning they are big enough to affect a company's profitability.[4] That would damage investor confidence in companies that have not taken the right steps, and perhaps customer confidence as well. That might shift the cost-benefit calculus in the boardroom—what if protecting our data was actually more cost effective than hiring legions of lawyers, insurance firms, and cybersecurity companies?

Another option for changing corporate decision making would be to hold directors and officers in certain critical industries personally liable for negligence in securing their networks, as Soble argues. While this may seem a burdensome requirement, the Delaware Supreme Court and the Delaware Court of Chancery have developed a standard for director and officer accountability for risk oversight that can be directly applied to cybersecurity.

In 1996, the Delaware Court of Chancery ruled in *In re Caremark International* that directors of corporations bear responsibility to establish a reporting mechanism to exercise oversight of the functions of a company. "Utter failure to attempt to assure a reasonable information and reporting system exists . . . will establish the lack of good faith that is a necessary condition to liability," the court in *Caremark* held.[5] In June 2019, the Delaware Supreme Court sharpened the *Caremark* duty in another landmark case, *Marchand v. Barnhill*, which ratcheted up the scrutiny of boards who breach their duties to oversee the mission-critical areas of an organization operating in a highly regulated industry.[6] In October 2019, the Delaware Supreme Court further refined the *Caremark* standard in the third case, *In re Clovis Oncology*, by imposing not only a duty to make a good-faith effort to establish a reporting system or controls to ensure oversight, but also a responsibility to provide adequate monitoring of the oversight system once implemented.[7]

Taken together, these three cases stand for the proposition that directors and officers of companies in highly regulated industries bear the responsibility for both creating and monitoring processes for the oversight of areas critical to the mission of their organization. There is little doubt that IT systems fall squarely in the "mission-critical" arena for every organization. For companies incorporated in Delaware (and most publicly traded companies are incorporated there), boards of directors in critical infrastructure that fail to fulfill their cybersecurity oversight responsibilities may be held liable for breach of duty.

Given the scale of the cybersecurity crisis, courts have the opportunity to enhance the enforcement of effective cybersecurity protocols and prevent ignorance of vulnerabilities from impacting America's critical infrastructure. By adopting the Delaware standard of liability for directors and officers of companies in critical infrastructure sectors, courts would send a clear message to corporate leaders: the burden for ensuring strict oversight and monitoring of cybersecurity protocols falls on the board of directors.

Elsewhere, it is important that companies learn to be more pro-active, not merely reactive. There are myriad techniques available. Most critical is for any network owner to reduce the "attack surface." That means limiting the number of points of contact between a company's IT systems and the open internet, which reduces the number of channels that malicious actors can exploit.

Accepting that a network's perimeter cannot be defended is absolutely essential. "The simple fact of the matter is that there is no perimeter," Cunningham argues. "The perimeter is everywhere. Every user presents a risk, every device presents a risk, every data transaction presents a potential risk, and it's all transiting an inherently dangerous environment." That's why the concept of "zero trust" is so important. If the castle's walls, meaning network perimeters, have been breached, what must be done? "The new, new concept if you want to continue with the medieval analogy is to make sure that everyone inside the castle is wearing a suit of armor instead of just kind of wandering around," said Cunningham. "What we're trying to do with micro-segmentation and isolation is make sure that every entity—every person, device, and bit of data—has got security controls around it. We are enveloping that entity in a sort of secure cocoon so that you're not an easy target." "Micro-segmentation" and "isolation" mean breaking down the different elements inside a computing system so that they can each be better defended.

Ted Schlein, a veteran of thirty-five years in information technology, including twenty-five years with the famous venture-capital firm Kleiner Perkins, agrees that "the whole landscape needs to be completely rethought." He told *The Record*, a news outlet owned by the cyber intelligence firm Recorded Future, that looking for signatures associated with malware at the network's boundary no longer works. "We have to rethink things that we took for granted if we're going to protect ourselves going forward," he said. "We will look for bad signatures, and I think we all realize that it just doesn't work."

Rather than trying to improve intrusion detection systems (aimed at defending a perimeter), he advocates greater use of artificial intelligence and machine learning to manage networks more securely. And rather than viewing security as an afterthought once a system has been built, security has to "be embedded in everything that we do."[8]

The new architecture requires multiple layers of protections. One tool for confusing an attacker is called "obfuscation" technology, which hides the original data and presents modified and hence falsified data to the would-be miscreant. One concept in which data obfuscation is used is called a "honeypot," which is the same euphemism used by spies who use attractive females to entrap and blackmail married diplomats, scientists, or high-ranking military officers in exchange for their secrets. A digital honeypot, by contrast, is an "attractive" folder of seemingly important data that resides in an easily accessible part of the network. The data, which can include a beacon or a watermark to assist law enforcement after the breach, is intended to be compromised by an attacker. By offering up useless data in an area with weak security, net defenders are able to identify attributes of an attacker in order to strengthen their network against future attacks, but also to preserve the "crown jewels" in a better-protected part of the network. A similar concept is called "canary files," which sing like a bird, so to speak, by alerting net defenders when they are accessed by an attacker, revealing the presence of malicious actors.

It goes without saying that until better software practices can become widespread, companies need to be much more active in patching their known vulnerabilities, even in older legacy equipment.

Better training of all employees, not just the IT staff, is also essential. Knowing how to recognize spear-phishing attacks is key, as is spotting fellow employees who may be making mistakes on their systems or, worse, cooperating with outside parties posing as allies, when in fact they are penetrating the company's systems. That is a frequent trick that hackers use.

All Americans and their companies need to be aware of the security hazards created during the pandemic. With so many Americans working from home, moving back and forth from personal devices to their corporate networks, security has taken a backseat to convenience. That has to change. Various arms of the U.S. government such as CISA and the NSA have posted security and safety guidelines on their websites, but they have gone largely unnoticed by the general public. We need an old-fashioned World War II–style campaign of posters and propaganda even—possibly including social media influencers—to spotlight best practices. In Taiwan, for example, the government has encouraged the slogan "Think before You Click."

"Sometimes we as a society are careless about the importance of software that's well made," NIST's Black told us. "It's not just about companies going after profits. It's society as a whole. Governments, engineering firms, users, everybody has a role to play in insisting on software being written better and built better."

SUMMARY OF RECOMMENDATIONS IN CHAPTER 11

- The government should subsidize companies that are introducing thousands of low-altitude satellites to expand and strengthen the American and allied information ecosystems.

- Management and boards of companies must emphasize building secure systems rather than playing a circular blame game with lawyers, insurance companies, and cybersecurity firms after their systems are breached.

- The era of defending "the castle" is over. Network boundaries are going to be breached. Companies need new strategies in response.

- The government should follow through on an executive order requiring that software companies selling to it take responsibility for the software. Similarly, the government could reverse an existing law that exempts software companies from responsibility for security vulnerabilities that exist in their software or that are created after it is sold.

- The Securities and Exchange Commission should follow through on the proposal to require publicly traded companies to disclose cyber incidents that are "material" to their earnings.

- The software industry should consider a licensing program for software developers, perhaps in conjunction with government, to educate them about best practices and to guarantee that those best practices are put to use.

CHAPTER 12

Government Action

What the Public Sector Must Do

THE U.S. FEDERAL GOVERNMENT APPEARS TO BE ON A WAR FOOTING when it comes to cyber threats. Since 2018, the United States has established the Cybersecurity and Infrastructure Security Agency (CISA) within the Department of Homeland Security as the leading organization for securing federal networks and critical infrastructure cybersecurity. That same year, the Defense Department's Cyber Strategy laid out its aggressive "Defend Forward" plan to enable the military to eliminate cyber threats abroad before they can target domestic networks. In 2021, President Biden signed the Executive Order on Improving the Nation's Cybersecurity, which established the government as the standard-bearer for cybersecurity best practices. And between January 2021 and January 2022, Congress submitted or passed more than eighty pieces of cyber legislation, including the establishment of a national cyber director to lead the nation's cyber efforts from the White House.[1]

However, appearances can be deceiving. There are 101 federal departments or agencies, and many of them are saddled with systems and software dating back to the 1970s and 1980s. Each agency has the incentive to compete for funding rather than coalescing into a common cyber front. "If you don't have 'cyber' or 'security' in the title of your department, like CISA, Cyber Command, or the NSA, you probably don't prioritize cybersecurity," executive director of the Cyberspace Solarium Commission and retired navy rear admiral Mark Montgomery told us. "The government over the years was slow to properly resource IT modernization and slow to properly resource the installation of effective cybersecurity.

"When you are catching up for years of underfunding or unrecognized funding, it's hard," Montgomery continued. Despite the focus on cyber issues of late, the federal government continues to struggle to keep pace with the ever-changing threat landscape. "I'm disappointed to see that legislation continues to focus on the same traditional areas: reporting and punishing," Tyler Young, director of security at Relativity told the Cyber Policy Institute in early 2022. "Reporting and disclosures are only interesting if we learn from them and take action. Nothing in the legislation calls that out."[2]

Similarly, the federal government's cyber strategy remains limited by self-imposed restrictions on what powers different agencies possess, a lack of information sharing across agencies and with the private sector, and redundant missions. Simply put, the federal government, with its incredible spending power and broad access to exquisite sources of intelligence, is not structured appropriately for the battle in cyberspace. Information silos, redundancies, skill gaps, antiquated acquisition processes, and unregulated cryptocurrency markets—to name but a few—greatly hinder the government from getting to where it needs to be.

Further exacerbating the problem is the common misconception that cybersecurity can be achieved by simply throwing humans at a problem who can respond to an attack, flip a switch, and make the problem disappear. Even if this were true, the federal government and the private sector both lack the human capital and the supporting educational system necessary to fill present cybersecurity roles, let alone address future threats.

Moreover, both the federal government and the larger cybersecurity community are failing to attract and tap into female and minority talent pools. As a nation, we need more people from every demographic studying software engineering, machine learning, cybersecurity, and data analytics. We need foundational education reform at every level—from elementary school to trade schools to universities—to make training and retraining more accessible. The cyber workforce shortage is far more than a human capital problem; it is a pervasive national security problem.

For the United States to be fully armed in this battle, it needs to make organizational reforms within the federal government, take legislative action to better ensure domestic cybersecurity, and flex its considerable muscle to partner with, and place pressure on, the private sector. "But information sharing isn't enough," argues former NSA general counsel Glenn Gerstell. "It would be hamstrung from the start if the government cannot seamlessly and quickly track malicious cyber activity from its foreign source to its intended domestic victims."[3] Beyond mere improved partnerships and information sharing, Americans must be willing to embrace a federal government with the authority to pursue adversaries onto private networks without a warrant or court order. By the time the FBI is able to lawfully act on intelligence the NSA has collected about foreign actors operating on U.S. networks, it is already too late, as General Nakasone testified. In the name of privacy, the federal government has largely left the private sector to fend for itself. "Like a property owner who has put up a fence a few feet inside his property line just to be safe, Congress has established more restrictive structures and rules in our current system than what the Constitution would require for reasonable, warrantless monitoring," Gerstell writes. The gap between the public and private sectors—which is enshrined in our ideals as how we as a nation function—is at the same time a critical weakness.

Organizational Reforms

In the 2021 National Defense Authorization Act, Congress gave CISA the power to issue administrative subpoenas to internet service providers and to conduct threat-hunting operations on federal networks.[4] While this designation solidifies CISA's position as the focal point for securing federal government and critical infrastructure networks, it did not provide CISA with powers that would encroach upon those of the military or law enforcement agencies like the FBI. And while a clear distinction in powers is important, it can create inefficiencies when rapidly responding to threats in the cyber domain. In early 2022, Deputy Attorney General Lisa Monaco, in a rare breach of protocol, criticized a provision in an omnibus spending bill for creating such inefficiencies, arguing that the law actually "makes us less safe."

Monaco's position at the Justice Department includes administration of the FBI. The new law—the Cyber Incident Reporting for Critical Infrastructure Act of 2022—requires operators of critical infrastructure to report cyber incidents to CISA but does not require simultaneous reporting to the FBI. This is surprising given that the FBI's actions in response to cyber incidents have led to spectacular successes, such as clawing back much of Colonial Pipeline's $4.4 million ransom payment and using federal warrant procedures to remotely clean hundreds of computers infected by China's compromise of Microsoft Exchange. The law "leaves one of our best tools, the FBI, on the sidelines and makes us less safe at a time when we face unprecedented threats," Monaco said in a statement. Government officials do not normally comment on pending legislation.

Chinese and Russian hackers care little which agency is designated as lead for which type of incident. In fact, there is ample evidence that both Russian and Chinese cyber strategies operate precisely at the seams where government agencies are unclear as to who is responsible.

Suppose a hacker affiliated with Russia's intelligence services uses a backdoor that it previously established through a software supply-chain compromise to target hundreds of organizations across dozens of sectors. Which agency leads? Well, it depends. If those organizations are federal agencies or critical infrastructure, then CISA would lead. If those organizations are comprised solely of military networks or the defense industrial base, then the Defense Department would lead. If they are private companies or universities, the FBI would lead.

The problem is that large-scale cyber incidents do not align themselves to *our* organizational construct. Moreover, companies rarely understand the federal government's organizational hierarchy for cyber incident response. If a company is hit by ransomware, their first call is likely going to be to their attorney. If the attorney is good, she will know the precise reporting requirements for the specific industry in which the company operates (which differ dramatically from sector to sector). But what if the attorney is unfamiliar with cyber incident reporting? Or what if the company believes they will receive better support from the feds by calling the FBI instead of CISA? Law enforcement investigations have specific requirements, such as an evidentiary chain of custody, that are outside CISA's authority. The federal government is tying itself in knots trying to determine which agency has the lead role and what information can be shared with whom—greatly hindering any sort of "real-time" government support. "Instead of going to five or six different agencies, there needs to be a front door that is clearly visible," former CISA director Chris Krebs said during his keynote address at the Black Hat conference in August 2022.

The root cause of friction between government agencies when it comes to cyberspace is that the government is attempting to overlay traditional authorities and delineations designed for the physical world onto a domain where no such separation exists. The federal government wants Cyber Command to wage war in cyberspace, the FBI to investigate crimes and espionage, and CISA to serve as the focal point for threats to nonmilitary government networks and critical infrastructure. The only problem is that's not the way our adversaries see the battle space.

To better align U.S. government efforts to the threats facing America, the government should make two very large, sweeping changes. The first is to remove CISA from the Department of Homeland Security and elevate it to a cabinet agency—the Department of Digital Services—with the national cyber director at its helm. The second is to establish a Cyber Force that operates under both the Department of Digital Services and the Department of Defense, with sufficient military, intelligence, and law enforcement authority to take on the full scope of threats in cyberspace.

Department of Digital Services

Presently, responsibility for cybersecurity, digital policy, cyber defense, cyber intelligence, and cyber warfare are spread broadly across the federal government. Writing this book, we've spoken to dozens of officials from many agencies and departments. Each has a unique role to play, but each answers to an entirely different chain of command. By establishing a cabinet-level agency headed by the national cyber director, the federal government would be able to consolidate the national strategy, oversight, and enforcement mechanisms into a single organization. Such a consolidation would allow for better management and implementation of necessary protocols to ensure digital security across all sectors.

We have certainly witnessed the shortcomings of the present system. For instance, in 2015, NIST first published its landmark guidance for defense contractors aimed at securing defense supply-chain networks. NIST Special Publication 800–171 detailed more than one hundred steps it deemed necessary to protect unclassified defense information on nonfederal networks. In 2016, Congress modified the Defense Federal Acquisition Regulation Supplement—the regulation that governs all defense contracts—to require that contractors implement the security steps outlined in the NIST special publication. Five years later, in October 2021, Deputy Attorney General Monaco announced that the Justice Department was establishing a Civil Cyber-Fraud Task Force to "pursue cybersecurity related fraud by government contractors."[5] In other words, from the time NIST published its guidelines, it took the Department of Justice *five years* to begin enforcing contractual cybersecurity protocols for companies handling national security information. This failure to consolidate the policy, regulation, and enforcement arms of government has resulted in an insecure defense supply chain and an unacceptable risk to U.S. national security.

As head of the Digital Services Department, the national cyber director would be responsible for the functioning of an operational agency with regulatory responsibilities and enforcement authorities in coordination with the Department of Justice. The department would continue CISA's responsibilities for federal network and critical infrastructure security while also taking on new functions. These would include absorbing NIST's role in establishing standards for cybersecurity and data privacy, serving as cochair of the Committee on Foreign Investment in the United States (CFIUS), and leading the review of American technology exports with Commerce's Bureau of Industry and Security, among others.

Establishing a Digital Services Department would also allow the federal government to expand its investment in new and critical technologies. In 1999, the CIA chartered the establishment of In-Q-Tel, a privately held nonprofit organization charged with identifying and investing in cutting-edge technologies to support U.S. national security. Some of In-Q-Tel's early successes include the precursor to Google Earth, Palantir Technologies, and Wickr secure communications. Similarly, in 2016, the Defense Department chartered a "digital embassy" in Silicon Valley, named the Defense Innovation Unit. DIU, as it is known, is focused on identifying critical technologies being developed by the private sector and rapidly adapting them to military use. DIU works exclusively to bring artificial intelligence, autonomy, cyber, energy, human systems, and space technologies to the military.

Within the Digital Services Department, the federal government could establish a federally chartered venture-capital firm and technology incubator designed to further national security objectives in cyberspace. In this way, the federal government could more efficiently cultivate critical technologies to compete with China's state-owned enterprises while reinforcing competition in the market that has given American technology an edge.

Finally, a Digital Services Department could also serve the function of human resources management for civilians across the federal government. This does not apply only to cybersecurity, but to a cadre of digital services employees. In 2021, the National Security Commission on Artificial Intelligence detailed in its report the pressing need to rapidly increase digital talent in government. "The government needs new talent pipelines, including a U.S. Digital Services Academy to train current and future employees. It needs a civilian National Digital Reserve Corps to recruit people with the right skills—including industry experts, academics, and recent college graduates."

While the report makes a compelling argument for the establishment of such a civilian corps, it places the management of such a cadre with the Office of Management and Budget. Instead, human capital management for digital talent across the federal government—including the National Digital Reserve Corps—should reside in the Digital Services Department. The Digital Services Department also needs an operational element with sufficient authority, training, and personnel to confront modern cyber threats.

UNITED STATES CYBER FORCE[6]

During World War II, airpower tipped the scale of victory in favor of the Allies, as aviation proved to be an indispensable war-fighting capability.[7] From air-to-air engagements and tactical bombing campaigns to aircraft carrier–centered naval combat and the delivery of nuclear munitions, for the first time in history the air became a significant war-fighting domain.[8] After the war, America's military and political leaders recognized the inefficacy of having all the nation's airpower subordinated as components of the army and navy.[9] Nearly two years after the end of hostilities, the National Security Act of 1947 officially established the United States Air Force as its own military service within the Department of Defense.[10]

The creation of the U.S. Air Force was predicated on the notion that a "realistic understanding of the new weapon, of its implications in terms of national security, of its challenge to America, is not a matter of choice" but one of the conditions on which national survival rested, wrote aviation pioneer Alexander de Seversky.[11] Today, cyber superiority has wider implications to U.S. national security than air superiority meant at the close of World War II, as every facet of life in America has become reliant on cyberspace.[12]

However, threats in cyberspace are inherently different from traditional national security threats. Malicious cyber actors recognize neither physical borders nor the distinction between military and nonmilitary targets.[13] Nation-states frequently blend criminal activities, espionage, and military operations to conduct malicious activities and impose costs upon businesses, governments, and individuals.[14] To address the novel legal and operational challenges of cyber warfare and cyber-enabled malicious activities, the United States needs to move beyond the current monolithic military, intelligence, and law enforcement constructs to imagine a new Cyber Force.

Within the U.S. Code, there are several unique titles that, if combined, would imbue a Cyber Force with authorities commensurate with the evolving threats in cyberspace.[15] While different organizations within the federal government are authorized to conduct various activities under multiple titles, no single organization can leverage all requisite authorities for effectively combating malicious cyber actors and activities. However, the government is not without adequate models—the U.S. Coast Guard and the National Guard offer prime examples for how the United States can overcome this obstacle.

The Coast Guard operates at the intersection of homeland defense, law enforcement, intelligence activities, and military operations.[16] It is the only element within the federal government where individual personnel can conduct activities simultaneously under authorities traditionally reserved for individual governmental agencies. The Coast Guard's unique composition offers a particularly good model for addressing the challenges inherent in cyberspace, where lines between domestic security, law enforcement, and warfare are often blurred.

Following 9/11, the Homeland Security Act of 2002 transferred the U.S. Coast Guard to the Department of Homeland Security.[17] As the agency responsible for the maritime sector within DHS, the Coast Guard maintains broad authority over the navigable waters of the United States. These powers include the ability to prescribe how private and commercial vessels operate,[18] control over the anchorage and movement of vessels to ensure the safety and security of U.S. naval vessels,[19] and the ability to prescribe regulations for the inspection and certification of vessels.[20] To fulfill its role in the maritime domain, the Coast Guard is authorized to operate as a law enforcement organization.[21] Coast Guard personnel have federal law enforcement authorities to board any vessel subject to the jurisdiction of the United States, whether on the high seas or on waters over which the United States has jurisdiction, and make arrests for violations of U.S. laws.[22]

In addition to its role as a sector-specific agency within DHS, the Coast Guard is also "a military service and a branch of the armed forces of the United States at all times."[23] As such, the president may direct elements of the Coast Guard transferred to the Department of the Navy to execute operations consistent with the authorities of the armed forces.[24] For example, in April 2021, two Coast Guard cutters deployed to the Middle East to operate under the U.S. Navy's Fifth Fleet in Bahrain. The Coast Guard has continuously conducted such military deployments to the U.S. Central Command area of responsibility since 2002.

Among its myriad functions, the Coast Guard also operates as a member of the U.S. intelligence community.[25] In this role, the Coast Guard has the authority to "collect, analyze, produce, and disseminate foreign intelligence and counterintelligence" and to "conduct counterintelligence activities."[26]

These characteristics make the Coast Guard an effective model on which to establish a new branch of the military as well as an operational arm of the Department of Digital Services. However, the Coast Guard model alone would be inherently limited in its scope due to its size and placement within the federal government. To complement the active component of the Cyber Force, the government should simultaneously establish a cyber reserve force modeled on the National Guard.

The National Guard currently consists of the Army National Guard and the Air National Guard and operates either as organizations under the control of the governors of individual states and territories or as elements of the Defense Department when activated by the president.[27] Comprising over half of the total force strength of the entire reserve component of the armed forces, the National Guard is a crucial component of both national defense and disaster response and recovery.[28] For example, when natural disasters such as Hurricane Katrina or Superstorm Sandy devastated major metropolitan areas, state governors activated their National Guard personnel to rapidly provide assistance.

Unfortunately, this resource has not been used well to combat cyber threats at the state level. Despite the size and broad powers of the National Guard operating under state authority, it has only been leveraged in limited scope to "prepare for, respond to, and recover from cybersecurity incidents that overwhelm state and local assets."[29] Congress has recognized a lack of standardization and efficient employment of the National Guard for responding to cyber events.[30] In the 2021 National Defense Authorization Act, Congress directed the secretary of defense to evaluate the "statutes, rules, regulations and standards that pertain to the use of the National Guard for the response to and recovery from significant cyber incidents."[31] Congress went on to direct an update to the National Cyber Incident Response Plan to reflect improved use of the National Guard.[32]

The United States should establish a Cyber Force with an active component modeled on the U.S. Coast Guard and a reserve component modeled on the National Guard. The active component would serve as the operational component of the Department of Digital Services and "a military service and a branch of the armed forces of the United States at all times."[33] The reserve component would form a third National Guard component—designated the Cyber National Guard of the United States—and would operate alongside each of the fifty-four National Guard organizations nationwide.

Within the Digital Services Department, the Cyber Force would be responsible for responding to cyber incidents affecting federal government and critical infrastructure networks. The Cyber Force would retain operational control over all U.S. Computer Emergency Response Teams (US-CERTs) and the Industrial Control Systems Cyber Emergency Response Team (ICS-CERT). The Cyber Force would focus its efforts to engage with the private sector, monitor networks, and hunt for threats on both government and private-sector networks.

The Cyber Force would be granted federal law enforcement powers for the "prevention, detection, and suppression of violations of laws of the United States" in cyberspace similar to those of the Coast Guard in the maritime domain.[34] To limit an overly broad interpretation of this authority, the Cyber Force's law enforcement functions could be limited to those unlawful activities that target or affect the federal government or critical infrastructure networks. The Cyber Force could use these authorities and the warrant process to mitigate cyber threats on domestic networks when acting with a warrant.[35] Law enforcement authorities would also permit the Cyber Force to apply for and serve warrants and subpoenas to domestic entities wittingly or unwittingly used by malicious cyber actors, such as virtual private servers and cryptocurrency exchanges. Finally, these authorities would allow the Cyber Force to integrate with and support other federal law enforcement agencies as well as state, local, tribal, and territorial law enforcement elements without violating the Posse Comitatus Act.

Similar to the Coast Guard, the Cyber Force would also be an individual member of the intelligence community, which currently comprises seventeen different agencies. This would enable the training and development of cyber-specific intelligence and counterintelligence collectors, analysts, and operational personnel. The Cyber Force would have the authority to conduct counterintelligence activities, operations, and investigations in direct support of national cyber missions and requirements. As a member of the intelligence community, the Cyber Force would also be able to conduct foreign intelligence liaison relationships and exchange programs with partners to improve the collective cyber defense posture of the United States and its allies.

When operating as part of the Defense Department, the Cyber Force would serve as the force provider for Cyber Command's Cyber National Mission Force. In this role, the Cyber Force would train and equip personnel to conduct full-spectrum cyberspace operations against malicious cyber actors. Under the operational control of U.S. Cyber Command at the Pentagon, Cyber Force personnel would be able to execute offensive and defensive cyber operations targeting malicious cyber actors outside of the United States. Rotational assignments would ensure that personnel supporting U.S. Cyber Command can benefit from the operational experience of performing sector-specific functions for the Digital Services Department and vice versa. Additionally, mobilization of the Cyber National Guard to support Cyber Command would ensure that experience is continuously shared between state defenders and the Defense Department. Importantly, the establishment of a Cyber Force would not supplant the cyber components of the other military services. U.S. Cyber Command's service component commands would maintain their respective offensive and defensive missions in the same way as U.S. Space Command's service component commands maintain their areas of operation despite the existence of the U.S. Space Force.

As the reserve component of the Cyber Force, the Cyber National Guard would serve primarily as a digital militia for individual states and territories while providing a ready pool of cyber professionals in the event of a national emergency. The establishment of a Cyber National Guard would standardize the training and equipping of a state-level cybersecurity response force. This stand-alone force could be leveraged by governors to respond, using state police powers, to significant cyber incidents affecting state and local governments, critical infrastructure, and private entities. A Cyber National Guard would also enable the individual states and the federal Cyber Force to tap into the talent pool across the private sector by allowing for part-time state and federal service without requiring those individuals to join the regular military.

These two sweeping organizational changes will require significant political will and for different agencies within the federal government to set aside their individual interests in the name of national security. This will require sacrifice and compromise because centralizing all cyber functions in a single department means that other government agencies will lose funding. However, the current organizational structure is grossly inefficient. The government is already reeling from years of underfunding cyber priorities; nothing short of sweeping changes will right the ship.

LEGISLATION

In 2019, the government commissioned a blue-ribbon panel to study America's cyber challenges and issue recommendations. It was modeled on the Solarium task force that President Dwight D. Eisenhower created in 1953 in response to the rise of the Soviet Union. In March 2020, the Cyberspace Solarium Commission issued eighty-two proposals—many of which have made their way into legislation. However, most of these reforms, as well as the vast majority of cyber legislation over the past five years, have used the annual defense budget as their legislative vehicle. In fact, the 2020 and 2021 national defense acts saw 179 cyber provisions, dwarfing the paltry fourteen cybersecurity bills passed during the entire 116th session of Congress.[36]

According to Third Way, a Washington think tank, the 2020 and 2021 national defense acts accounted for 60 percent of all cyber legislation during those years.[37] Of course, congressional action addressing cyber issues is a positive indication that the cyber domain is receiving more attention at the federal level. Indeed, the 2021 national defense act had nearly four times as many cyber provisions as its 2017 equivalent did, Third Way reported. However, while Congress has grown comfortable addressing cyber-related issues annually in the defense budget, this creates a disproportionate focus on—and funding for—defense-related programs at the expense of other elements of the federal and state governments.

Presently, the 101 federal agencies of the federal government are all vying for resources from a limited pool. If the Department of Agriculture is making budgetary decisions between cybersecurity and its primary role of ensuring viability of the food chain, cybersecurity is going to be slashed. "If you're the Department of Agriculture and you are down to your last couple of dollars, and you have a shortage of food inspectors and a shortage of IT administrators, I'm pretty sure which way you lean, and it's going to be the food inspectors," Mark Montgomery told us. Congress needs to shift its legislative focus to tackling hard problems that cannot be resolved by merely reallocating resources.

One of the benefits of establishing the national cyber director with an appropriately staffed office in the executive branch is the ability to properly manage the cybersecurity budgets of all 101 agencies. The national cyber director should also be responsible for ensuring proper investment in cyber talent and technology to protect these networks. However, as previously discussed, one of the major cybersecurity issues plaguing the federal government is the cyber workforce gap. "The workforce problem has been a consistent challenge for the twenty-three years I've been involved in this," Montgomery continued. "We've done workforce studies in 2000, 2010, and 2015, and our commission did one in 2020. We all identified the same issues. Very few things were getting properly addressed."

According to the Cyberspace Solarium Commission, the United States presently has a seven-hundred-thousand-person shortfall in cybersecurity, with the federal government missing nearly fifty thousand from its required strength. "What happens where you are two-thirds manned? Any military organization will tell you that you don't do as well. You've got two-thirds of the people trying to do the work of three-thirds," Montgomery said.

But simply filling positions with trained personnel is only the beginning. Cyber is a unique field that requires constant reeducation to remain technically competent. Consider how frequently operating systems change or the government acquires new hardware or software. Every update or installation requires training of cybersecurity and IT personnel to secure and operate the network. Typically this type of training is self-taught or is conducted through on-the-job training. This results in cybersecurity professionals spending their personal time or overtime trying to learn new skills to stay ahead of threats. This leaves little time for training and education to attain the advanced certifications required to move up in an organization. And when federal government agencies are manned at two-thirds, the likelihood that managers will be able to allow their workforce to take an extended leave of absence to go through training is less likely.

This creates a negative spiral where the federal government is left with an overworked, underperforming, and poorly trained workforce. With the private sector facing similar personnel shortages while having the ability to offer far more lucrative salaries, the federal government workforce challenges will only continue to grow more dire as personnel opt to leave government for greener pastures.

Part of the problem is a lack of information about the scope of the workforce problem. "Despite the fact that we have the Cybersecurity Workforce Assessment Act, we still don't get good data," Montgomery explained. That act is about to expire. One immediate step Congress can take to address the workforce issue is to extend and amend the Workforce Assessment Act to ensure that the government has full visibility into the issue. In which agencies are the shortages most acute? What types of positions? What pay grades? Why are personnel departing? What training is required for personnel to attain different levels? These questions, among many others, help the national cyber director and individual agency heads to best allocate the resources at hand. Without accurate data, national leadership is left to make ill-informed decisions. Ultimately, meeting this challenge may "require a greater reliance in general on the private sector, since government alone does not possess the requisite expertise," former NSA general counsel Glenn Gerstell argued in a landmark op-ed for the *New York Times*.[38]

Another area where Congress can legislate solutions is the establishment of a Digital Services Academy. This idea was promoted by the National Security Commission on Artificial Intelligence as a parallel to the military service academies. However, this idea should be expanded to address the ability of the cyber workforce to not only gain entry-level training but also to move from apprentice to journeyman. Many of the shortfalls within the federal government are not at entry-level positions but are after the government has made an initial investment in training its personnel who are ready to move to the next level. It is at this point that the private sector hires away cyber talent for higher salaries and advanced training. A Digital Services Academy that offers continuing education for all levels of the cyber workforce would provide the opportunity for improved technical training, upward mobility, and reskilling.

Congress can also address the disparate compensation packages between the private sector and the federal government. While the government will never be able to compete dollar for dollar with the private sector, it can increase salaries, pay signing bonuses, and offer other non-monetary incentives—such as free training through the Digital Services Academy, student loan repayments, and increased hiring at higher pay grades for executives and cyber personnel with unique skill sets.

Equally important is for Congress to address the underlying education and digital literacy problem across all demographics. Despite exceeding their male counterparts in overall college enrollment, women only represent 25 percent of the cybersecurity workforce according to a 2021 study by Pew Research. Within the federal cyber workforce, that number drops to 14 percent. Across all computer-related occupations, Black and Hispanic people represent 7 and 8 percent, respectively. Bachelor's degrees among Black and Hispanic college students reflect this same underrepresentation, with Black students earning 7 percent and Hispanic students earning 12 percent of science, technology, engineering, and mathematics (STEM) degrees.

Where the nation is facing a cyber workforce shortage, the U.S. cannot afford to disclaim or marginalize any group. For Congress to address this issue, it should address the digital redlining that renders many areas of the country wholly without access to resources necessary to become proficient in technical fields. Digital redlining occurs where internet service providers selectively underinvest in communities that are lower income. These are business decisions driven by profit margins—wealthier, whiter communities generally have a higher rate of high-speed internet usage. More households in a geographic area subscribing to high-speed internet yields a greater return on investment for internet service providers. The result is that lower-income communities, which are disproportionately communities of color, have limited access to high-speed internet or are charged higher rates for the same speed offered to wealthier communities. "The market doesn't work in lower-income areas, and the problem with the market analogy in general is that Internet is now an essential service," Vinhcent Le, senior legal counsel of tech equality for the Greenlining Institute, told Government Technology. "The way we designed our broadband systems doesn't account for everyone needing Internet and needing it at fast speed."[39]

However, everyone *does* need internet at fast speed. The COVID-19 pandemic has revealed the power of remote work and remote education to make physical location nearly irrelevant. What this means for the future of the cyber workforce is that the education system can retool itself to provide on-demand STEM education to K–12 classrooms all over the country. CISA is currently piloting a train-the-trainer program to educate STEM teachers across the country. Altogether, there are more than five hundred thousand teachers to whom the program aims to provide resources and training. Presently, CISA is training only around eighteen thousand—between 10 and 12 percent of the teachers that America *needs* to be trained each year.

To close the education gap, Congress should address digital redlining, also called the "digital divide." Congress, through the FCC, should require reports by each major internet service provider regarding their high-speed internet coverage and rates charged. This granular detail will enable government to target resources to rapidly expand access. One way to do this would be to subsidize access to satellite-based internet by providers such as SpaceX's StarLink, Viasat, or Amazon. This would have the added benefit of supporting domestic satellite-based internet technology companies to expand access globally, as well as to drive traditional internet service providers to compete for customers in historically marginalized communities.

Congress has ample tools at its disposal to address the myriad issues affecting America's ability to secure the cyber domain. Importantly, Congress needs to ensure that the cyber issues remain bipartisan. In the increasingly polarized political climate in which the United States finds itself, addressing cyber threats should be a lightning rod around which compromises can be made. Threats to cyberspace affect every American, and Congress needs to put the interests of cybersecurity and national security above partisan politics.

MODERNIZING INTERNATIONAL CYBER LAW

Considering the destabilizing effect Russian aggression has on the international community, international law must evolve to address not just *individual* actions but *campaigns* of cyber-enabled malicious activities. Such an evolution would afford victims the ability to aggregate the consequences of multiple breaches conducted by a single aggressor to most effectively defend themselves.[40]

The principle of aggregation is well understood when applied to other areas, such as criminal law. For example, an individual who follows his coworker home on a single occasion may draw the coworker's ire but likely would not violate a criminal statute. If the individual continues to follow his coworker home on multiple occasions after having been asked to stop, he might be liable for harassment.[41] If the individual follows his coworker home on multiple occasions, makes threatening comments, and generally instills a reasonable fear of bodily harm in his coworker, the aggregation of individual wrongful acts could elevate the actions to the crime of stalking.[42] This is called *normative aggregation*, and it occurs where two or more claims—the individual normative weights of which are insufficient to establish liability—are aggregated and the combined weight of all claims is sufficient.[43]

When applied to malicious cyber activities in the context of international law, normative aggregation may be appropriate where a series of acts can be attributed to a single state. As with normative aggregation in domestic criminal law, individual malicious cyber activities do not have to constitute a stand-alone wrongful act if, in the aggregate, the consequences of state action constitute a breach of an international obligation.[44] Under international law, this theory of aggregation is called the accumulation of events theory, or *Nadelstichtaktik* (needle prick).[45]

During the 1970s, Israel invoked Nadelstichtaktik to justify its bombardment of Palestine Liberation Organization (PLO) strongholds in Lebanon as being in response to a series of small-scale attacks by the PLO. Under Israel's theory, though each individual act of terrorism by the PLO may not have risen to the level of armed attack triggering an Article 51 right to self-defense, the sum of the combined consequences of the campaign of terrorist attacks crossed that threshold. The primary thrust of this theory is that the actions taken in self-defense to a series of wrongful acts should not be judged through the limited scope of an immediate response to an isolated attack; rather, the actions should be viewed as a response to the totality of attacks.

For Israel's claim, the Security Council refused to aggregate the PLO's series of attacks and deemed Israel's actions to be in violation of international law. Conducting a strict reading of the language of Article 51, the Security Council could only scrutinize Israeli action taken in response to particularized attacks by the PLO. However, in 2002, the United Nations adopted the Articles on Responsibility of States for Internationally Wrongful Acts, which asserts that a "breach of an international obligation by a State through a series of actions or omissions defined in aggregate as wrongful occurs when the action[,] . . . taken with the other actions or omissions, is sufficient to constitute the wrongful act."[46] This resolution gives significant support to the application of the accumulation of events theory.

Unfortunately, an adequate body of international law does not exist to determine whether normative aggregation of the consequences of cyber operations can be used to establish grounds for self-defense options or countermeasures.[47] However, since the mass adoption of the internet worldwide—and certainly since Israel's failed Nadelstichtaktik claim—the types and scale of belligerent actions that are executed in the digital gray zone of international law continue to increase significantly. As evidenced in multiple International Court of Justice rulings and enshrined in the UN rulings, a general rule has coalesced regarding the aggregation of actions under international law.[48] Where there exists a series of connected acts that are cumulative in nature and attributable to a state, a breach of an international obligation occurs when the combined consequences of the acts are sufficient to constitute an internationally wrongful act. Whether the internationally wrongful act constitutes an armed attack depends on the scale and effect of the consequences.[49]

To this end, the International Court of Justice has provided a patchwork of guidance from which a framework may be discerned by implication. In *Nicaragua*, the court indicated that when determining the existence of an armed attack, "customary international law continues to exist alongside treaty law. The areas governed by the two sources of law thus do not overlap exactly, and the rules do not have the same content."[50] The court further explained that there exist varying degrees of uses of force, not all of which constitute an armed attack.[51] To invoke the right of self-defense by aggregating the consequences of multiple cyber-enabled malicious activities, the court provides insight into several key notions.

First, uses of force are governed by the UN Charter and other treaties, as well as by customary international law. Laws on the use of force can be interpreted, reinterpreted, or even superseded by subsequent state practice pointing to emerging customary international law. This allows for some flexibility in the evolution of the right to self-defense against cyberattacks.

Second, the gravity of different uses of force lies on a spectrum, with the "most grave" form consisting of armed attack. While the gravest forms of the use of force would, by definition, trigger a right to self-defense (or collective self-defense), less grave forms may be aggregated if the individual actions are connected and have a common source.

Third, it is not required that actions being aggregated consist solely of uses of force. The court in *Nicaragua* pointed to the Declaration on Principles of International Law concerning Friendly Relations and Co-operation among States to describe actions that may constitute less grave uses of force. The resolution is a far-reaching statement on international norms and includes principles such as "the duty to refrain from the threat or use of force to violate the existing international boundaries of another State" and "the duty to refrain from organizing, instigating, assisting or participating in acts of civil strife or terrorist acts in another

State." However, the consequences of accumulated acts must still reach the de minimis threshold of armed attack in order to satisfy the UN Charter's requirement for invoking the right to self-defense.

The foundational test for when a cyberattack constitutes an armed attack triggering a right to self-defense is whether the consequences are comparable with those resulting from a traditional military weapon. To aggregate the cumulative effects of cyber-enabled malicious activities that do not individually reach this threshold, the consequences and actions must be related and attributed to a single source. The accumulation of events begins with the first identifiable wrongful act in the series and continues until the activity ceases. Any action taken in self-defense must be both proportionate and necessary to the effective exercise of self-defense. In responding to cyber events, proportionality and necessity are predicated on that which is required to affect either the ability or the will of the nation in violation to continue its wrongful actions.

Despite the understandable reluctance by nation-states to respond to cyber activities with what might constitute a use of force, it is crucial for global leaders to be reminded that international law was not intended to be a suicide pact. Nation-states are expected to enforce international obligations by inflicting an adequate punishment for violations of international law. It is therefore incumbent upon nations to enforce the guiding principles underpinning the international community where there exist gray zones consistently being exploited.

Malicious cyber activities by states such as Russia persist because their leaders perceive there to be an insufficient risk of blowback. To this end, Russia has consistently tested legal boundaries for signs of resistance and, finding none, has proceeded to execute increasingly unrestrained cyber-enabled malicious activities against nations and organizations worldwide. And Russia's blueprint is being followed by Iran and North Korea, among others. It is impractical for the international community to hope for a change in this strategy. To remedy the failure of international law and adequately deter and punish egregious campaigns of cyber-enabled malicious activities requires that states be able to respond with something more than sanctions and indictments. The application of the accumulation of events theory to such campaigns might reshape the calculus of other nations seeking to replicate Russia's brand of low-intensity cyber warfare.

SUMMARY OF RECOMMENDATIONS IN CHAPTER 12

- The Cybersecurity and Infrastructure Security Agency (CISA) should be removed from the Department of Homeland Security and made into a separate cabinet-level agency called the Digital Services Department.

- Congress should create both a Cyber Force patterned on the U.S. Coast Guard and a reserve body patterned on the U.S. National Guard to assist in responding to cyber incidents at both the state and federal level.

- Congress should create a Digital Services Academy to assist in the training and retraining of federal information technology workers.

- Congress must address the digital divide that separates those Americans with access to high-speed internet from those who do not.

- The United States should aggressively pursue a modernization of international law with other techno-democracies to allow for the aggregation of the consequences of Russia and China's gray-zone cyber warfare, thereby permitting a more forceful set of responses.

CHAPTER 13

Collective Defense

How the Public and Private Sectors Must Work Together

WHILE IT MAY APPEAR THAT THE UNITED STATES IS FACING DEFEAT IN this vast and endless cyber battle space, we have been here before. Most Americans know that President Franklin D. Roosevelt officially entered U.S. forces into World War II in December 1941 after the "day of infamy," on which Japanese military forces attacked Pearl Harbor. But few Americans understand that the way Roosevelt tipped the scales of war in favor of the Allies was actually established the following month, in January 1942. It was then that Roosevelt issued an executive order creating a War Production Board headed by a Sears, Roebuck and Co. executive named Donald M. Nelson.

The War Production Board, which included both government and nongovernment members who did their jobs for $1 a year, had extraordinary powers to impose rations on how civilians used gasoline and heating oil, metals, rubber, and other materials that the war effort would require. It established regional headquarters across the United States. Factories that made silk ribbons started making parachutes. Automobile factories built tanks. Typewriter manufacturers produced rifles. Undergarment clothiers sewed mosquito netting. And a roller-coaster manufacturer converted to the production of bomber repair platforms. The surge of industrial production aiding the war effort was so profound that Soviet dictator Joseph Stalin—then a U.S. ally—said in 1943, "Without American production, the Allies could never have won the war."[1]

The collaboration also set the stage for American companies to dominate the world's economy starting in the 1950s. The nation won, but so did business interests.

That is the type of mind-set that is necessary today to resist Chinese and Russian efforts to dismantle the American democratic capitalistic system and its position as a global technology leader. There has not been one shocking, galvanizing moment like Pearl Harbor or 9/11, but anyone who has read this book understands by now that the scale of the challenge is historic. Once again, partnership between the public and private sectors is the absolute key to whether the government can secure its own systems and those of the entire country.

So far, progress has been slow. "Where we've struggled and where we've had less success is in the [Solarium Commission's] recommendations to build a good public-private collaboration," Mark Montgomery acknowledged to us.

There are two primary arenas of concern—defending critical infrastructure and helping the defense industrial base resist digital penetrations.

One area where Congress has found common ground is in the protection of critical infrastructure. The Cyber Incident Reporting for Critical Infrastructure Act of 2022 specifies that companies in sixteen different critically important sectors such as chemicals, communications, dams, energy, food and agriculture, and others must report cyber incidents to the Cybersecurity and Infrastructure Security Agency within seventy-two hours. The law, which primarily targets ransomware attacks like the one on Colonial Pipeline, also requires companies to disclose any payments they make to the attackers.

However, the new law does not provide the operators of critical infrastructure with support or enhanced tools for cyber defense. One of the Cyberspace Solarium Commission's recommendations was the establishment of a joint collaborative environment in which cyber elements of the federal government and the private sector could rapidly identify attack signatures and tactics used by adversaries to alert companies about incoming malicious activities. But the data exchange between the public and private sectors is not happening with the speed required for an adequate response.

Unfortunately, this has been a persistent problem. In 2009, the Obama White House reported in its Cyberspace Policy Review that "government and private-sector personnel, time, and resources are spread across a host of bodies engaged in sometimes duplicative or inconsistent efforts. Partnerships must evolve to clearly define the nature of the relationship [and] the roles and responsibilities of various groups and their participants."[2]

Then, in 2015, President Obama signed into law the Cybersecurity Information Sharing Act.[3] Congress designed this law to encourage and facilitate the sharing of threat indicators, defensive measures, and best practices between public- and private-sector entities.[4] However, in November 2018, the Defense Department's inspector general found that the military had taken only limited actions to implement the act's requirements.[5] Federal guidelines direct government agencies to make unclassified cyber threat indicators broadly available to other agencies as well as to nonfederal entities as quickly as operationally practicable.[6]

The inspector general found that the military did not have the internal controls necessary for sharing cyber threat indicators and defensive measures with the private sector as required by the act.[7] Information "silos" also prevent the integration of different types of intelligence and operational activities that would otherwise enable the military to help private-sector companies to harden their cyber defenses and mitigate the risk of compromise.

By failing to effectively work with the private sector, the government is acquiescing to a demarcation that doesn't really exist. In cyberspace, the line between government and private network security has evaporated. Even if federal agencies were able to unilaterally secure federal networks, the government is still entirely reliant on the private sector for everything from research and development to contractor personnel to weapon systems. Federal facilities are still reliant on private energy companies that deliver electricity, internet service providers that carry government communications, cloud service providers that store sensitive and classified information, and a financial sector that underpins every aspect of America's capitalist society. The SolarWinds compromise proved that the notion that the private sector and the government can secure their networks independently is dead wrong. The belief that everyone can work unilaterally through their own mechanisms to secure their individual networks is not only unrealistic but also incredibly dangerous.

U.S. private-sector cybersecurity providers such as Mandiant and CrowdStrike possess network traffic logs and continuously scan for indicators of compromise—they have *domestic access*. The U.S. intelligence community monitors, aggregates, and analyzes threats from across a broad spectrum of both classified and unclassified information sources—the intelligence community collects *threat intelligence*. The Defense Department maintains resources to execute military activities against adversary targets at the timing and tempo of military commanders—the military maintains *operational capability*. And the broader federal government provides policy responses such as sanctions or criminal options for decision makers—whole-of-government *federal response options*. By combining the elements of domestic access, threat intelligence, operational capability, and federal response options, the United States can leverage the strengths of each component in a best-athlete approach to cybersecurity and respond to adversary aggression.

"Corporations are a major force in our lives, and a few digital superpowers act like consequential actors, at times on par with governments," the *New York Times* technology columnist Shira Ovide wrote.[8] "They have a responsibility beyond profits, whether any of us like it or not." But that responsibility does not translate well to a profit-and-loss statement. The private sector has "many more times the quantity of data about individuals and commercial activity than governments could ever obtain," wrote Glenn Gerstell. "The larger antivirus vendors, with their sensors connected to their global corporate clients, already know more at any given moment about the state of networks around the world than does any government agency."[9] The key is identifying ways to make public-private partnerships advantageous for the private sector beyond patriotism and good-will.

* * *

How Taiwan's Government Works with Its Private Sector on Cybersecurity

Taiwan is dramatically different from the United States in terms of culture, language, and history, but it is remarkably similar in other ways because Americans helped shape its government and society. It is a democracy with different branches of government, and it recognizes the distinction between government and the private sector. But because it is under constant digital assaults from China, it has developed a number of mechanisms to defend itself. Here is the conclusion of Bill Holstein's interview with Howard Jyan, director-general of the Department of Cybersecurity under Taiwan's Executive Yuan, or cabinet. This department supervises cybersecurity for all government agencies in Taiwan.

Q. What recommendations do you have for the United States?

A. For each government, no matter the country, cross-agency cooperation is difficult. The [Taiwanese] cabinet has set up this cybersecurity department. We cooperate with the other agencies, and we cooperate with the National Security Council and the intelligence agencies. We play as the heart of all this. We do policy analysis and make proposals to the cabinet. The most important part is the coordination mechanism. No matter which country, if a government wants to have good protection, all the agencies must join together. They must identify the role of who can be the hub. Secondly, we have a Cybersecurity Management Act. Under this act, we ask all the agencies, government-owned enterprises, and critical infrastructure providers to report [cyberattacks] to us. They also must have a chief information security officer.

Q. What kind of relationship have you established with your private sector?

A. We are still working on the public-private partnership and how to invite the public and private sectors to cooperate. We must build out the mutual trust for each side. In Taiwan, we set up an organization called TW Cert. If the private sector has any cybersecurity incidents, they can contact this organization. This organization will provide them with technical support. It will become a positive [feedback] circle. The private sector provides incident information, and this organization provides them technical support. We think this will result in tighter cooperation.

Q. Can you, as a government, look into the systems of private-sector companies?

A. If a private-sector company has a contract with a government agency, we have asked for the right to audit it, and the company has agreed. We have two kinds of auditing. One is annual. I can audit a company once per year. The second kind is if the company has faced a cybersecurity incident. We can cooperate to set up an auditing group to do outside auditing to make sure the incident will not affect the government. We have a very clear statement that the government agency can audit the contractor. The supply chain security is very important. If the government agency cannot audit the contractor, how can you manage the risk?

Q. What is your position on using Chinese-made products?

A. A few years ago, we passed an executive order that says agencies cannot use Chinese brands, like Huawei and Hikvision, in their working environment. We gave all the agencies six months to one year to clarify how many of these products they have used and to remove all those products from their environment. Right now, most of the government agencies have removed all Chinese-brand products. We think those products can connect to their [mainland China's] networks. It is a potential risk. We have to defend not only our networks from attack but also be careful about our products. Each one of them can become a backdoor inside our environments.

One American effort to create tighter cooperation between the public and private sectors is CISA's Joint Cyber Defense Collaborative, or JCDC for short. JCDC is responsible for developing the nation's cyber defense plans for securing critical infrastructure networks. The collaborative includes over twenty big-name companies from the private sector, including Amazon Web Services, Verizon, Google Cloud, Mandiant, and Microsoft. "Simply put," CISA's fact sheet states, "the work of the JCDC is about seeing the dots, connecting the dots, and collectively driving down risk to the nation at scale."

This is a good start, argues Montgomery. "We hope that will give some of the structure for how you exchange data at high speed between critical infrastructure companies and the federal government and within the federal government itself."

But the speed is not there yet. With twenty of the most profitable technology companies sitting around a table, the incentive to share proprietary data in the room is still lacking.

Moreover, any information that is exchanged is occurring at the unclassified level. The next step would be to establish a process by which indicators of compromise and signatures derived from classified sources can be mingled with proprietary, anonymized data from tech companies. "Another portion is a deeper analytical look where the private sector and public sector can get their analysts together for a classified discussion and ask, 'What did that mean?' 'Why do we see the adversary attempting to do this?'" Montgomery continued. "The government has an insight into what an adversary is doing, but the private sector has an insight into why they're doing it. That collaboration hasn't happened. That's a big one."

Anyone who lived through Hurricane Katrina or Superstorm Sandy understands what happens when a weather event immediately knocks out the essential services that everyone depends on to live—telephone service, gasoline distribution, food supplies, access to ATMs, air travel, and electricity. The experts who worry about America's critical infrastructure getting taken down by the Chinese or Russians realize that the only way to truly be sure they cannot do that is to build in redundancy and therefore resilience.

The Department of Defense, for example, has the budget to examine the power grids that supply its major bases in the United States and fund those electricity companies to build extra capacity. But doing that for America's entire critical infrastructure would cost hundreds of billions of dollars, perhaps trillions, triggering the question: Who pays? "The challenge here is that when someone in government identifies a problem, the company looks at it and says, 'Hey, I don't need a redundant fourteen-thousand-volt transformer outside of this city. I don't need redundant water piping,'" Montgomery points out.

But if the piece of infrastructure is so critically important to national security and therefore vulnerable to the malware already inserted into its control systems, what must be done? "You have to have an agreement with the private sector where maybe [the government] funds the construction of that facility and [the private sector] funds its long-term life-cycle maintenance," Montgomery suggests. "What you can't do is just sit there and say there is a single point of failure that company X has to fix. Company's X's shareholders will say, 'Why? We don't need that redundancy. If you're saying a foreign adversary is going to attack us, where are you as the U.S. government here to assist with that?' We haven't closed the loop on that." In other words, very little progress has been made.

That means it could take years to sort out a full public-private strategy. In the meantime, the federal government should establish more than a collaborative, such as the JCDC. The Cyberspace Solarium Commission noted that "there is much that the U.S. government can do to improve its defenses and reduce the risk of a significant attack, but it is clear that government action alone is not enough." The United States needs a threat fusion center to rapidly ingest data feeds from cybersecurity vendors, analyze threats through all-source analysis, and maintain a common operating picture of threats to critical infrastructure. "If we had a real fusion center, we would have caught SolarWinds," Gilman Louie, founder of In-Q-Tel, told us.

To establish such a fusion center, the government needs to first establish a "marketplace" of validated cybersecurity vendors certified to provide cybersecurity services to critical infrastructure organizations. Coauthor Michael McLaughlin argued for the establishment of such a marketplace to secure the defense industrial base in an article for *Lawfare* in August 2022.[10] But the concept also could apply to critical infrastructure organizations.

The United States is the largest cybersecurity services market in the world, valued at over $21 billion and accounting for 0.1 percent of U.S. gross domestic product (GDP).[11] Yet domestic cybersecurity vendors such as Mandiant, Symantec, and CrowdStrike have not been leveraged to support U.S. national security. To do so, the federal government must partner with domestic cybersecurity vendors to enable the rapid sharing of threat indications and warnings and finished threat intelligence.

There would be myriad benefits to such a marketplace, including addressing threats to the defense industrial base (DIB):

Certification. The federal government could establish a set of heightened certification standards that would serve as a baseline for DIB cybersecurity. These could include standards for cloud computing providers, managed detection and response, endpoint detection and response, firewall solutions, and insider threat detection, among many others. This would allow for a standardized process by which the government conducts risk-management assessments for cybersecurity companies and would ensure that each vendor can handle sensitive defense information and technology. This would also enable the government to conduct background checks and certifications of all cybersecurity vendors charged with protecting DIB networks. Such a marketplace would allow the government to establish and maintain a list of "best in class" cybersecurity providers authorized to secure DIB networks.

Each contract between a defense contractor and the Defense Department would stipulate that the selected cybersecurity vendor enter into an agreement with the federal government for an uninhibited exchange of threat information. DIB companies would not have to self-report cyber-security breaches and would be able to improve the overall security of their networks—better securing both their federal and their commercial information. For cybersecurity vendors, this would place them on a select list of cybersecurity companies that receive specialized alerts and reports of cyber threat intelligence directly from the government. The alerts and threat intelligence could include signatures or indicators of compromise derived from sensors deployed across the Defense Department informa-tion network, analysis from across the agencies involved, or identified behavioral traits of malicious cyber actors, among many others.

For the government, this would enable real-time data flow from the defense industrial base to allow for the identification of large-scale threats and vulnerabilities, as well as targeting of individual companies—all without the need for the Defense Department to purchase and man-age more than a quarter million government-installed network sensors. By screening data through cybersecurity vendors under contract with the DIB companies, this model provides the government a cost-effective way to resolve its inability to "see the dots" without impinging on DIB companies' right to privacy.

Improved Cybersecurity Nationwide. As the saying goes, "a rising tide lifts all ships." Cybersecurity vendors would compete for the opportunity to be on a discrete list of authorized vendors required to be patronized by the more than three hundred thousand defense contractors. By imple-menting a high threshold for certification, the government would be able to set the bar for cybersecurity across the country. Cybersecurity vendors within the marketplace would be able to use threat information exclu-sively shared with them by the government to update their definitions, improve their monitoring capabilities, and direct their threat-hunting teams, benefiting their DIB and non-DIB customers alike. The nation's overall cybersecurity would improve.

The beauty of this model is that it taps into the profit-seeking moti-vation of the private sector. In other words, it plays to the strengths of the American model rather than seeking to impose top-down authoritarian control as both Xi and Putin have done. Companies of many descriptions could make money by more effectively guarding America's systems than by allowing those systems to be thoroughly penetrated.

National security expert Doowan Lee says the U.S. government has three possible ways to shape corporate behavior. "Number one is an idealistic appeal to CEOs so that they will do the right thing," Lee explains. "I don't think that has ever worked."

A second approach is to enact laws and regulations and authorize government agencies to investigate whether companies are adhering to the laws and regulations. "We have a lot of this already. The Commerce Department has different programs that investigate [foreign] companies that may invest in American tech companies. The Treasury Department has multiple investigative units doing this. However, it's very slow because you have to investigate too much and then, once you investigate everything, fixing these issues is also very time consuming."

The third approach is creating a different incentive structure by appealing to a company's bottom line. "This is the best incentive structure for corporate behavioral modification," Lee argued. "If you have more investments by technology companies that serve our national security or public good, then there might be some kind of financial benefits or tax benefits that would be appealing to corporations' bottom line. We can bring all the tech companies closer to the public good and closer to national security."

An effective, collaborative response to threats to the United States requires the federal government to create a network of networks—both in the technical sense and in the operational sense, leveraging the strengths of government and private-sector entities while respecting the private sector's rights to privacy and profit. American military, economic, and technological capabilities and ingenuity are predicated on a strong relationship between the federal government and the private sector. So, too, must be their defense.

SUMMARY OF RECOMMENDATIONS IN CHAPTER 13

- The different arms of the federal government must create a system in which they can exchange threat information with private-sector entities, even involving classified information in some cases. The government should have a single "fusion center" where information can be shared quickly.

- The government could create a "marketplace" of approved cybersecurity companies with whom it could exchange information about cyber threats.
- Those approved cybersecurity companies could then work for the defense industrial base to make sure their systems are protected.
- They could also be an important conduit in communicating threats that the government sees to the private-sector companies that operate critical infrastructure.

Conclusion

The Metaverse, Education, and Restoring the Political "Center"

COMPANIES THROUGHOUT THE WORLD ARE AGGRESSIVELY EXPLORING ways to use artificial intelligence for commercial gain. You can feel it if you call American Express to pay your monthly bill or download your boarding pass from an airline. Machines and robots with their velvety human voices possess an increasingly surprising range of capabilities, and they can actually "chat" with you online. As a society and as a government, we have not even begun to prepare a policy framework that can govern the uses of AI.

Instead, policies are being established piecemeal, as in early August 2022, when the U.S. Court of Appeals ruled that AI cannot be an inventor under U.S. patent law.[1] Regulations and laws surrounding the use of artificial intelligence are still in their infancy; however, in the same way that privacy laws are limiting the tools available to the federal government to protect private networks, laws governing artificial intelligence will determine how rapidly net defenders and war fighters are able to leverage AI in the battle for cyberspace.

Along with augmented reality and virtual reality, AI will be the cornerstone of the next-generation internet, and nowhere is this becoming more apparent than in the rising metaverse. More and more devices will be connected to the internet, and faster speeds will occur when the United States figures out how to make the leap to 5G wireless technology, which is roughly one hundred times faster than today's connections. Online experiences will become infinitely more immersive. Mark Zuckerberg is betting so heavily on artificial intelligence and the metaverse that he refashioned Facebook as Meta Platforms. He obviously sees profits. McKinsey & Company estimates that global investment in the metaverse hit $120 billion in the first five months of 2022.[2] Predictably, Meta, Microsoft, and the other tech giants are positioning themselves to dominate, partly through acquisitions, such as Microsoft's $69 billion purchase of Activision Blizzard, which the federal government is suing in an effort to halt.[3] Millions of virtual reality headsets have already been sold.

But this coming technological surge will create more opportunities for foreign penetration and influence. It is also going to make the American population more vulnerable to disinformation and disruption. Imagine a teenager whose head is inside a helmet or behind a visor where he can see a virtual world with stunning clarity. Perhaps he is watching TikTok videos or playing games. A falsified video image appears. He has a visceral reaction to it but continues to play. When he finally reenters the real world, will that image stick in his mind as being real? Experts are beginning to worry that young people, in particular, will lose their ability to distinguish between their fictional worlds and the real world.

National security expert Doowan Lee is worried about the creation of a "fully immersive biophysical and psychological environment." A company, political party, or government that pays to advertise on a meta entertainment or news platform "can track your biometrics. They can track your pupil movements. They can track your stimulus response. Just imagine the social engineering they could engage in." Some educational classes are already available in the metaverse, he said.

"I always try to think like a bad person," Lee continued, "and if I wanted to manipulate a space for political purposes—oh my God. I'm going to have a field day. I could do so many awful things in that environment. I could get all the users hyped up and then just give them specific instructions. 'Hey, let's all gather at this location at this time and then smash into this building and then hang Mike Pence or something like that.' That's the kind of possibility that keeps me awake at night, and there is nothing—no framework, no safety net, and no guardrails—in the metaverse at this point." Obviously, there is much work to be done.

EDUCATION

In public discussions among experts, a panel member or speaker will argue that the solution to a major technological issue they can't solve or don't have an answer for is to better educate the public. "Ninety-nine percent of the time, people will say, 'Oh, we have to educate the public,'" Lee told us. "I think that's mostly bullshit."

It's easy to be cynical, but here we disagree with Lee. America's entire educational system needs a reboot. In addition to recovering from the lost learning inflicted by the pandemic, we need one hundred thousand more people with cyber knowledge just to operate our IT systems, says Google. (The Solarium Commission put the number at seven hundred thousand, as cited.) Clearly recognizing the challenge, the National Security Agency is trying to foster cyber interest among young people by creating Centers for Academic Excellence.

In the final analysis, only trained humans can keep computers secure, no matter what hardware and software they use. This is one enormous advantage the Chinese possess over the United States. Since ancient times, their culture encourages and rewards those who strive for education. As a result, they have more operators and more hackers than we can keep track of. This will require a shifting of resources from four-year liberal arts colleges to more technically inclined vocational schools and community colleges. The Chinese also possess a linguistic advantage— even adjusted for the size of their population, proportionately far more speak or read English than Americans speak or read Chinese.

K–12 education has not adapted its course work in the past twenty-five years to recognize how technology has changed so many aspects of American society. K–12 students should stage competitions to hack one another so that they can begin to learn the skills to attack, but also to defend themselves and the institutions they care most about. There should be coding competitions in the same way that schools hold track meets. Coding and technical literacy needs to become a universal skill. Foreign language programs, currently a national embarrassment, must be enhanced.

Civics classes should hammer home that students cannot believe everything they see on social media. They need to learn more "critical thinking," social engineering expert Chris Hadnagy told us. They need to be trained to find a reliable source to confirm something they have seen online, rather than assuming it is real. Often that requires finding a mainstream media source. Reading should be encouraged in schools because, at current trend lines, young people will soon consume all their education and entertainment visually. The ability to sit and reflect on a well-crafted essay, let alone write one, could be lost.

High-school-level courses need to be created to discuss virtually every theme of this book. Young people should be taught about how to maintain their privacy and better control their data. Doing those things requires more sophistication than the vast majority of American adults possess. Young people need to learn more about the history of technology—how the printing press, steam engine, and other inventions altered human behavior and required societal and governmental action in response. At the same time they are mastering the technology, they need to understand how current technology works and the impact it is having on society and on human psychology. For instance, pornography has become so readily available online that some psychologists wonder if it will alter the perceptions of young people about what healthy romantic relationships really are.

Helping Americans become true "digital citizens" who are aware of all the joys—and dangers—of new technologies will require years of education. It is not a throwaway punch line.

The reason it is important to get these issues right is that the technological revolution is not over. The National Security Commission on Artificial Intelligence led by former Google CEO Eric Schmidt said that China is already a peer of the United States in some areas of AI and is funneling those advancements to the People's Liberation Army. Quantum computing, although unproven, could be another game changer. The United States faces a technological challenge across all key industries, including electric batteries, solar power, rare earth elements, semiconductors, and wireless communications. Education will be key to prevailing.

Establishing a Political "Center"

At times it has seemed that the American political system has become so polarized, so poisonous, so dysfunctional that it could not take rational action on behalf of the nation. We Americans have helped create that situation, partly as a result of social media's algorithms that fuel divisiveness and because some people—such as InfoWars' Alex Jones—found ways to make millions of dollars from sheer lies. But it is also partly because our adversaries have exacerbated the centrifugal forces pushing us apart. The passage of the $280 billion CHIPS and Science Act in the summer of 2022, however, demonstrated that government is still capable of sensible compromise. The process was frustrating and, as President Biden remarked, often infuriating—but in the final analysis, the system worked.

Vladimir Putin's invasion of Ukraine has helped create the sense that a middle ground can be found. A 95–1 vote in the U.S. Senate approving Finland's and Sweden's admission to NATO only a few short years after a sitting president threatened U.S. withdrawal from NATO was a welcomed display of bipartisanship.

Perversely, the Chinese have also helped the U.S. political system recover at least a measure of cohesion. China's outburst of military threats surrounding House Speaker Nancy Pelosi's visit to Taiwan—and the firing of missiles over the island after she had departed—were intended to intimidate the United States, just as Beijing has sought to intimidate Lithuania and Australia following political decisions counter to the Chinese global agenda. It is clear that Xi Jinping wants to impose his belligerence more broadly, just as he did in wiping out Hong Kong's democratic infrastructure. He has made it clear to the entire world, and American politicians on both sides of the aisle can see it plainly.

Another theme that can unify rather than divide is the urgent need for greater cybersecurity in all aspects of American society and the economy. Pragmatism runs deeply through our nation's history.

Reestablishing a political center is an extremely tall order in view of the prevailing tone in American politics today. It will require political leaders who are dedicated to finding solutions rather than riding wedge issues into power. It will also require less corruption. For Democrats to enact the Fighting Inflation legislation, which included environmental goals and other priorities, they had to appease two Democratic senators, Joe Manchin of West Virginia and Kyrsten Sinema of Arizona. Both senators were, in effect, influenced by different industries—the pipeline industry for Manchin and the private equity industry for Sinema. In a different era, that would have been shocking, but it has become business as usual. As long as members of Congress represent corporate interests at the expense of American interests, the U.S. government will never be able to enact legislation to, among other things, check the power of Big Tech.

In this book, we have offered a portrait of how China and Russia are taking advantage of America's political dysfunctionality and seeking to exacerbate it. The challenges are steep, but we have outlined what we think are clear solutions. The Sino-Russian strategy is working, but there is still time to stop it. The American system is capable of remarkable achievement when it coalesces around a common objective. This is the existential question of our generation: can the American democratic capitalist system, along with its techno-democratic allies, prevail over an authoritarian axis?

It has before—and it can again.

Notes

Introduction

1. Shira Ovide, "Digital Threads between the U.S. and China," *New York Times*, May 30, 2022, https://www.nytimes.com/2022/05/25/technology/us-china-internet.html.

2. Kate Benner and Kate Conger, "U.S. Accuses Russians of Hacking Infrastructure, Including Nuclear Plant," *New York Times*, March 25, 2022, https://www.nytimes.com /2022/03/24/us/politics/russians-cyberattacks-infrastructure-nuclear-plant.html. See also U.S. Department of Justice, "Four Russian Government Employees Charged in Two Historical Hacking Campaigns Targeting Critical Infrastructure Worldwide," March 24, 2002, https://www.justice.gov/usao-dc/pr/four-russian-government-employees-charged -two-historical-hacking-campaigns-targeting.

3. Sumner Lemon, "China Gets Access to Microsoft Source Code," IDG News Service, March 3, 2003, https://www.infoworld.com/article/2681548/china-gets-access-to -microsoft-source-code.html.

4. Tripp Mickle, "Apple Says Factory Disruptions in China Will Limit iPhone Supply," *New York Times*, November. 7, 2022, https://www.nytimes.com/2022/11/06/technology/ apple-iphones-shortage.html.

5. George Bowden, "MI6 Boss Warns of China 'Debt Traps and Data Traps,'" BBC News, November 30, 2021, https://www.bbc.com/news/uk-59474365.

6. James Ball, "Russia Is Risking the Creation of a 'Splinternet'—and It Could Be Irreversible," *MIT Technology Review*, March 17, 2022, https://www.technologyreview .com/2022/03/17/1047352/russia-splinternet-ris.

Chapter 1

1. Yaakov Katz, "Stuxnet Virus Set Back Iran's Nuclear Program by Two Years," *Jerusalem Post*, December 15, 2010, https://www.jpost.com/iranian-threat/news/stuxnet-virus -set-back-irans-nuclear-program-by-2-years/amp (accessed October 14, 2020).

2. Andy Greenberg, "The Untold Story of NotPetya, the Most Devastating Cyberattack in History," *Wired*, August 22, 2018, https://www.wired.com/story/notpetya -cyberattack-ukraine-russia-code-crashed-the-world (accessed October 14, 2020).

3. *United States v. Yuriy Sergeyevich Andrienko, et al.*, No. 20–316 (WDPA) [hereinafter: "Sandworm Indictment"].

4. Sandworm Indictment, para. 31.

5. See Sandworm Indictment.

6. Greenberg, "The Untold Story of NotPetya."

7. Critical infrastructure is defined in Presidential Policy Directive 21 (PPD-21) and consists of sixteen sectors deemed crucial to national security. These sixteen sectors are chemical; commercial facilities; communications; critical manufacturing; dams; defense industrial base; emergency services; energy; financial services; food and agriculture; government facilities; health care and public health; information technology; nuclear reactors, materials, and waste; transportation systems; and water and wastewater systems.

8. David E. Sanger, *The Perfect Weapon: War, Sabotage, and Fear in the Cyber Age* (New York: Penguin, 2018), 158.

9. Sandworm Indictment.

10. David E. Sanger and Kate Conger, "West Ties Russia to Cyberattack on Ukraine's Satellites in Run-Up to Invasion," *New York Times*, May 11, 2022, https://www.nytimes.com/2022/05/10/us/politics/russia-cyberattack-ukraine-war.html.

11. Winnona DeSombre, Testimony before the U.S.-China Economic and Security Review Commission Hearing on "China's Cyber Capabilities: Warfare, Espionage, and Implications for the United States," February 17, 2022, https://www.uscc.gov/sites/default/files/2022-02/Winnona_DeSombre_Testimony.pdf.

12. Scott Henderson and Cristiana Kittner, Mandiant telephone interview, May 2022.

13. Henderson and Kittner, telephone interview, May 2022.

14. H.R. 117–36, "Defending the U.S. Electric Grid against Cyber Threats," July 27, 2021, https://www.congress.gov/event/117th-congress/house-event/LC67058.

15. Patrick Howell O'Neill, "How China Built a One-of-a-Kind Cyber-Espionage Behemoth to Last," *MIT Technology Review*, February 28, 2022, https://www.technologyreview.com/2022/02/28/1046575/how-china-built-a-one-of-a-kind-cyber-espionage-behemoth-to-last.

16. U.S. Department of Defense Cyber Strategy (2018), https://media.defense.gov/2018/Sep/18/2002041658/-1/-1/1/cyber_strategy_summary_final.pdf.

17. https://www.afcea.org/signal-media/us-cyber-command-hunts-forward.

18. U.S. Cyber Command, "U.S. Conducts First Hunt Forward Operation in Lithuania," CyberCom.mil, May 4, 2022, https://www.cybercom.mil/Media/News/Article/3020430/us-conducts-first-hunt-forward-operation-in-lithuania.

19. U.S. Cyber Command, "'Partnership in Action': Croatian, U.S. Cyber Defenders Hunting for Malicious Actors," CyberCom.mil, August 18, 2022, https://www.cybercom.mil/Media/News/Article/3131961/partnership-in-action-croatian-us-cyber-defenders-hunting-for-malicious-actors.

20. U.S. Cyber Command, "U.S. Conducts First Hunt Forward Operation in Lithuania."

21. Shannon Vavra, "US Lacks Visibility into Digital Espionage at Home, NSA Boss Says," *CyberScoop*, March 25, 2021, https://www.cyberscoop.com/nsa-solarwinds-russia-china-nakasone.

22. Glenn S. Gerstell, "I've Dealt with Foreign Cyberattacks: America Isn't Ready for What's Coming," *New York Times*, March 4, 2022, https://www.nytimes.com/2022/03

/04/opinion/ive-dealt-with-foreign-cyberattacks-america-isnt-ready-for-whats-coming
.html.

CHAPTER 2

1. Federal Bureau of Investigation, "Ransomware," https://www.fbi.gov/scams-and
-safety/common-scams-and-crimes/ransomware (accessed March 24, 2022).

2. SonicWall, *2022 SonicWall Cyber Threat Report*, 2022, https://www.sonicwall.com
/2022-cyber-threat-report; Chainalysis Team, *Russian Cybercriminals Drive Significant Ransomware and Cryptocurrency-Based Money Laundering Activity*, February 14,
2022, https://blog.chainalysis.com/reports/2022-crypto-crime-report-preview-russia
-ransomware-money-laundering.

3. Cybersecurity and Infrastructure Security Agency, Alert (AA21–265A), "Conti
Ransomware" (last revised March 9, 2022), https://www.cisa.gov/uscert/ncas/alerts/aa21
-265a.

4. Brian Krebs, "Conti Ransomware Group Diaries, Part I: Evasion," *KrebsOnSecurity*,
March 1, 2022, https://krebsonsecurity.com/2022/03/conti-ransomware-group-diaries
-part-i-evasion.

5. SonicWall, *2022 SonicWall Cyber Threat Report*, 2022, https://www.sonicwall.com/
medialibrary/en/white-paper/2022-sonicwall-cyber-threat-report.pdf.

6. U.S. Department of the Treasury, "Treasury Sanctions North Korean State-Sponsored
Malicious Cyber Groups," September 13, 2019, https://home.treasury.gov/news/press
-releases/sm774.

7. MITRE Corporation, "Lazarus Group," https://attack.mitre.org/groups/G0032.

8. Microsoft Threat Intelligence Center (MSTIC), "Evolving Trends in Iranian Threat
Actor Activity—MSTIC Presentation at CyberWarCon 2021," Microsoft, November 16,
2021, https://www.microsoft.com/security/blog/2021/11/16/evolving-trends-in-iranian
-threat-actor-activity-mstic-presentation-at-cyberwarcon-2021.

9. Kiral Avramov, "Ransomware Attacks Are Another Tool in the Political Warfare
Toolbox," *The Hill*, September 26, 2021, https://thehill.com/opinion/cybersecurity
/573794-ransomware-attacks-are-another-tool-in-the-political-warfare-toolbox.

10. "Internet of the 1980s," Computer History Museum, https://www.computerhistory
.org/internethistory/1980s (accessed May 10, 2022); "Providence Population by Year,"
BiggestUsCities.com, https://www.biggestuscities.com/city/providence-rhode-island
#byyear (accessed May 10, 2022).

11. "History of AIDS," History.com, February 21, 2021, https://www.history.com/
topics/1980s/history-of-aids.

12. Alina Simone, "The Strange History of Ransomware: Floppy Disks, AIDS
Research, and a Panama P.O. Box," Medium, March 26, 2015, https://medium.com/@
alinasimone/the-bizarre-pre-internet-history-of-ransomware-bb480a652b4b.

13. Bill Whitaker, "Shields Up: U.S. Officials Preparing for Potential Russian Cyberattacks," *60 Minutes*, April 17, 2022, https://www.cbsnews.com/news/russia-cyberattacks
-60-minutes-2022-04-17.

14. "Working Together: Priorities to Enhance the Quality and Security of Independent Work in the United States," Uber, August 10, 2020, https://www.uber.com/newsroom/working-together-priorities.

15. Brett Helling, "How Many Uber Drivers Are There in 2022?," Ridester.com, July 18, 2022, https://www.ridester.com/how-many-uber-drivers-are-there; "Uber Announces Results for Fourth Quarter and Full Year 2019," Uber Investor, February 6, 2020, https://investor.uber.com/news-events/news/press-release-details/2020/Uber-Announces-Results-for-Fourth-Quarter-and-Full-Year-2019/default.aspx.

16. China's Great Firewall, known in China as the Golden Shield, is a combination of legislative and technical implementations that allow China's Ministry of Public Security (MPS) to monitor and control access to China's domestic cyberspace. Russia's System for Operative Investigative Activities, known by its Russian acronym SORM, is the vast surveillance system that gives Russia's Federal Security Service (FSB) legal authority to intercept, analyze, and store all data that traverses Russian networks.

17. "History," TorProject.org, https://www.torproject.org/about/history (accessed May 10, 2022).

18. "Membership," TorProject.org, https://www.torproject.org/about/membership (accessed May 10, 2022).

19. "Network Size," TorProject.org, https://metrics.torproject.org/networksize.html (accessed May 10, 2022).

20. The authors do not condone illegal activity of any sort and provide this site for illustrative purposes only.

21. "BBC News Launches 'Dark Web' Tor Mirror," BBC.com, October 23, 2019, https://www.bbc.com/news/technology-50150981.

22. "Top Dark Web Sites Links List," Darkweblink.com, https://darkweblink.com/search-hacker-forums-dark-web/#Top-Dark-Web-Forum-Sites-Links-List (accessed July 12, 2022).

23. "Silk Road and the Dark Web: One of the 21st Century's Most Famous Crime Stories," PointPark.edu, May 26, 2021, https://online.pointpark.edu/criminal-justice/silk-road-busts.

24. "Ransomware as a Service: Understanding the Cybercrime Gig Economy and How to Protect Yourself," Microsoft.com, May 9, 2022, https://www.microsoft.com/security/blog/2022/05/09/ransomware-as-a-service-understanding-the-cybercrime-gig-economy-and-how-to-protect-yourself.

25. "Ransomware as a Service," Microsoft.com.

26. Zach Budryk et al., "5 Takeaways from Attack on Colonial Pipeline," *The Hill*, May 10, 2021, https://thehill.com/policy/energy-environment/552751-5-takeaways-from-attack-on-colonial-pipeline.

27. Joe Panettieri, "Colonial Pipeline Cyberattack: Timeline and Ransomware Attack Recovery Details," MSSP Alert, June 7, 2021, https://www.msspalert.com/cybersecurity-breaches-and-attacks/ransomware/colonial-pipeline-investigation.

28. Taylor Telford et al., "Fuel Shortages Crop Up in Southeast, Gas Prices Climb after Pipeline Hack," *Washington Post*, March 11, 2021, https://www.washingtonpost.com/business/2021/05/11/gas-shortage-colonial-pipeline.

29. Cathy Bussewitz, "Colonial Pipeline Confirms It Paid $4.4M to Hackers," AP News, May 19, 2021, https://apnews.com/article/hacking-technology-business-ed15565 56c7af6220e6990978ab4f745.

30. Satoshi Nakamoto, "Bitcoin: A Peer-to-Peer Electronic Cash System," 2008, https://bitcoin.org/bitcoin.pdf.

31. Zachary Halaschak, "Colonial Pipeline attack: How did the FBI recover the ransom money?" June 9, 2021, https://news.yahoo.com/colonial-pipeline-attack-did-fbi-103000117.html.

32. Mitnick Security, "An Overview of the 2021 JBS Meat Supplier Ransomware Attack," MitnickSecurity.com, June 3, 2021, https://www.mitnicksecurity.com/blog/an-overview-of-the-2021-jbs-meat-supplier-ransomware-attack.

33. Brian Fung, "JBS Says It Paid $11 Million Ransom after Cyberattack," CNN, June 9, 2021, https://www.cnn.com/2021/06/09/business/jbs-cyberattack-11-million/index.html.

34. David Uberti, "Iowa Grain Cooperative Hit by Cyberattack Linked to Ransomware Group," *Wall Street Journal*, September 20, 2021, https://www.wsj.com/articles/iowa-grain-cooperative-hit-by-cyberattack-linked-to-ransomware-group-11632172945.

35. Uberti, "Iowa Grain Cooperative Hit."

36. Dan Lohrmann, "Lincoln College Closure Is Just Another Ransomware Milestone," *Governing.com*, May 17, 2022, https://www.governing.com/security/lincoln-college-closure-is-just-another-ransomware-milestone.

37. United States Department of Commerce, "Sanctions," *Russia—Country Commercial Guide*, March 4, 2022, https://www.trade.gov/country-commercial-guides/russia-sanctions.

38. Isabelle Bousquette, "Russian Tech Spending Declines as Sanctions Take Toll," *Wall Street Journal*, April 8, 2022, https://www.wsj.com/articles/russian-tech-spending-declines-as-sanctions-take-toll-11649410200.

39. Bousquette, "Russian Tech Spending Declines."

40. James Andrew Lewis, "A Dangerous Moment for Russian Cybercrime May Get Worse," *Barron's*, February 15, 2022, https://www.barrons.com/articles/a-dangerous-moment-for-russian-cybercrime-may-get-worse-51644936090.

41. Stuart Panensky, "Why War in Ukraine Has Put Cyber Risk Center Stage for Clients," *National Law Journal*, April 11, 2022, https://www.law.com/nationallawjournal/2022/04/11/why-war-in-ukraine-has-put-cyber-risk-center-stage-for-clients.

42. *United States v. Evgeny Viktorovich Gladkikh*, No. 1:21-cr-0042-CJN (D.D.C. 2021).

43. *Gladkikh*, at 6.

44. *Gladkikh*, at 8.

45. See National Institute of Standards and Technology, "Operational Technology Security," https://csrc.nist.gov/projects/operational-technology-security (accessed April 25, 2022): "Operational technology (OT) encompasses a broad range of programmable systems or devices that interact with the physical environment (or manage devices that interact with the physical environment). These systems/devices detect or cause a direct change through the monitoring and/or control of devices, processes, and events.

Examples include industrial control systems, building automation systems, transportation systems, physical access control systems, physical environment monitoring systems, and physical environment measurement systems."

46. *Gladkikh*, at 9.

47. Cybersecurity and Infrastructure Security Agency, Alert (AA22–103A), "APT Cyber Tools Targeting ICS/SCADA Devices" April 14, 2022, https://www.cisa.gov/uscert/ncas/alerts/aa22-103a.

48. Joseph Menn, "U.S. Warns Newly Discovered Malware Could Sabotage Energy Plants," *Washington Post*, April 13, 2022, https://www.washingtonpost.com/technology/2022/04/13/pipedream-malware-russia-lng.

49. Menn, "U.S. Warns."

50. Matt Burgess, "Leaked Ransomware Docs Show Conti Helping Putin from the Shadows," *Wired*, March 18, 2022, https://www.wired.com/story/conti-ransomware-russia.

51. Tom Balmforth and Maria Tsvetkova, "Russia Takes Down REvil Hacking Group at U.S. Request—FSB," Reuters, January 14, 2022, https://www.reuters.com/technology/russia-arrests-dismantles-revil-hacking-group-us-request-report-2022-01-14.

Chapter 3

1. Natalie Obiko Pearson, "Did a Chinese Hack Kill Canada's Greatest Tech Company?," *Bloomberg BusinessWeek*, July 1, 2020, https://www.bloomberg.com/news/features/2020-07-01/did-china-steal-canada-s-edge-in-5g-from-nortel.

2. Brian Shields, emails and telephone interview, April and May 2022.

3. Shields, emails and interview.

4. Chuin-Wei Yap, "State Support Helped Fuel Huawei's Global Rise," *Wall Street Journal*, December 25, 2019, https://www.wsj.com/articles/state-support-helped-fuel-huaweis-global-rise-11577280736.

5. General Keith Alexander, "Greatest Transfer of Wealth in History," July 9, 2012, https://www.youtube.com/watch?v=JOFk44yy6IQ.

6. IP Commission, "The Theft of American Intellectual Property," February 2017, 2, https://www.nbr.org/wp-content/uploads/pdfs/publications/IP_Commission_Report_Update.pdf.

7. Cyberreason Nocturnus, "Operation CuckooBees: Cyberreason Uncovers Massive Chinese Intellectual Property Theft Operation," May 4, 2022, https://www.cybereason.com/blog/operation-cuckoobees-cybereason-uncovers-massive-chinese-intellectual-property-theft-operation.

8. John Hayward, "Report: Chinese Hackers Stole Trillions in Intellectual Property from Multinational Companies," Breitbart, May 5, 2022, https://www.breitbart.com/asia/2022/05/05/report-chinese-hackers-stole-trillions-in-intellectual-property-from-multinational-companies.

9. IEEE Communications Society, undated profile of Wen Tong, https://www.comsoc.org/wen-tong.

10. Tom Blackwell, "Exclusive: Did Huawei Bring Down Nortel? Corporate Espionage, Theft, and the Parallel Rise and Fall of Two Telecom Giants," *National Post*,

February 20 and 24, 2020, https://nationalpost.com/news/exclusive-did-huawei-bring
-down-nortel-corporate-espionage-theft-and-the-parallel-rise-and-fall-of-two-telecom
-giants.

11. Siobhan Gorman, "Chinese Hackers Suspected in Long-Term Nortel Breach," *Wall
Street Journal*, February 14, 2012; https://www.wsj.com/articles/SB100014240529702033
63504577187502201577054.

12. Dan McWhorter, "APT1: Exposing One of China's Cyber Espionage Units," 2013,
https://www.mandiant.com/sites/default/files/2021-09/mandiant-apt1-report.pdf.

CHAPTER 4

1. See Jonathan E. Hillman, *The Digital Silk Road: China's Quest to Wire the World and
Win the Future* (New York: Harper Business, 2021).

2. Ellen Nakashima, "Chinese Hack of Federal Personnel Files Included
Security-Clearance Database," *Washington Post*, June 12, 2015, https://www.washingtonpost
.com/world/national-security/chinese-hack-of-government-network-compromises
-security-clearance-files/2015/06/12/9f91f146-1135-11e5-9726-49d6fa26a8c6_story
.html; see also William J. Holstein, *The New Art of War: China's Deep Strategy Inside the
United States* (New York: Brick Tower Press, 2019).

3. Natasha Bertrand, "The Suspected Chinese Hack on United Airlines Makes
the CIA's Job 'Much More Difficult,'" *Business Insider*, July 29, 2015, https://www
.businessinsider.com/chinese-hack-on-united-airlines-affects-the-cia-2015-7.

4. Katie Benner, "Justice Dept. Charges 4 Chinese in Equifax Hack," *New York
Times*, February 11, 2020, https://www.nytimes.com/2020/02/10/us/politics/equifax
-hack-china.html.

5. Ian Smith, "Bolton Confirms China was Behind OPM Data Breaches," FedSmith,
September 21, 2018, https://www.fedsmith.com/2018/09/21/bolton-confirms-china
-behind-opm-data-breaches.

6. *United States v. Wu Zhiyong, et al.*, 2:20-CR046 (N.D. Ga.), January 28, 2020, https:
//www.justice.gov/opa/press-release/file/1246891/download.

7. U.S. Department of Justice, Office of Public Affairs. "Two Chinese Hackers Associated with the Ministry of State Security Charged with Global Computer Intrusion
Campaigns Targeting Intellectual Property and Confidential Business Information." Dec.
20, 2018. https://www.justice.gov/opa/pr/two-chinese-hackers-associated-ministry-state
-security-charged-global-computer-intrusion.

8. Michael McLaughlin and William J. Holstein, "Is China Seeking a Secretive Permanent Presence in America's Computers?," *National Interest*, November 27, 2020, https:
//nationalinterest.org/feature/china-seeking-secretive-permanent-presence-america%E2
%80%99s-computers-173292.

9. Summer Lemon, "China Gets Access to Microsoft Source Code," IDG News Service, March 3, 2003, https://www.infoworld.com/article/2681548/china-gets-access-to
-microsoft-source-code.html.

10. Samantha Hoffman, "The U.S.-China Data Fight Is Only Getting Started," Australian Strategic Policy Institute, July 22, 2021, https://www.aspi.org.au/opinion/us-china
-data-fight-only-getting-started.

11. Samantha Hoffman, "How to Avoid Falling into China's Data Trap," TechCrunch, December 26, 2021, https://techcrunch.com/2021/12/26/how-to-avoid-falling-into -chinas-data-trap.

12. Mara Hvistendahl, "How China Surveils the World," *MIT Technology Review*, August 19, 2020, https://www.technologyreview.com/2020/08/19/1006455/gtcom -samantha-hoffman-tiktok.

13. Garrett M. Graff, "China's Hacking Spree Will Have a Decades-Long Fallout," *Wired*, February 11, 2020, https://www.wired.com/story/china-equifax-anthem-marriott -opm-hacks-data.

14. Paul Mozur, "Forget TikTok: China's Powerhouse App Is WeChat, and Its Power Is Sweeping," *New York Times*, September 4, 2020, https://www.nytimes.com/2020/09/04 /technology/wechat-china-united-states.html.

15. Amnesty International, "Hong Kong's National Security Law: 10 Things You Need to Know," July 17, 2020, https://www.amnesty.org/en/latest/news/2020/07/hong-kong -national-security-law-10-things-you-need-to-know.

16. Antoinette Siu, "TikTok Can Circumvent Apple and Google Privacy Protections and Access Full User Data, 2 Studies Say," *The Wrap*, February 14, 2022, https://www .yahoo.com/video/tiktok-circumvent-apple-google-privacy-140000271,html.

17. Tyler Sonnemaker, "TikTok's New Privacy Policy Lets It Collect Your Biometric Data, Including Faceprints and Voice Prints," *BusinessInsider*, June 3, 2021, https: //www.businessinsider.com/tiktok-privacy-policy-update-lets-it-collect-users-biometric -data-2021-6#:~:text=TikTok%20rolled%20out%20major%20updates%20to%20its %20privacy,as%20faceprints%20and%20voiceprints%2C%20from%20your%20User %20Content.

18. Richard Nieva, "TikTok's In-App Browser Includes Code That Can Monitor Your Keystrokes, Researcher Says," *Forbes*, August 18, 2022, https://www.forbes.com/sites/ richardnieva/2022/08/18/tiktok-in-app-browser-research.

19. Emily Baker-White, "Leaked Audio from 80 Internal TikTok Meetings Shows That US User Data Has Been Repeatedly Accessed from China," *BuzzFeed News*, June 17, 2022, https://www.buzzfeednews.com/article/emilybakerwhite/tiktok-tapes-us-user -data-china-bytedance-access.

20. David McCabe, "An F.C.C. Commissioner Pushes Apple and Google to Remove TikTok from Their App Stores," *New York Times*, June 29, 2022, https://www.nytimes .com/2022/06/29/technology/apple-google-tiktok.html.

21. John D. McKinnon, "Lawmakers Add to Call for Probe of TikTok," *Wall Street Journal*, July 9, 2022, https://www.wsj.com/articles/calls-for-tiktok-probe-widen-adding -to-pressure-on-biden-to-weigh-in-11657281927.

22. "Technical Analysis of TikTok App," Internet 2.0, July 4, 2022, https://internet2-0 .com/technical-analysis-of-tiktok-app.

23. James Griffiths, "The Global Internet Is Powered by Vast Undersea Cables. But They're Vulnerable," CNN, July 26, 2019, https://www.cnn.com/2019/07/25/asia/ internet-undersea-cables-intl-hnk/index.html.

24. H. I. Sutton, "Russian Spy Ship Yantar Loitering Near Trans-Atlantic Internet Cables," *Naval News*, August 19, 2021, https://www.navalnews.com/naval-news/2021/08 /russian-spy-ship-yantar-loitering-near-trans-atlantic-internet-cables.

25. Larry Clinton, president, Internet Security Alliance, "Krebs Tells Black Hat 'Time to Rethink Cybersecurity.' He Is Right," *Pulse*, August 15, 2022, https://www.linkedin .com/pulse/krebs-tells-black-hat-time-rethink-cybersecurity-he-right-clinton.

26. Danielle Cave et al., "Mapping China's Tech Giants," Australian Strategic Policy Institute, April 18, 2019, https://www.aspi.org.au/report/mapping-chinas-tech-giants.

27. Eric Cheung et al., "How Taiwan Is Trying to Defend against a Cyber 'World War III.'" CNN Business, July 23, 2021, https://edition.cnn.com/2021/07/23/tech/taiwan -china-cybersecurity-intl-hnk/index.html.

28. Samantha Hoffman, "Producing Policy-Relevant China Research and Analysis in an Era of Strategic Competition," Australian Strategic Policy Institute, February 28, 2022, https://www.aspi.org.au/report/producing-policy-relevant-china-research-and -analysis-era-strategic-competition.

29. Charlie Savage, "Report Shows N.S.A. Use of Court-Approved Domestic Surveillance Fell to a New Low," *New York Times*, April 30, 2022, https://www.nytimes.com /2022/04/29/us/politics/national-security-surveillance-2021.html.

CHAPTER 5

1. Mason Walker and Katerina Eva Matsa, "News Consumption across Social Media in 2021," Pew Research Center, September 20, 2021, https://www.pewresearch.org/ journalism/2021/09/20/news-consumption-across-social-media-in-2021.

2. SafeGuard Cyber, "Contactless Actions against the Enemy: How Russia Is Deploying Misinformation on Social Media to Influence European Parliamentary Elections," 2019.

3. National Academies of Sciences, Engineering, and Medicine, *Cryptography and the Intelligence Community: The Future of Encryption* (Washington, DC: National Academies Press, 2022).

4. See Robert S. Mueller III, U.S. Department of Justice, Office of Special Counsel, *Report on the Investigation into Russian Interference in the 2016 Presidential Election*, 2019, 4, https://www.justice.gov/storage/report.pdf.

5. Mueller, *Report on the Investigation into Russian Interference*.

6. Mueller, *Report on the Investigation into Russian Interference*, 5; see, for example, Jennifer Palmieri, "Re: NYT Hillary Clinton's Use of Private Email at State Department Raises Flags," Wikileaks.com, October 7, 2016, https://wikileaks.org/podesta-emails/ emailid/1038 (accessed November 26, 2020); see also Sam Frizell, "What Leaked Emails Reveal about Hillary Clinton's Campaign," *Time*, October 7, 2016, https://time.com /4523749/hillary-clinton-wikileaks-leaked-emails-john-podesta (accessed November 26, 2020).

7. Sen. Rep. No. 116-XX, *Report of the United States Senate Select Committee on Intelligence on Russian Active Measures Campaigns and Interference in the 2016 U.S. Election, Volume 2: Russia's Use of Social Media with Additional Views*, 36.

8. Sen. Rep. No. 116-XX, at 36.

9. *United States v. Internet Research Agency, et al.*, No. 18-cr-32 (D.D.C.), at 3–4.

10. Clint Watts, *Messing with the Enemy: Surviving in a Social Media World of Hackers, Terrorists, Russians, and Fake News* (New York: HarperCollins, 2018).

11. Max Glicker and Clint Watts, "Russia's Propaganda & Disinformation Ecosystem," February 15, 2022, https://miburo.substack.com/p/russias-propaganda-and-disinformation.

12. "SIEGESEC Targets Pro-Life State Governments," DarkOwl, June 27, 2022, https://www.darkowl.com/blog-content/darkowl-cyber-group-spotlight-siegedsec-and-leaked-data.

13. Patricia Mazzei, "Russian Charged with Spreading Propaganda through U.S. Groups," *New York Times*, July 30, 2022, https://www.nytimes.com/2022/07/29/us/russian-indictment-florida.html.

14. Ellen Barry, "Trolls in Russia Schemed to Divide Women's March," *New York Times*, September 18, 2022, https://www.nytimes.com/2022/09/18/us/womens-march-russia-trump.html.

15. Ellen Barry, "How Russian Trolls Helped Keep the Women's March Out of Lock Step," *New York Times*, September 18, 2022, https://www.nytimes.com/2022/09/18/us/womens-march-russia-trump.html.

16. Sheera Frenkel and Stuart A. Thompson, "How Russia and Right-Wing Americans Converged on War in Ukraine," *New York Times*, March 23, 2022, https://www.nytimes.com/2022/03/23/technology/russia-american-far-right-ukraine.html.

17. Stuart A. Thompson, "How Russia Argues Case with Help of Fox News," *New York Times*, April 19, 2022, https://www.nytimes.com/2022/03/23/technology/russia-american-far-right-ukraine.html.

18. Julia Davis, "Russia Airs Its Ultimate 'Revenge Plan' for America," *Daily Beast*, April 11, 2022, https://www.thedailybeast.com/russian-state-media-airs-its-ultimate-revenge-plan-for-2024-us-presidential-elections.

19. Sana Sekkarie, "A Global Tour through Russian Propaganda," Substack, May 6, 2022.

20. Chris Buckley, "Beijing Campaign Casts Russia as the West's Longtime Victim," *New York Times*, April 5, 2022, https://www.nytimes.com/2022/04/04/world/asia/china-russia-ukraine.html.

21. Ingram Niblock et al., "Chinese and Russian Propaganda Work in Tandem to Blame the West for War in Ukraine," Australian Strategic Policy Institute, May 26, 2022, https://www.aspistrategist.org.au/chinese-and-russian-propaganda-work-in-tandem-to-blame-the-west-for-war-in-ukraine.

22. Resolution of the Central Committee of the Communist Party of China on the Major Achievements and Historical Experience of the Party over the Past Century," *China Daily*, November 17, 2021, https://global.chinadaily.com.cn/a/202111/17/WS61944b49a310cdd39bc75c01_12.html.

23. Thomas Daigle, "Canadian Professor's Website Helps Russia Spread Disinformation, Says US State Department," CBC, October 21, 2020, https://www.cbc.ca/news/science/russian-disinformation-global-research-website-1.5767208.

24. Muyi Xiao, Paul Mozur, et al., "Buying Influence: How China Manipulates Facebook and Twitter," *New York Times*, December 20, 2021, https://www.nytimes.com/interactive/2021/12/20/technology/china-facebook-twitter-influence-manipulation.html.

25. Steven Lee Myers and Paul Mozur, "Musk's Ties to China Could Create Headaches for Twitter," *New York Times*, April 29, 2022, https://www.nytimes.com/2022/04/29/technology/elon-musk-china-tesla.html.

26. SafeGuard Cyber, "Contactless Actions."

27. SafeGuard Cyber, "How Russian Twitter Bots Weaponize Social Media to Influence & Disinform," 2017.

28. A. J. Agrawal, "How to Optimize Your SEO Results through Content Creation," *Forbes*, August 30, 2017, https://www.forbes.com/sites/ajagrawal/2017/08/30/how-to-optimize-your-seo-results-through-content-creation.

29. "China Discreetly Paid for U.S. Social Media Influencers to Tout Beijing Winter Olympics," CBS News, April 8, 2022, https://www.cbsnews.com/news/china-us-social-media-influencers-tiktok-instagram-beijing-winter-olympics.

30. Christopher Paul, "How China Plays by Different Rules—at Everyone Else's Expense," *The Hill*, February 6, 2022, https://thehill.com/opinion/technology/592998-how-china-plays-by-different-rules-at-everyone-elses-expense.

31. Joseph Thai, "The Right to Receive Foreign Speech," *Oklahoma Law Review* 71, no. 1 (2018).

32. Cate Cadell, "China Harvests Masses of Data on Western Targets, Documents Show," *Washington Post*, December 31, 2011, https://www.washingtonpost.com/national-security/china-harvests-masses-of-data-on-western-targets-documents-show/2021/12/31/3981ce9c-538e-11ec-8927-c396fa861a71_story.html.

33. Foreign minister spokesperson Zhao Lijian's regular press conference on April 14, 2022, https://www.mfa.gov.cn/eng/xwfw_665399/s2510_665401/2511_665403/202204/t20220414_10668055.html.

34. Ryan Serabian and Lee Foster, "Pro-PRC Influence Campaign Expands to Dozens of Social Media Platforms, Websites, and Forums in at Least Seven Languages, Attempted to Physically Mobilize Protesters in the U.S.," Mandiant report, September 7, 2021, https://www.mandiant.com/resources/pro-prc-influence-campaign-expands-dozens-social-media-platforms-websites-and-forums.

35. Edward Wong, "How China Uses LinkedIn to Recruit Spies Abroad," *New York Times*, August 27, 2001, https://www.nytimes.com/2019/08/27/world/asia/china-linkedin-spies.html.

36. Bradley Honigberg, "The Existential Threat of AI-Enhanced Disinformation Operations," Center for Security and Emerging Technology, July 8, 2022, https://www.justsecurity.org/82246/the-existential-threat-of-ai-enhanced-disinformation-operations.

37. Ezra Klein, "TikTok May Be More Dangerous than It Looks," *New York Times*, May 15, 2022, https://www.nytimes.com/2022/05/08/opinion/tiktok-twitter-china-bytedance.html.

CHAPTER 6

1. Patrick Howell O'Neill, "The US Military Wants to Understand the Most Important Software on Earth," *MIT Technology Review*, July 14, 2022, https://www.technologyreview.com/2022/07/14/1055894/us-military-sofware-linux-kernel-open-source.

2. Santiago Torres-Arias, "What Is Log4j? A Cybersecurity Expert Explains the Latest Internet Vulnerability, How Bad It Is and What's at Stake," *The Conversation*, December 22, 2021, https://theconversation.com/what-is-log4j-a-cybersecurity-expert-explains-the-latest-internet-vulnerability-how-bad-it-is-and-whats-at-stake-173896.

3. Liza Lin and David Uberti, "Alibaba Employee First Spotted Log4j Software Flaw but Now the Company Is in Hot Water with Beijing," *Wall Street Journal*, December 22, 2021, https://www.wsj.com/articles/china-halts-alibaba-cybersecurity-cooperation-for-slow-reporting-of-threat-state-media-says-11640184511.

4. Jen Easterly, "CISA Director: The LOG4J Security Flaw is the 'Most Serious' She Has Seen in Her Career," CNBC, December 21, 2021, https://www.youtube.com/watch?v=XC3Oqn_yADk.

5. Patrick Howell O'Neill, "The Internet Runs on Free Open-Source Software. Who Pays to Fix It?," *MIT Technology Review*, December 17, 2021, https://www.technologyreview.com/2021/12/17/1042692/log4j-internet-open-source-hacking.

6. Brian Fung and Geneva Sands, "Former SolarWinds CEO Blames Intern for 'solarwinds123' Password Leak," CNN, February 26, 2021, https://www.cnn.com/2021/02/26/politics/solarwinds123-password-intern.

7. Dina Temple-Raston, "A 'Worst Nightmare' Cyberattack: The Untold Story of the SolarWinds Attack," NPR, April 16, 2021, https://www.npr.org/2021/04/16/985439655/a-worst-nightmare-cyberattack-the-untold-story-of-the-solarwinds-hack.

8. Brian Carlson, "The Microsoft Exchange Server Hack: A Timeline," CSO, May 6, 2021, https://www.csoonline.com/article/3616699/the-microsoft-exchange-server-hack-a-timeline.html.

CHAPTER 7

1. In 1988, a Cornell University graduate student and son of the chief scientist of the NSA's National Computer Security Center brought down 10 percent of all computers then connected to the internet. On November 2, 1988, Robert Tappan Morris created and released his worm exploiting the most common email systems in use at the time.

2. Chase Cunningham, *Cyber Warfare—Truth, Tactics, and Strategies: Strategic Concepts and Truths to Help You and Your Organization Survive on the Battleground of Cyber Warfare* (Packt Publishing, 2020).

3. Aaron Tilley, "Amazon, Microsoft, Google Strengthen Grip on Cloud," *Wall Street Journal*, July 2, 2022, https://www.wsj.com/articles/amazon-microsoft-google-strengthen-grip-on-cloud-11657018980.

4. White House, E.O. 14028, "Executive Order on Improving the Nation's Cyber Security," May 12, 2021, https://www.whitehouse.gov/briefing-room/presidential-actions/2021/05/12/executive-order-on-improving-the-nations-cybersecurity.

5. Kyle Alspach, "6 'Nightmare' Cloud Security Flaws Were Found in Azure in the Last Year. Does Microsoft Have Work to Do?," *Protocol*, June 1, 2022, https://www.protocol.com/amp/microsoft-azure-vulnerabilities-cloud-security-2657422221.

6. "Chinese State-Sponsored Cyber Operations: Observed TTPS (tactics, techniques and procedures)," National Security Agency, Cybersecurity and Infrastructure Security Agency, and the Federal Bureau of Investigation, July 2021, https://media.defense.gov/2021/jul/19/2002805003/-1/-1/1/csa_chinese_state-sponsored_cyber_ttps.pdf.

7. U.S. Department of Justice, "Two Chinese Hackers Associated with the Ministry of State Security Charged with Global Computer Intrusion Campaigns Targeting Intellectual Property and Confidential Business Information," December 20, 2018.

CHAPTER 8

1. University of Maryland Applied Research Laboratory for Intelligence and Security, *NCIIN: National Cyber Information Integration Network* (unpublished), 2021.

2. National Defense Industrial Association, "Vital Signs," February 2022, https://www.ndia.org/-/media/vital-signs/2022/vital-signs_2022_final.pdf.

3. National Defense Industrial Association, "Vital Signs."

4. Cameron Holt, Keynote, Seventh Annual Government Contract Pricing, June 15, 2022.

5. Qiao Liang and Wang Xiangsui, *Unrestricted Warfare* (PLA Literature and Arts Publishing House, February 1999).

6. Brendan Carr, Testimony before the Subcommittee on National Security of the United States House of Representatives Committee on Oversight and Reform, July 13, 2022, https://oversight.house.gov/sites/democrats.oversight.house.gov/files/Carr%20Testimony.pdf.

7. Alexandra Alper, "Exclusive: U.S. Probes China's Huawei over Equipment Near Missile Silos," Reuters, July 21, 2022, https://www.reuters.com/world/us/exclusive-us-probes-chinas-huawei-over-equipment-near-missile-silos-2022-07-21.

8. U.S. Department of Defense Interagency Task Force in Fulfillment of Executive Order 13806, *Assessing and Strengthening the Manufacturing and Defense Industrial Base and Supply Chain Resiliency of the United States*, September 2018, 39, https://media.defense.gov/2018/oct/05/2002048904/-1/-1/1/assessing-and-strengthening-the-manufacturing-and-defense-industrial-base-and-supply-chain-resiliency.pdf.

9. 2021 DOD CMSD, p. 49. See also pp. vi and 48, and 2019 DIA CMP, p. 63.

10. Anders Corr, "China's New Aircraft Carrier Uses Catapult Tech Stolen from US," *Epoch Times*, June 28, 2022, https://www.theepochtimes.com/chinas-new-aircraft-carrier-uses-catapult-tech-stolen-from-us_4557632.html.

11. Daniel R. Coats, "Statement for the Record: Worldwide Threat Assessment of the U.S. Intelligence Community," Senate Select Committee on Intelligence, May 11, 2017, https://www.dni.gov/files/documents/Newsroom/Testimonies/SSCI%20Unclassified%20SFR%20-%20Final.pdf.

12. "Former Boeing Engineer Sentenced to Nearly 16 Years in Prison for Stealing Aerospace Secrets for China," U.S. Attorney's Office for the Central District of

California, February 8, 2010, https://archives.fbi.gov/archives/losangeles/press-releases/2010/la020810.htm.

13. "A List of the U.S. Weapons Designs and Technologies Compromised by Hackers," *Washington Post*, May 27, 2013, https://www.washingtonpost.com/world/national-security/a-list-of-the-us-weapons-designs-and-technologies-compromised-by-hackers/2013/05/27/a95b2b12-c483-11e2-9fe2-6ee52d0eb7c1_story.html.

14. *United States v. Su Bin*, No. SA CR 14–131 (C.D. Cal. Mar. 22, 2016).

15. *United States v. Su Bin*.

16. *United States v. Wang Dong, et al.*, Crim. No. 14–118 (WDPA 2014).

17. *United States v. Wang Dong, et al.*

18. Mandiant, "APT1: Exposing One of China's Cyber Espionage Units," 2021, https://www.mandiant.com/sites/default/files/2021-09/mandiant-apt1-report.pdf.

19. Mandiant, "APT1: Exposing One of China's Cyber Espionage Units."

20. "APT3 Is Boyusec, a Chinese Intelligence Contractor," Intrusiontruth, May 10, 2017, https://intrusiontruth.wordpress.com/2017/05/09/apt3-is-boyusec-a-chinese-intelligence-contractor.

21. Ellen Nakashima and Paul Sonne, "China Hacked a Navy Contractor and Secured a Trove of Highly Sensitive Data on Submarine Warfare," *Washington Post*, June 8, 2018, https://www.washingtonpost.com/world/national-security/china-hacked-a-navy-contractor-and-secured-a-trove-of-highly-sensitive-data-on-submarine-warfare/2018/06/08/6cc396fa-68e6-11e8-bea7-c8eb28bc52b1_story.html.

22. "Secretary of the Navy Cyber Readiness Review," United States Navy, 2019, https://www.wsj.com/public/resources/documents/CyberSecurityReview_03-2019.pdf.

23. James Risen and Jeff Gerth, "Breach at Los Alamos: A Special Report; China Stole Secrets for Bombs, U.S. Aides Say," *New York Times*, March 6, 1999, https://www.nytimes.com/1999/03/06/world/breach-los-alamos-special-report-china-stole-nuclear-secrets-for-bombs-us-aides.html.

CHAPTER 9

1. Julian E. Barnes, "China Seeks to Pre-empt Sanctions in Case of Taiwan Clash, F.B.I. Chief Says," *New York Times*, July 7, 2022, https://www.nytimes.com/2022/07/06/world/asia/fbi-china-taiwan-sanctions.html.

2. Sopan Deb, "After a Boycott, Chinese Television Is Again Airing N.B.A. Games," *New York Times*, March 31, 2022, https://www.nytimes.com/2022/03/31/sports/basketball/nba-china.html.

3. Michael Martina, "Chinese Embassy Lobbies U.S. Business to Oppose China Bills—Sources," Reuters, November 15, 2021, https://www.reuters.com/business/exclusive-chinese-embassy-lobbies-us-business-oppose-china-bills-sources-2021-11-12.

4. Paul Mozur et al., "'The Eye of the Storm': Taiwan Is Caught in a Great Game over Microchips," *New York Times*, August 29, 2022, https://www.nytimes.com/2022/08/29/technology/taiwan-chips.html.

5. Ben Murphy, "Chokepoints: China's Self-Identified Strategic Technology Import Dependencies," Center for Security and Emerging Technology, May 2022.

6. Andre Barbe and Will Hunt, "Preserving the Chokepoints: Reducing the Risks of Offshoring among U.S. Semiconductor Manufacturing Equipment Firms," Center for Security and Emerging Technology, https://cset.georgetown.edu/publication/preserving-the-chokepoints.

7. William J. Holstein and David B. H. Denoon, "US Needs a Coherent Tech Strategy for China," *Asia Times*, August 19, 2021, https://asiatimes.com/2021/08/us-needs-a-coherent-tech-strategy-for-china.

8. David E. Sanger, "China Has Leapfrogged the U.S. in Key Technologies. Can a New Law Help?," *New York Times*, July 28, 2022, https://www.nytimes.com/2022/07/28/us/politics/us-china-semiconductors.html.

9. Don Clark, "The Tech Cold War's 'Most Complicated Machine' That's out of China's Reach," *New York Times*, July 4, 2021, https://www.nytimes.com/2021/07/04/technology/tech-cold-war-chips.html.

10. Liam Gibson, "Sanction Semiconductors to Deter China's Taiwan Ambitions," *Asia Nikkei*, May 30, 2022 https://asia.nikkei.com/Opinion/Sanction-semiconductors-to-deter-China-s-Taiwan-ambitions.

11. Amanda Lee, "Japan Alliance Restricting Vital Tech Exports to China Risks 'Major Impact' on Trade, Supply Chains," *South China Morning Post*, January 25, 2022, https://www.scmp.com/economy/china-economy/article/3164537/us-japan-alliance-restricting-vital-tech-exports-china-risks.

12. Melissa Eddy, "Germany, Taking a Firmer Line on China, Blocks 2 Foreign Investment Deals," *New York Times*, November 10, 2022, https://www.nytimes.com/2022/11/09/world/europe/germany-china-investment.html.

13. "President Biden Signs Executive Order to Ensure Robust Reviews of Evolving National Security Risks by the Committee on Foreign Investment in the United States," White House Fact Sheet, September 15, 2022, https://www.whitehouse.gov/briefing-room/statements-releases/2022/09/15/fact-sheet-president-biden-signs-executive-order-to-ensure-robust-reviews-of-evolving-national-security-risks-by-the-committee-on-foreign-investment-in-the-united-states.

14. John VerWey, "Re-Shoring Advanced Semiconductor Packaging," Center for Security and Emerging Technology, June 2022, https://cset.georgetown.edu/publication/re-shoring-advanced-semiconductor-packaging.

15. Ryan Redasiuk, Karson Elmgren, and Ellen Lu, "Silicon Twist: Managing the Chinese Military's Access to AI Chips," June 2022, https://cset.georgetown.edu/publication/silicon-twist.

16. "Why Is China So Concerned at the Prospect of South Korea Joining a US-Led Chip Alliance?," *South China Morning Post*, July 23, 2022, https://finance.yahoo.com/news/why-china-concerned-prospect-south-093000358.html.

17. Ana Swanson, "Biden Administration Outlines Indo-Pacific Economic Framework," *New York Times*, September 10, 2022, https://www.nytimes.com/2022/09/09/business/ipef-framework-asia-trade.html.

18. Gibson, "Sanction Semiconductors to Deter China's Taiwan Ambitions."

19. Ellen Nakashima, "White House Wants Transparency on American Investment in China," *Washington Post*, July 13, 2022, https://www.washingtonpost.com/national -security/2022/07/13/china-investment-transparency.

20. Debby Wu et al., "US Quietly Tightens Grip on Exports of Chipmaking Gear to China," *Bloomberg*, July 29, 2022, https://www.bloomberg.com/news/articles/2022-07-29 /us-pushes-expansion-of-china-chip-ban-key-suppliers-say.

21. Alexandra Alper and Karen Freifeld, "U.S. Considers Crackdown on Memory Chips in China," Reuters, August 1, 2022, https://finance.yahoo.com/news/u-considers -crackdown-memory-chip-100425288.html.

22. Zeyi Yang, "Inside the Software That Will Become the Next Battle Front in US-China Chip War," *MIT Technology Review*, August 18, 2022, https://www .technologyreview.com/2022/08/18/1058116/eda-software-us-china-chip-war.

23. Ana Swanson, "U.S. Targeting China's Access to Technology," *New York Times*, October 8, 2022, https://www.nytimes.com/2022/10/07/business/economy/biden-chip -technology.html.

24. Matt Turpin, "Crafting a Competitive Response: A Framework for Countering China's Digital Ambitions," chapter 6 in National Bureau of Asian Research, *China's Digital Ambitions* (March 2022).

25. Don Clark, "Intel to Invest at Least $20 Billion in New Chip Factories in Ohio," *New York Times*, January 21, 2022, https://www.nytimes.com/2022/01/21/technology/ intel-chip-factories-ohio.html.

26. Dion Rabouin, "U.S. Firms Bring Home Overseas Jobs," *Wall Street Journal*, August 20, 2022, https://www.wsj.com/articles/u-s-companies-on-pace-to-bring-home-record -number-of-overseas-jobs-11660968061.

27. VerWey, "Re-Shoring Advanced Semiconductor Packaging."

28. "China Accuses US of 'Technological Terrorism' as Chip Curbs Grow," *Bloomberg News*, July 6, 2022, https://www.bloomberg.com/news/articles/2022-07-06/china-calls -us-pressure-on-chipmakers-technological-terrorism.

29. Cocol Feng, "Apple Supplier Foxconn Expands India iPhone Production, Further Diversifying Supply Chain away from Mainland China," *South China Morning Post*, August 5, 2022, https://internet2-0.com/technical-analysis-of-tiktok-app.

30. Tripp Mickle et al., "China Turning into a Liability for the iPhone," *New York Times*, November 8, 2022, https://www.nytimes.com/2022/11/07/business/apple-china -ymtc.html.

31. Rajesh Roy and Newley Purnell, "Apple to Cut New iPhone 14 Production Lag between India and China," *Wall Street Journal*, August 23, 2022, www.wsj.com/articles/ apple-to-cut-new-iphone-14-production-lag-between-india-and-china-11661251562.

32. Jack Nicas et al., "To Get in China, Apple Swallowed Hard Bargain," *New York Times*, May 18, 2021, https://www.nytimes.com/2021/05/17/technology/apple-china -censorship-data.html.

33. "Apple Says China's Uighurs Targeted in iPhone Attack," GeoTV, September 7, 2019, https://www.geo.tv/latest/246980-apple-says-uighurs-targeted-in-iphone-attack.

34. Dan Harris, "Preparing for China Decoupling Should Start NOW," *China Law Blog*, June 6, 2022, https://harrisbricken.com/chinalawblog/preparing-for-china -decoupling-should-start-now.

35. "Reshoring Initiative IH 2022 Data Report," August 15, 2022, https://reshorenow .org/blog/reshoring-initiative-1h-2022-data-report.

36. Phelim Kine and Gavin Bade, "China Blowback Looms for Schumer's Innovation and Competition Act," *Politico*, November 28, 2021, https://www.politico.com/news /2021/11/28/china-schumers-innovation-and-competition-act-523414.

37. Ana Swanson, "Law Fighting Forced Labor to Hit Trade," *New York Times*, June 22, 2022, https://www.nytimes.com/2022/06/22/us/politics/xinjiang-uyghur-forced-labor -law.html.

CHAPTER 10

1. *McIntyre v. Ohio Elections Comm'n*, 514 U.S. 334 (1995).

2. Pub. L. No. 104–104, Tit. V, 110 Stat. 133 (1996).

3. Jeff Kosseff, *The Twenty-Six Words That Created the Internet* (Ithaca, NY: Cornell University Press, 2019).

4. "Section 230 of the Communications Decency Act," Electronic Frontier Foundation, n.d., https://www.eff.org/issues/cda230.

5. "About Verified Accounts," Twitter.com, https://help.twitter.com/en/managing-your -account/about-twitter-verified-accounts (accessed July 16, 2022).

6. https://twitter.com/king_langabi.

7. "Warner, Hirono, Klobuchar Announce the Safe Tech Act to Reform Section 230," February 5, 2021, https://www.warner.senate.gov/public/index.cfm/2021/2/warner -hirono-klobuchar-announce-the-safe-tech-act-to-reform-section-230.

8. Adam Satariano, "E.U. Takes Aim at Social Media's Harms with Landmark New Law," *New York Times*, April 22, 2022, https://www.nytimes.com/2022/04/22/technology /european-union-social-media-law.html.

9. Frances Haugen, "I Blew the Whistle on Facebook. Europe Showed Us the Next Step," *New York Times*, April 29, 2022, https://www.nytimes.com/2022/04/28/opinion/ social-media-facebook-transparency.html.

10. John Rindone, "China and America's Social Media Paradox," Georgetown University, January 29, 2020, https://uschinadialogue.georgetown.edu/responses/china-and -america-s-social-media-paradox.

11. Emily Baker-White, "Leaked Audio from 80 Internal TikTok Meetings Shows That US User Data Has Been Repeatedly Accessed from China," *BuzzFeed News*, June 17, 2022, https://www.buzzfeednews.com/article/emilybakerwhite/tiktok-tapes-us-user -data-china-bytedance-access.

12. Aaron Tilley, "TikTok User Data Is Routed to Oracle," *Wall Street Journal*, June 18, 2022, https://www.wsj.com/articles/tiktok-says-all-data-for-u-s-users-now-routed -to-oracle-cloud-11655503707.

13. U.S. Const., Art. 1, Sec. 8, Cl. 3.

14. Kimberly Adams and Daniel Shin, "How FTC Chair Lina Khan Wants to Modernize the Watchdog Agency," Marketplace Tech, June 17, 2022, https:

//www.marketplace.org/shows/marketplace-tech/how-ftc-chair-lina-khan-wants-to
-modernize-the-watchdog-agency.

15. David McCabe and Stephanie Lai, "Clock Is Running Out on an Antitrust Bill Targeting Big Tech Companies," *New York Times*, August 6, 2022, https://www.nytimes .com/2022/08/05/business/antitrust-bill-klobuchar.html.

16. Cecillia Kang, "As Europe Approves New Tech Laws, the U.S. Falls Further Behind," *New York Times*, April 22, 2022, https://www.nytimes.com/2022/04/22/ technology/tech-regulation-europe-us.html.

CHAPTER 11

1. David Sanger, "As Revolt Rises in Iran, U.S. Takes Different Tack," *New York Times*, September 27, 2022, https://www.nytimes.com/2022/09/26/us/politics/biden -iran-protesters.html.

2. Kent Walker, "Why We're Committing $10 Billion to Advance Cybersecurity," Google blog, August 25, 2021, https://blog.google/technology/safety-security/why-were -committing-10-billion-to-advance-cybersecurity.

3. Office of Management and Budget Memorandum, "Enhancing the Security of the Software Supply Chain through Secure Software Development Practices," M-22–18, September 14, 2022.

4. U.S. Securities and Exchange Commission, "SEC Proposes Rules on Cybersecurity Risk Management, Strategy, Governance, and Incident Disclosure by Public Companies" (press release, March 9, 2022), https://www.sec.gov/news/press-release/2022-39.

5. *In re Caremark Int'l Inc. Derivative Litig.*, 698 A.2d 959, 971 (Del. Ch. 1996).

6. *Marchand v. Barnhill*, 212 A.3d 805, 823–24 (Del. 2019).

7. *In re Clovis Oncology, Inc. Derivative Litig.*, 2019 Del. Ch. LEXIS 1293, at 29 (Ch. October 1, 2019).

8. Adam Janofsky, "Cybersecurity Investor Ted Schlein: 'I Think the Whole Landscape Needs to Be Completely Rethought," *The Record*, April 23, 2021, https://therecord .media/cybersecurity-investor-ted-schlein-i-think-the-whole-landscape-needs-to-be -completely-rethought.

CHAPTER 12

1. Cyber Policy Institute, "Cybersecurity Bills in the 117th Congress," February 2022, https://cyberpolicyinstitute.org/wp-content/uploads/2022/03/CybersecurityBills -117Congress-final.pdf.

2. Cyber Policy Institute, "Cybersecurity Bills in the 117th Congress."

3. Glenn Gerstell, "There's a Big Gap in Our Cyber Defenses. Here's How to Close It," *Politico*, April 19, 2021, https://www.politico.com/news/magazine/2021/04/19/theres -a-big-gap-in-our-cyber-defenses-heres-how-to-close-it-483111.

4. Pub. L. 116–283. Title XVII, section 1716, U.S. Congress, January 1, 2021, https:// www.congress.gov/bill/116th-congress/housebill/6395/text/enr.

5. https://www.justice.gov/opa/pr/deputy-attorney-general-lisa-o-monaco-announces -new-civil-cyber-fraud-initiative.

6. Portions of this section appeared in the Fall 2022 edition of *Cyber Defense Review*, published by the Army Cyber Institute at the U.S. Military Academy at West Point. Reprinted with permission.

7. Arthur W. Tedder, *Air Power in War* (Tuscaloosa: University of Alabama Press, 2010), 87–124.

8. Tedder, *Air Power in War*, 29.

9. Alexander P. de Seversky, *Victory through Air Power* (New York: Simon and Schuster, 1942), 254.

10. Pub. L. 80–253, 61 Stat. 495, enacted July 26, 1947.

11. De Seversky, *Victory through Air Power*, 254.

12. White House, *National Cyber Strategy of the United States of America*, 2018, 1: "America's prosperity and security depend on how we respond to the opportunities and challenges in cyberspace."

13. Michael Daniel, "Why Is Cybersecurity So Hard?," *Harvard Business Review*, May 22, 2017, https://hbr.org/2017/05/why-is-cybersecurity-so-hard: "Our physical-world mental models simply won't work in cyberspace. For example, in the physical world, we assign the federal government the task of border security. But given the physics of cyberspace, everyone's network is at the border. If everyone lives and works right on the border, how can we assign border security solely to the federal government?"

14. See *United States v. Yuriy Sergeyevich Andrienko, et al.*, No. 20–316 (WDPA). On October 15, 2020, a grand jury in the Western District of Pennsylvania returned an indictment against six Russian intelligence officers. These officers, members of GRU Military Unit 74455—more commonly referred to as "Sandworm"—were charged with executing a pervasive and continuous destructive malware campaign against nations worldwide since at least 2015.

15. U.S.C. Title 6, Domestic Security, governs the Department of Homeland Security and the Cybersecurity and Infrastructure Security Agency; U.S.C. Title 10, Armed Forces, governs the military; U.S.C. Title 14, Coast Guard, governs the activities of the U.S. Coast Guard; U.S.C. Title 18, Crimes and Criminal Procedure, governs law enforcement; U.S.C. Title 32, National Guard, governs the functions of the National Guard Bureau; U.S.C. Title 50, War and National Defense, governs the activities of the U.S. Intelligence Community.

16. 14 U.S.C. § 101.

17. Pub. L. 107–296.

18. 33 U.S.C. § 1223.

19. 14 U.S.C. § 91.

20. 46 U.S.C. § 3306.

21. 14 U.S.C. § 89.

22. 14 U.S.C. § 89.

23. 14 U.S.C. § 101.

24. 14 U.S.C. § 103.

25. Pub. L. 80–253 (amended December 28, 2001).

26. EO 12333.

27. EO 12333; 32 U.S.C. § 104.

28. Defense Manpower and Data Center, "Selected Reserve Personnel by Reserve Component and Rank/Grade (Updated Monthly): September 2021," DoD Personnel, Workforce Reports and Publications, https://dwp.dmdc.osd.mil/dwp/app/dod-data -reports/workforce-reports. As of September 2021, the combined strength of the Army National Guard and Air National Guard is 446,008 personnel.

29. U.S. Cyberspace Solarium Commission, "U.S. Cyberspace Solarium Commission Report." Senator Angus King and Representative Mike Gallagher, March 2020, https://doc-14-ac-prod-02-apps-viewer.googleusercontent.com/viewer2/prod -02/pdf/muo37o9at8cdi5009i0fiuuhh5l0lnkb/a3aji1224n30ekcedbcfch3me0nhd9eq /1671564750000/3/105440943537035326434/APznzaZhI04CqvfOIZrHXslcgV ocvQ2wVu_Zphym3rFiUsvhqVXSa7ZqioVNU5XdyRuAHoLdqjnWvLTV2Lm -sTCGk7d8aOwHMkOJpFrjKa1__uhAhovvF5rja_j7jYLZzamen3RasQ286OTA2uA XCuak9jfkmXuen-_dg6j264uU4yU5U9RXpSXJk5c3OaGaghbGmrFlyvJkf9x7PGqc Nx46VcEbe9fCIAaCjmXYNDSn2KIia6bU1AVvPsYCoE302hCPZ8qBl5LY9q9UUl JzfvzKNm548tRvePqPDNDn2bcTXJGTEUFfYoJ6G3Oc-6pVZoT1UHihOitVVFLj -byyHXBVtKjjrv9eXb_8sXWpAZ6fe8Ntn0l6QNo=?authuser=0&nonce=guhba83ipjjr2 &user=105440943537035326434&hash=gr810v00onn78ruvuspeedjvq8mnqc9i: "Examples of states relying on National Guard units to deal with cybersecurity incidents include Colorado, Louisiana, and Texas, where the governors declared state of emergencies to activate their National Guard."

30. Pub. L. 116–283 § 1729.

31. Pub. L. 116–283 § 1729.

32. Pub. L. 116–283 § 1729.

33. 14 U.S.C. § 101.

34. See 14 U.S.C. § 89.

35. Federal Rules of Criminal Procedure 41(6)(b)(6); see April Falcon Doss, "We're from the Government, We're Here to Help: The FBI and the Microsoft Exchange Hack," JustSecurity.org, April 16, 2021, https://www.justsecurity.org/75782/were-from -the-government-were-here-to-help-the-fbi-and-the-microsoft-exchange-hack. The FBI used this authority to remove malware from networks affected by the Microsoft Exchange server vulnerability exploited by Hafnium—malicious cyber actors associated with the Chinese government.

36. Michael Garcia, "The Militarization of Cyberspace? Cyber-Related Provisions in the National Defense Authorization Act," Third Way, April 5, 2021, https: //thirdway.imgix.net/pdfs/the-militarization-of-cyberspace-cyber-related-provisions-in -the-national-defense-authorization-act.pdf.

37. Garcia, "The Militarization of Cyberspace?"

38. Glenn Gerstell, "I Work for N.S.A. We Cannot Afford to Lose the Digital Revolution," *New York Times*, September 10, 2019, https://www.nytimes.com/2019/09/10/ opinion/nsa-privacy.html.

39. Zack Quaintance, "What Is Digital Redlining? Experts Explain the Nuances," GovTech.com, March 28, 2022, https://www.govtech.com/network/what-is-digital -redlining-experts-explain-the-nuances.

40. G.A. Res. 56/83, annex, Art. 8, Responsibility of States for Internationally Wrongful Acts (January 28, 2002).

41. Md. Code, Crim. Law § 3–803.

42. Md. Code, Crim. Law § 3–802.

43. Ariel Porat and Eric A. Posner, "Aggregation and Law," *Yale Law Journal* 122, no. 2 (2012): 6.

44. G.A. Res. 56/83, annex, Art. 8, Responsibility of States for Internationally Wrongful Acts (January 28, 2002).

45. Yaroslav Shiryaev, "The Right of Armed Self-Defense in International Law and Self-Defense Arguments Used in the Second Lebanon War," *Acta Societatis Martensis* 3 (2007/2008): 80, 95.

46. G.A. Res. 56/83, annex, Art. 8, Responsibility of States for Internationally Wrongful Acts (January 28, 2002).

47. *Case Concerning Armed Activities on the Territory of the Congo (Democratic Republic of the Congo v Uganda)*, Judgment-Merits 2005 I.C.J. 116, para. 146 (December 19, 2005).

48. International Court of Justice, *Case Concerning the Military and Paramilitary Activities in and against Nicaragua (Nicaragua v. United States of America)*, Merits, June 27, 1986, ICJ 14.

49. International Court of Justice, *Case Concerning the Military and Paramilitary Activities in and against Nicaragua (Nicaragua v. United States of America)*, Merits, June 27, 1986, ICJ 14.

50. International Court of Justice, *Case Concerning the Military and Paramilitary Activities in and Against Nicaragua (Nicaragua v. United States of America)*, Merits, June 27, 1986, ICJ 14.

51. In ruling on *Nicaragua*, the International Court of Justice (ICJ) analyzed whether incursions by Nicaragua "singly or collectively" amounted to an armed attack. Ultimately, the court found the information provided to be insufficient to make a determination. Similarly, in the *Oil Platforms* case, the ICJ analyzed whether an Iranian attack, "either in itself or in combination with the rest of the 'series of . . . attacks' cited by the United States can be categorized as an 'armed attack' on the United States justifying self-defence." Ultimately, the ICJ ruled that Iran's actions, "taken cumulatively . . . do not seem to the Court to constitute an armed attack on the United States, of the kind that the Court, in the case concerning Military and Paramilitary Activities in and against Nicaragua, qualified as a 'most grave' form of the use of force."

CHAPTER 13

1. "War Production Board," Wikipedia, https://en.wikipedia.org/wiki/War_Production_Board.

2. White House, *Cyberspace Policy Review: Assuring a Trusted and Resilient Information and Communications Infrastructure*, 2009, 18, https://nsarchive.gwu.edu/document/21424-document-28.

3. Pub. L. 114–113, "Division N—Cybersecurity Act of 2015, Title I—Cybersecurity Information Sharing," December 18, 2015.

4. 6 U.S.C. § 1502.

5. DODIG-2019–016.

6. DODIG-2019–016, at 11, citing "Sharing of Cyber Threat Indicators and Defensive Measures by the Federal Government under the Cybersecurity Information Sharing Act of 2015," February 16, 2016, https://www.cisa.gov/sites/default/files/publications/Federal%20Government%20Sharing%20Guidance%20under%20the%20Cybersecurity%20Information%20Sharing%20Act%20of%202015_1.pdf.

7. DODIG-2019–016, at 5, citing "Sharing of Cyber Threat Indicators."

8. Shira Ovide, "Tech Is Not Representative Government," *New York Times*, July 7, 2022, https://www.nytimes.com/2022/07/07/technology/big-tech-abortion.html.

9. Glenn Gerstell, "I Work for N.S.A. We Cannot Afford to Lose the Digital Revolution," *New York Times*, September 10, 2019, https://www.nytimes.com/2019/09/10/opinion/nsa-privacy.html.

10. Michael McLaughlin and Harvey Rishikof, "Seeing the Dots, Connecting the Dots: How the Government Can Unify Cybersecurity Efforts," *Lawfare*, August 4, 2022, https://www.lawfareblog.com/seeing-dots-connecting-dots-how-government-can-unify-cybersecurity-efforts.

11. *Cybersecurity Services Market Report 2020–30: COVID-19 Growth and Change*, Business Research Company, December 2020, https://www.thebusinessresearchcompany.com/report/cybersecurity-services-market.

CONCLUSION

1. *Thaler v. Vidal*, No. 2021–2347 (4th Cir., August 5, 2022).

2. Matthew Ball, "What the Metaverse Will Mean," *Wall Street Journal*, August 13–14, 2022, https://www.wsj.com/articles/what-the-metaverse-will-mean-11660233462.

3. Karen Weise and David McCabe, "F.T.C. Sues to Prevent Acquisition by Microsoft," *New York Times*, December 9, 2022, https://www.nytimes.com/2022/12/08/technology/ftc-microsoft-activision.html.

Index

About the Authors

Michael G. McLaughlin and William J. Holstein collectively have over fifty years of experience at the center of this war.

McLaughlin is an American attorney in Washington, DC, where he concentrates on cybersecurity, government contracting, and national security law. He left active-duty military service in 2022 after a career leading clandestine operations around the world. In his most recent assignment, McLaughlin served as the senior counterintelligence adviser for U.S. Cyber Command, where he was responsible for the coordination of all Department of Defense counterintelligence operations in cyberspace.

Holstein was based in Hong Kong and Beijing for United Press International and has been following U.S.–China relations for more than forty years. He also has specialized in covering technology since joining *U.S. News & World Report* in 1996. He has worked for or written for *BusinessWeek*, the *New York Times*, *Business 2.0*, *Fortune*, and other top publications. He has written nine previous books, most recently *The New Art of War: China's Deep Strategy inside the United States* (2019) and *A Grand Strategy: Countering China, Taming Technology, and Restoring the Media* (2021).

Holstein lived in China and studied the language and culture. He is one of the few China watchers who is deeply versed in technology. He also has a lifetime of experience in explaining complicated global, business, and technology issues to a lay audience. As editor in chief of *Chief Executive* magazine for three years, he has had extensive exposure to the belief system of American CEOs.